OUTSIDE
LOOKING IN

OUTSIDE
LOOKING IN

Lobbyists' Views on Civil Discourse in U.S. State Legislatures

Edited by Nicolas P. Lovrich,
Francis A. Benjamin, John C. Pierce,
and William D. Schreckhise

WSU
PRESS

Washington State University Press
Pullman, Washington

Washington State University Press
PO Box 645910
Pullman, Washington 99164-5910
Phone: 800-354-7360
Email: wsupress@wsu.edu
Website: wsupress.wsu.edu

Library of Congress Cataloging-in-Publication Data

Names: Lovrich, Nicholas P., editor. | Benjamin, Francis A., 1961- editor.
  | Pierce, John C., 1943- editor. | Schreckhise, William Dean, 1969-
  editor.
Title: Outside looking in : lobbyists' views on civil discourse in U.S.
  state legislatures / edited by Nicholas P. Lovrich, Francis A. Benjamin,
  John C. Pierce, William D. Schreckhise.
Description: Pullman, Washington : Washington State University Press, 2021.
  | Includes bibliographical references and index.
Identifiers: LCCN 2021003576 | ISBN 9780874224061 (hardcover)
Subjects: LCSH: Legislative bodies--United States--States. | Civil
  society--United States--States. | Polarization (Social
  sciences)--Political aspects--United States--States. | Political
  culture--United States--States. | Lobbyists--United States--States.
Classification: LCC JK2488 .O87 2021 | DDC 328.73--dc23
LC record available at https://lccn.loc.gov/2021003576

The Washington State University Pullman campus is located on the homelands of the Niimíipuu (Nez Perce) Tribe and the Palus people. We acknowledge their presence here since time immemorial and recognize their continuing connection to the land, to the water, and to their ancestors. WSU Press is committed to publishing works that foster a deeper understanding of the Pacific Northwest and the contributions of its Native peoples.

Cover design by Patrick Brommer. iStock Photo

Contents

Dedication

This book is dedicated to Dr. Martha (Marty) Mullen. As a tireless educator in student affairs working with countless student leaders and their organizations, Marty taught the values of civil discourse and respectful debate to many Washington State University students for three decades. Many of these appreciative students went on to careers in public affairs, ever-enriched by the experience of getting to know the always engaging, ever-insightful and unfailingly sympathetic Marty. As a major benefactor of political science at Washington State University, Marty promoted excellence in teaching by supporting the annual William F. Mullen Teaching Award. As a benefactor of the Thomas S. Foley Institute for Public Policy and Public Service, Marty took an active role in promoting the scholarship and the civic education work of the Institute. In the tributes to Marty penned by Karen Kiessling and Bill Marler, the great depth of her character and mirth of kind spirit both shine through.

• • •

TRIBUTE TO MARTY MULLEN

When I heard of Marty's death, my thoughts went back nearly 43 years to a city council candidate forum where I met Marty, perpetually young, and Frank, prematurely professorial. As the forum ended, both Marty and Frank came up to talk—Marty with a wide smile and Frank with a quizzical gaze. As a 19-year-old candidate, with less than a year living in Pullman, that night I had struggled with the issues. However, ignoring that, Marty told me what a great job I had done, while Frank had a list of suggestions on how I could improve my chances of a less-humiliating future performance.

Through Frank's untimely death and through her years of service at WSU, Marty stayed that same perpetually young woman, always with an outward smile and always with support—real or imagined. For those who were lucky enough to have known Marty, our lives were made more joyful by her optimism. That perpetually young woman is missed.

William D. Marler, Esq.
Marler Clark LLP PS
The Food Safety Law Firm
Former Washington State University Regent

• • •

TRIBUTE TO MARTY MULLEN

I know that Marty would be very pleased indeed to have this book dedicated to her. She was a fan and financial supporter of the Foley Institute, and Marty took part in many of the activities there and in the Department of Political Science where she both espoused and practiced civil discourse. I have known Marty for over 50 years, as we came to Pullman near the time that she and her husband Frank did. We both lived on College Hill and savored the pleasures and the frustrations of being in the heart of student land.

My favorite and most personal memory of Marty is when she came to visit my husband Nick and me in Casablanca, Morocco, in the summer of 2003. After we had showed her our favorite things there, Marty and I took the train to Marrakesh, where we settled into a luxurious apartment. On one of our days we visited a souk and a rug gallery called The Dune Gallerie. An old rug seller there showed us his wares and told us stories of the desert and how he missed the night sky. Marrakesh had so much light he could never see the spangle of stars he knew well. Marty and I both spied a small rug that featured stylized palm trees in a line and then speckles of light throughout the dark blue weave. The desert sky. We both loved it. She bought it, took it home and hung it on her bedroom wall, where it was the last thing she saw at night and the first thing in the morning. I would visit it for a look when we met to play canasta at her house once every few months.

When Marty died, she left me the rug, along with her letter of farewell and her wonderful photo album of all those Moroccan pictures. She left a postcard saying how she had loved our time together and that she knew I would savor "our rug." I do. It hangs in my entry hall and I see it whenever I enter the house. It is Marty, still with me, sharing joy and beauty and loving the good things of life, but knowing when, for her, it was time to say goodbye.

Karen Kiessling
Former Mayor, City of Pullman
Former President, Pullman League of Women Voters
Former member, League of Women Voters of Washington
    Education Fund Board of Directors
Civic Leader
Pullman, WA

Acknowledgments

Publication of this work has been supported by donations from individuals and institutions. The editors wish to acknowledge and offer sincere thanks for the contributions made in the name of:
- In honor of John Pierce
- The Department of Political Science at Bradley University
- The J. William Fulbright College of Arts and Sciences at the University of Arkansas
- The Division of Governmental Studies at Washington State University

We also thank the Next Generation and Research programs at the National Institute for Civil Discourse for supporting this book and the promotion of civil discourse in state legislatures. More about their programs can be found at NextGenUSA.org.

The editors wish to thank readers James Thurber and Max Neiman for their thoughtful and thorough reviews of the manuscript. Their recommendations have been integrated into this work, and readers will benefit from the expanded introduction and conclusion that resulted from their feedback.

Thanks are also due to Steven Stehr and Sam Reed of the Thomas S. Foley Institute for Public Policy and Public Service at Washington State University for preparing the foreword and supporting the public presentations derived from the national survey of state legislative lobbyists. The editors likewise wish to thank the preface authors Megan Remmel, Bradley McMillan, Craig Curtis, James R. Hanni, and Richard Kimball for their thoughtful framing of the timeliness of this work. Finally, the editors wish to thank the chapter contributors for their efforts to promote understanding of the dynamics of civil discourse and how it affects the ability of our 50 state legislatures to engage in productive legislative deliberations on behalf of the people of their states.

Foreword

CIVILITY AND INCIVILITY IN THE STATES: LESSONS FROM 50 STATE LEGISLATURES

There is a widespread belief among Americans of all political persuasions that a serious "crisis of civility" has infected the body politic. As students of American history understand, however, this concern is nothing new. As political scientist Cornell Clayton has noted, "There never was a golden age of American political civility, and history is replete with periods that rival or surpass the bitterness and incivility of today's debates" (Clayton, 2012, p. 1). To some observers it appears that the period of general consensus (or at least the illusion of consensus) and bipartisanship that followed the end of World War II and lasted until the early 1960s was, in retrospect, an exception. Rather, it should be seen that the current state of "nasty politics" more closely adheres to a normal state of affairs (Shea and Sproveri, 2012). While many people wring their hands and decry negative political discourse, no one seems to do anything about it. This book offers some important lessons learned from the experiences gleaned from an impressive study that encompasses all 50 state legislatures. These lessons include some admirable stories, successful efforts to promote bipartisanship and productive dialogue from which political leaders at the national level might learn. It is important to remember that civil discourse is important in a democracy. The lobbyists participating in the survey conducted for this book are in strong agreement with this belief. Civil discourse can lead to increased trust in valued political institutions and to more effective problem solving through public policies that have been leavened by several competing points of view.

As we write this in late summer 2020, the United States faces a wide-ranging set of problems. The immediate challenges are mitigating the impacts of the worst public health crisis in a century, a renewed debate regarding racial and social justice in the aftermath of the death of George Floyd at the hands of the police, and fears that the near-term health of the national economy is in grave danger. These challenges join a number of other long-term issues that have been emerging since at least the early 1980s, such as a propitious decline in trust in American political and social institutions, persistent levels of deficits and debt in the public finances of the national government, extreme levels of income inequality and persistent income stagnation among the bottom 80% of the work force, and a level of partisan political polarization not observed since the Civil War. Scientist Peter Turchin has documented the levels of political stress in the United States and has concluded that we are living in the "Age of Discord" (Turchin, 2016). One of the consequences of these high levels of political and social stress is a disquieting increase in the negative tone and tenor of political debate (Shea and Sproveri, 2012).

The increasingly hostile nature of discourse in the public sphere is partly due to a rise in what has been called "tribal politics" in which distaste for members of the opposite political party has driven a pronounced change in political civility. Clearly, the general public is concerned. A recent national survey conducted by the Pew Research Center found that fully 85% believe that the tone and nature of political debate have become more negative and less respectful in the last several years (Drake and Kiley, 2019). Another survey reported the responses to the following question: "How concerned are you that the negative tone and lack of civility in Washington will lead to violence or acts of terror?" The results show that 45% were "very concerned" and 34% were "concerned" (Montanaro, 2018). Finally, on March 1, 2019, the *Washington Post* featured the following headline: "In America, talk turns to something unspoken for 150 years: Civil War" (Jaffe and Johnson, 2019). This phenomenon has not escaped the attention of learned observers of American politics as they examine the causes and consequences of the rise in "nasty" politics (Boatright, et al., 2019; Clayton and Elgar, 2012; Hebst, 2010; Mutz, 2016). These trends have also infiltrated national political institutions. Benjamin Franklin believed that Congress should be a mirror of the American people, so it is not surprising that the contemporary United States House and Senate have reached near historically high levels of polarization and political incivility (Mann and Ornstein, 2016; Uslaner, 1993). An important and heretofore understudied question is: What impact have these trends had on the 99 state legislative assemblies (recall that Nebraska employs a unicameral form of government)?

The research reported in this volume examines the following questions from a variety of perspectives: Has the crisis in civic discourse and political civility in the population at large and the U.S. Congress been replicated in the state legislatures in the 50 states? What factors are most closely associated with both positive and negative civil discourse in statehouses around the country? There has been a large number of studies and reports on the topic of political polarization in state legislatures, but none we have found focus specifically on the topic of political civility.[1]

Political scientists Boris Shor and Nolan McCarty mapped the ideological distance between the parties in each state legislature from 1993 until 2016. According to their findings, first published in 2011, at least 34 state legislatures were more polarized than the U.S. Congress at the time of their study, with California, Colorado, Washington, Arizona, and Michigan being the most polarized (Shor and McCarty, 2011). Among the least polarized legislatures, according to the Shor and McCarty data, were Arkansas, Rhode Island, Louisiana, and Delaware. In February 2018, the National Conference of State Legislatures released a revised version of a report titled *State Legislative Policymaking in an Age of Political Polarization* (NCSL, 2018). This report focused on ten case studies of states to examine the extent to which polarization has had an impact on policymaking. The report concluded that most of the legislatures in their sample were able to negotiate differences and reach negotiated settlements on major policy issues. More recently, Seth Masket examined why some state legislatures have become more polarized (like California and Colorado) in the past few decades and why some (like Connecticut and Kentucky) have become depolarized (Masket, 2019). Among the factors he identifies as contributing to polarization in statehouses are the increase in economic inequality, the decline of state political journalism, and complex mixtures of district-level public opinion that cause some legislators to simplify their choices by following party cues.

1. It is common to think that polarization and incivility go hand in hand. While polarization certainly can contribute to incivility, it is possible to be polarized but respectful and civil. Indeed, chapter two of this volume reports the counterintuitive finding that members of more ideologically polarized legislatures appear to behave in a way that is more civil than members of legislatures that are less ideologically polarized.

"LABORATORIES OF DEMOCRACY"

Historically, state legislatures have been important centers of policy-making in the United States. Part of this importance is enshrined in the Constitution, in which government powers not expressly provided to the federal government are reserved for the states. Since the early 1960s a number of important changes have taken place that have increased the importance of state policymakers. One change was the creation of Medicare and Medicaid and other "entitlement" programs that began to alter the focus of the federal budget. Along with defense spending, these programs currently account for over 85% of all federal expenditures, leading Ezra Klein to quip that the U.S. government is an insurance company with a standing army (2011). More recently, partisan gridlock and policy inaction in the U.S. Congress have liberated states to adopt new policy initiatives, with the legalization of recreational marijuana as perhaps the best example. States have also had an important role in shaping policies related to the environment, climate change, public safety, and immigration. Clearly, state governments have become a new central locus of activity as policymakers struggle with pressing social, political, and financial problems.

ABOUT THIS BOOK

A portion of the institutional support for this book project and the data reported herein came from the Thomas S. Foley Institute for Public Policy and Public Service at Washington State University. This is most fitting, owing to Mr. Foley's reputation for encouraging civility and bipartisanship throughout his thirty years in the U.S. House of Representatives, the final six years as Speaker of the House. When he died in October 2013, many of his friends and colleagues, both Republicans and Democrats, came together for a memorial service in Washington, DC, at the U.S. Capital in Statutory Hall. An article that appeared in the *Washington Post* at the time captures the prevailing sentiments of the tributes.

In one of the most stirring moments, former House minority leader Robert H. Michel (R-Ill.) said that he and Foley knew "that there would always be a distinction and separation between campaigning for office and serving in office. We were, I guess, pupils of the old school." "He knew that if we wanted to be effective in the House, you just can't go around shouting your principles, you have to subject those principles to the test of open debate against those that don't share those principles," Michel said. "But true debate is not principled unless the 'Golden Rule' is applied, which simply means that you treat your fellow members the same way you want to be treated. Tom believed in that rule and he practiced it." Returning to the present, Michel added: "I only hope that the legislators who now walk through here each day so consumed by the here-and-now will feel his spirit, learn from it and be humbled by it" (O'Keefe and Rucker, 2013).

During the same memorial service, Rep. John Lewis (D-Ga.) said that Mr. Foley "believed that he should build and not tear down, reconcile and not divide. He stood for the principles of diplomacy and mutual respect even toward his opposition. He did not subscribe to the politics of personal destruction" (O'Keefe and Rucker, 2013).

In our view, civility is not the avoidance of conflict, the suppression of genuine and principled positions, nor is it a lack of disagreement. Rather, civil discourse, to our way of thinking, is a thoughtful inquiry into another person's assumptions and conclusions, and the presumption of goodwill despite disagreement. As we move forward in these difficult times, it is increasingly important that lawmakers, at all levels of government, discover ways to work together for the common good. We believe that the findings and conclusions set forth in this book will come to serve as an important contribution to the academic and practitioner dialogue regarding political civility in the United States.

Steven Stehr, Sam Reed Distinguished Professor in
    Civic Education and Public Civility
Washington State University
Pullman, Washington

Sam Reed, 14th Secretary of State (three terms of office)
State of Washington
Olympia, Washington

REFERENCES

Boatright, R., Shaffer, T., Sobieraj, S., & Young, D. G. (Eds.). (2019). *A crisis in civility? Political discourse and its discontents*. Routledge.

Clayton, C. (2012). Introduction: Historical perspectives on the role of civility in American democracy. In C. Clayton & R. Elgar (Eds.), *Civility and democracy in America: A reasonable understanding* (pp. 1–4). Washington State University Press.

Clayton, C., & Elgar, R. (Eds.). (2012). *Civility and democracy in America: A reasonable understanding*. Washington State University Press.

Drake, B., & Kiley, J. (2019). Americans say the nation's political debate has grown more toxic and 'heated' rhetoric could lead to violence. Pew Research Center, *FactTank*, July 18, 2019. https://www.pewresearch.org/fact-tank/2019/07/18/americans-say-the-nations-political-debate-has-grown-more-toxic-and-heated-rhetoric-could-lead-to-violence/.

Herbst, S. (2010). *Rude democracy: Civility and incivility in American politics*. Temple University Press.

Jaffe, G., & Johnson, J. (2019, March 1). In America, talk turns to something unspoken for 150 years: Civil war. *Washington Post*. https://www.washingtonpost.com/politics/in-america-talk-turns-to-something-unspoken-for-150-years-civil-war/2019/02/28/b3733af8-3ae4-11e9-a2cd-307b06d0257b_story.html.

Klein, E. (2011, February 14). The U.S. government: An insurance conglomerate protected by a standing army. *Washington Post*. http://voices.washingtonpost.com/ezra-klein/2011/02/the_us_government_an_insurance.html.

Mann, T., & Ornstein, N. (2012). *Worse than it looks: How the American constitutional system collided with the new politics of extremism*. Basic Books.

Masket, S. (2019). What is, and isn't, causing polarization in modern state legislatures. *PS: Political Science and Politics*, 52(3), 430–435.

Montanaro, D. (2018, November 1). Poll: Nearly 4 in 5 voters concerned incivility will lead to violence. *NPR.org*. https://www.npr.org/2018/11/01/662730647/poll-nearly-4-in-5-voters-concerned-incivility-will-lead-to-violence.

Mutz, D. (2016). *In-your-face politics: The consequences of uncivil media*. Princeton University Press.

National Conference of State Legislatures. (2018). *State legislative policymaking in an age of political polarization*. NCSL.

O'Keefe, E., & Rucker, P. (2013, October 29). Tom Foley remembered, as his colleagues beg for civility. *Washington Post*. https://www.washingtonpost.com/news/post-politics/wp/2013/10/29/tom-foley-remembered-as-his-colleagues-beg-for-civility/.

Shea, D., & Sproveri, A. (2012). The rise and fall of nasty politics in America. *PS: Political Science and Politics*, 45(3), 416–421.

Shor, B., & McCarthy, N. (2011). The ideological mapping of American legislatures. *American Political Science Review*, 105(3), 530–542.

Turchin, P. (2016). *Ages of discord: A structural-demographic analysis of American history*. Beresta Books.

Uslaner, E. (1993). *The decline of comity in Congress*. University of Michigan Press.

Preface I

A LEGACY OF PRINCIPLED LEADERSHIP IN CONGRESS: BOB MICHEL AND TOM FOLEY

Megan Remmel
Bradley McMillan
Craig Curtis

The second decade of the 21st century finds America at a crossroads. Many of the personal behavioral principles that were commonplace in the operation of our political system have been severely eroded. Partisan advantage now takes precedence over public good. Truth is sacrificed to temporary political advantage. Money to run a campaign is more important than having a vision for what candidates will do if they win election. Disinformation is knowingly and intentionally spread via social media. The president and partisan leaders in Congress snipe at each other in a personal way, something that never would have happened when Thomas S. (Tom) Foley of Washington was Speaker of the House or when Robert H. (Bob) Michel was the Minority Leader of the House. Neither of these honorable leaders would have tolerated that kind of behavior in their own caucuses.

Bob Michel and Tom Foley were political rivals with very different points of view about what was best for the nation, but they were also friends. They knew how to work together when the work of the nation needed to get done. For them, it was an honor to have a career in public *service*. Both of these leaders went to work each day with the idea that they could make America a better place to live, work, raise a family, start a business, and live your life. They were people who acted in good faith.

The founders created a government that only works well when run by people of good faith, by people committed to public service, by people who put the public welfare above party and above personal success. Tom

Foley and Bob Michel understood this necessity well. They served our country for many years in Congress, overlapping for thirty years from the time of Congressman Foley's election in 1964 until the end of both of their times in Congress in 1994. Despite being on opposite sides of the partisan divide and having quite significant policy disagreements, they were friends and allies in key times in our history. They valued truth. They valued public service. They did not stoop to personal attacks to gain temporary advantage in a policy battle or campaign. They would never call a political opponent a derogatory name, certainly not in public. They believed in civility, treating everyone with mutual respect and common courtesy. They did not lie to voters.

This is a book about the behavior of lobbyists. Lobbying has long been a part of our political system, one not always held in high esteem. Lobbyists often act as an interface between elected officials and the funding they need to campaign for their next election. While explicit vote-buying is forbidden, no one who pays attention to American politics is oblivious to the relationships between the patterns of giving and the way members of legislative bodies vote on policy issues. It may look like the privileged few gain access and influence the behavior of legislatures in their favor, and there is some truth to the criticism, but there is also another side to the coin.

Legislators are confronted with a myriad of public policy issues, and they cannot reasonably be expected to be experts or fully knowledgeable in every area. Lobbyists provide factual (though often one-sided) information to legislators and decision makers in administrative agencies that is both useful and difficult for the government to gather for itself. And a legislator is normally lobbied by interest groups both in favor of and against specific pieces of legislation. The legislator must then weigh the information presented by both sides and decide how to vote. Interest groups themselves play a role in the marketplace of ideas, a system in which policy ideas are tested by public exposure and criticism. It is not a perfect system, but so long as those who play a role in the system understand what the biases and the limits to the data are, there is some value to the way it works.

If those who participate in the system by which policy is made and implemented are people acting in good faith, the system's positives can outweigh the negatives. We can only understand whether the positive aspects of lobbying outweigh the negatives if we study the phenomenon.

Until this project, little has been done to study the way the system works in our state capitals. That fact in itself makes this project a meaningful contribution to our knowledge of how our governmental system works.

Both Tom Foley and Bob Michel understood that meeting with lobbyists was part of the job, and transfers of campaign cash were part of the process. They also understood that the process was not inherently corrupting when done with full understanding of the role interest groups play in the policy process and with respect for the public service ethic that lies at the center of working in government. So long as those who engage in lobbying, and those who are the recipients of those efforts, understand that there is a higher calling—public service—lobbying can play a beneficial role in the policy process. The key distinction between a fundamentally flawed system of lobbying and a healthy one is the principles held by those governmental officials and lobbyists engaged in the process.

It is our hope that the readers of this book will learn how the system can work to the best advantage of the residents of the nation. It is also our hope that the readers of the book will become more alert to the behaviors that indicate that the system is not functioning in a way that is fair, open, and honest. It is our hope that they will keep in mind the value of public service, something leaders of the caliber of Bob Michel and Tom Foley never forgot.

Preface II

James R. Hanni

Over a century and a half has passed since Abraham Lincoln visited Gettysburg, Pennsylvania, at the invitation of local attorney David Wills, to deliver the Gettysburg Address. Wills had been charged by Pennsylvania Governor Andrew Curtin with planning a new Soldier's National Cemetery for the interment of the Union dead at the battle of Gettysburg, as well as with organizing its dedication. Edward Everett had been secured as the keynote speaker for the November 19, 1863, dedication ceremony. Everett's resume was like no other: congressman, then governor, later senator of Massachusetts. In between, he served as ambassador to Great Britain, president of Harvard University, and U.S. secretary of state in the Fillmore administration. He was widely renowned as the finest orator in the country. In today's terminology, he was a "rock star." President Lincoln, on behalf of the nation as its chief executive, was invited and asked to provide "a few appropriate remarks."

Everett delivered an oration from memory of nearly 13,600 words, speaking for two hours. After a brief musical salute, the president rose and spoke 272 words in about two minutes. During Lincoln's brief speech, in a demonstration of humility, he said, "the world will little note nor long remember what we say here, but it can never forget what they did here." After he was finished, he is supposed to have remarked to his friend and marshal of the District of Columbia and the dedication ceremony, Ward Hill Lamon, "Lamon, that speech won't scour! It is a flat failure, and the people are disappointed."

Following the ceremony, public reaction was initially mixed. Republican papers were largely silent, if not complimentary, while Democratic papers were largely negative. However, Edward Everett later wrote to Lincoln, "I wish that I could flatter myself that I had come as near to the central idea of the occasion in two hours as you did in two minutes." The fact that Everett liked it was exceedingly satisfying to Lincoln, who very much admired Everett.

Part of the Gettysburg Address's greatness and fame is due to its brevity, as well as its poetic tone, but of course there are many other reasons. In time, people would agree that the address reshaped America. Its message rose above partisan politics. Lincoln exhibited empathy, consoling the many widows and orphans of the battle while also kindling a confidence that the dead were not forgotten and had not died in vain. There is no evidence of "us" versus "them." There is no gloating about a Union victory at Gettysburg. Lincoln does not malign the Confederates, the South. As a matter of fact, Lincoln does not even mention the other side. He never mentions slavery, Gettysburg, or himself. No, his brief remarks were of a civil nature and delivered in the spirit of unification.

Moreover, while remembering the sacrifices of the honored dead, Lincoln at Gettysburg challenged the living "to be dedicated here to the unfinished work," and take on the "great task remaining before us…that this nation, under God, shall have a new birth of freedom—and that government of the people, by the people, for the people, shall not perish from the earth." It is a perfect anthem for this volume, an example of civility. Lincoln spoke to the country in 1863, but his challenge to complete the "unfinished work" of the "great task remaining before us" speaks to all those involved in this research volume today.

As a matter of fact, in 1963 Dwight Eisenhower, then a former American president living at Gettysburg, spoke at the centennial of Lincoln's great address. He noted that the unfinished work of which Lincoln spoke in 1863 was still unfinished, and said, "We read Lincoln's sentiments, we ponder his words, but we have not paid to his message its just tribute until we, ourselves, live it."

Yes, clearly, those challenges called out by Lincoln and endorsed by Eisenhower have echoed through the decades to generations of American citizens since that November day in 1863 in Gettysburg; they call us still today. Over 20,000 members of the Friends of Gettysburg take seriously the call of the "unfinished work" and the "great task remaining before us," and "live it," as they support the preservation and education mission of the Gettysburg National Military Park and the Eisenhower National Historic Site.

It is fair to say Lincoln and Eisenhower would both be pleased with the work of the research professionals featured in this volume. Lovrich, Benjamin, Pierce, Schreckhise and their colleagues have taken up "the unfinished work," and an important piece of "the great task remaining before us." They are identifying and gaining greater understanding of the issues, problems, and opportunities at the heart of modern-day policymaking in state government, scientifically probing for insight into causes and effects of any dysfunctionality. They are seeking out best practices, enlisting the expertise of those studying civil discourse in policymaking so those best practices can be widely shared with practitioners, college students, and advocates of good government alike.

My generation is not turning over to the next generation a functioning democracy. However, we can be catalysts for improvement. The chapters of research and analysis here shine light on standards of practice, varying perceptions of the extent of issues in civility, term limits, differing experiences of lobbyists, party caucus functionality and the impact of a growing divide between rural and urban constituencies on civility. Professional perspectives on legislative civil discourse are provided, as well as observations of favorable outcomes in across-the-aisle cooperation and civil discourse in a broad cross section of state legislatures. It is hoped that this volume will serve as an essential guide to the continuation of Lincoln's resolve that "government of the people, by the people, for the people, shall not perish from the earth."

Preface III

THE CANDY DESK

Richard Kimball

Unknown to most citizens, the U.S. Senate has a Candy Desk. Generally staffed by Republican Senators and managed by tradition, it has existed for half a century and it is responsible for secreting sweet snacks onto the Senate floor. It is perhaps one of the longest-standing circumventions of their own laws—in this case, the Senate rule that prohibits food on the floor of the chamber. The Candy Desk started back when U.S. Senators once got along, even liked each other. But about 15 years into it, Democrats decided to have their own Candy Desk. Kindness, friendship, and cooperation left our Congress long ago.

The original Candy Desk was begun back when members of Congress and their families often lived in Washington full-time, instead of rushing back home at every opportunity to politic and raise the $10,000 a day, 365 days a year needed to win reelection. Back when money was not king and families and friendships were, the members of Congress got to know each other, even like each other. If you are old enough, you might even remember a few famously odd friends: Tip O'Neill and Ronald Reagan, or Jack Kennedy and Barry Goldwater.

Washington was different back then. Members of a congressperson's family often lived there. You were in the same social circles for dinner and embassy parties. Members stuck around Washington, DC, their children went to the same schools. You were just less likely to call the father of your kid's best friend a lying bastard. Civility won the day and won a lot of good government. What happened? Maybe not getting to know each other is part of it, maybe a big part. But there are also the mountains of cash, the success of attack ads, and social media's ability to drill fake news into those most persuadable and easily moved emotionally rather than intellectually. They all have a piece of this noxious pie.

Wherever one sticks the knife into what made this mess, the result seems clear. Fewer people of honor are willing to subject themselves, their families, and their lives to the slathering of sewage they will surely soak in should they dare offer themselves for public service. And that often leaves the road clear for the less honorable, for those inclined to act precisely as so many of our current leaders do.

It is hard to imagine people successfully applying to be your senator simply by providing you their background, their knowledge, and a sense of how they would deal with the work they are being hired for. That would work if you were applying to be a teacher, baker, or candlestick maker, or any other job for that matter, but not for these jobs. For political jobs, your own record is of modest consequence. You need to be a good butcher willing and able to carve up the other applicants.

This is, of course, behavior you would never accept from someone applying to mow your lawn, but it's tolerated, expected, even encouraged from those seeking the job of running our lives. We may long for civil behavior, but events have conspired to make it unlikely. Legislators are human and meet only for a few hours each week. All they really know of each other are the attacks on them yesterday by those they need to work with today.

I like the old days. Back then, when things got nasty, there were enough cool heads on board to salve the wounds, correct the egregious, and inch society forward, making it a bit fairer, a bit more just. I often think that maybe things would be different, perhaps a different standard set, the public's expectations put on a different better civil track had it not been for a fateful bullet.

In 1952, two men who would become political giants won election to the United States Senate and served together on the Labor and Public Welfare Committee where they became "unfailing friends." This friendship persisted despite the hostile parties they represented and their combative political philosophies. It was the fall of 1963 when they held a series of private conversations, much like you might have with one of your friends. Each liking the other, each trusting the other—only each was about to become his respective party's nominee for president of the United States.

It has become one of those dreamy "if only" aspects of history. If only it had happened. What if they had campaigned together, what if they had flown in tandem on Air Force One, what if their campaigns had been anchored by a series of debates with no moderators, no time limits? "They would have their say and be done with it"—after all, they were responsible adults. Consultants barked their opposition at Kennedy, but JFK would have none of it. Barry Goldwater has observed, "If Jack Kennedy had not been assassinated, our debates the following year would have shaken up the way we select our presidents thereafter...I enjoyed President Kennedy's humor, his intelligence and his obvious love for our country."

If you find dialogue like that between two opposing leaders today, give them help—a lot of help.

Editors' Introduction

Nicholas P. Lovrich
Francis A. Benjamin
John C. Pierce
William D. Schreckhise

TWO PRINCIPAL AUDIENCES

This book was conceived and produced for two distinct audiences. One audience is composed of participants in the process of state legislative politics in the 50 American states. That audience is comprised of state legislators, legislative staff, registered lobbyists and public agency legislative liaison officers, and those college- and university-based public affairs educators who routinely supply the state legislatures with college interns. Those educators likewise direct a good number of students to the many nonprofit advocacy groups such as the state Leagues of Women Voters, state chapters of Mothers Against Drunk Driving, and the state chapters of the American Civil Liberty Union. These organizations typically provide internship opportunities for college and law school students seeking to learn about the state public policy process through active engagement in legislative hearings, bill tracking, the offering of testimony and amendments, and face-to-face lobbying with legislators and their staff. Likewise, the many university-based public affairs educators in Cooperative Extension's longstanding "youth in government" programs in the nation's Land Grant colleges and universities who work with high school students interested in public affairs are seen as a key part of this first audience.

The second audience is composed of academics and their students for whom the preferred subject of study is the state legislative process. For scholars interested in state-level politics and the comparison of political processes across U.S. states, the advent of gridlock and hyper-partisanship

1

in the U.S. Congress has raised two key questions related to civil discourse. Those questions are addressed directly for readers in this book: (1) Is this same breakdown in the ability to reach bipartisan agreements and demonstrate comity and civility in the discussion of potentially divisive topics taking place in their own home states? (2) To the extent civility is breaking down in their own home states, what are the causes of this weakening of norms, customs, and traditions undergirding civil discourse?

ORIGINS OF THE STUDY: WASHINGTON STATE STUDIES

During the second of three terms of office as Washington's Secretary of State, Sam Reed, who served as the president of the National Association of Secretaries of State 2006–2007, noted some serious concerns beginning to mount among seasoned observers of the Washington State legislature. These concerns regarded adherence to some well-established norms, rules, and customs supportive of civility, comity, and mutual respect—and the public display of these qualities—in the Evergreen State. The training for newly elected legislators, commonly provided by the legislature with the active assistance of the state's research universities, was increasingly less well-attended and progressively viewed as less impactful than had been the case in the past. Secretary Reed made a request to the Division of Governmental Studies and Services at his alma mater Washington State University for active assistance in conducting research among the state's legislative community to assess the degree to which this concern for the well-being of the state legislative process was justified—and, if justified, in exploring what might be done to address it.

Working in collaboration with Secretary Reed, and later his successor in office Kim Wyman, researchers at WSU collaborated with the Office of Lieutenant Governor Brad Owens, Governor Jay Inslee and the leadership of both party caucuses in both houses. Their goal was to conduct a series of leadership-endorsed mail surveys of *legislators* (both current and those who had served over the course of the past 20 years), *legislative staff* (temporary caucus staff and permanent nonpartisan professional staff), *state legislative lobbyists* and public agency legislative liaison officers, and *legislative interns* (from the past 20 years). In 2013, the findings from those multiple surveys were presented at well-attended public events held in Olympia, Seattle, and Spokane, with reaction panels made up of current state legislators, past legislators, prominent lobbyists, and academics who commented on the findings.

The Thomas S. Foley Institute for Public Policy and Public Service at WSU and the William D. Ruckelshaus Center at the University of Washington cosponsored the public event in Olympia, held during a legislative session. The session featured the presentation of findings from the surveys and the commentaries of the panelists, and questions from the audience were recorded and archived by TVW (Washington state's equivalent to C-SPAN). The Seattle event was held in the law offices of K&L Gates, and the co-hosts were the Henry M. Jackson Foundation, K&L Gates, and the *Seattle Times*. The Spokane event was co-hosted by public affairs units of Gonzaga University, Whitworth University, Eastern Washington University, the Community Colleges of Spokane, the *Spokane Inlander* and Washington State University Spokane.

Upon retirement from office, Sam Reed was honored for his work by the creation of the Sam Reed Distinguished Professorship in Civic Education and Public Civility within the Foley Institute at WSU. This was done in recognition of his long record of public service. In due course, Professor Steven Stehr (founding director of the institute) was appointed to carry out the work associated with that Distinguished Professorship. The important outreach activities of the Foley Institute include promoting moderation and civility in political discourse; this work continues in many forms. Relatedly, the institute provided support for the development of this book and for the provision of a foreword authored by Steven Stehr and Sam Reed.

THE NATIONAL INSTITUTE FOR CIVIL DISCOURSE CONNECTION

Word of the state legislative work being carried out in Washington reached the National Institute for Civil Discourse founded by Representative Gabby Giffords and located at the University of Arizona. Ted Celeste and Director of Research Rob Boatright at the NICD were working with over a dozen state legislatures and were interested in teaming with researchers at WSU in the collection of survey data from state legislators in states beyond Washington. A meeting of key actors was arranged at the annual meeting of the New England Political Science Association held in Providence, Rhode Island, in April of 2017. Attending from the NICD were Ted Celeste and Rob Boatright, and attending from the WSU-connected team were

John Pierce (University of Kansas, founding dean of the WSU College of Liberal Arts), William Schreckhise (University of Arkansas, WSU PhD in 1999), Christopher Simon (University of Utah, WSU PhD in 1997), and Nicholas Lovrich (WSU Regents Professor Emeritus in the School of Politics, Philosophy, and Public Affairs). At that meeting it was agreed that survey data collected in Washington from *state legislative lobbyists* provided the most insightful information. This utility was the case in terms of the readiness of this group to participate in a survey and share their views, and in the substantial number of former legislators and legislative staff who were knowledgeable about changes and who had witnessed over a substantial time period the movement away from civility and comity.

At the meeting in Providence, the question arose about the potential for establishing an analytical baseline through a survey conducted in 2018–2019 which would gather data in all 50 U.S. states among legislative lobbyists and public agency legislative liaison personnel. That survey could then be replicated at a later time in those states where the NICD was engaged in across-the-aisle interventions and related work to reinforce norms supportive of civil discourse. Such surveys would assess the impact of these purposeful interventions. In due course, the NICD decided to provide a grant to researchers at WSU who undertook the tasks of generating contact lists for registered lobbyists and public agency legislative liaison officers in all 50 states, and who subsequently disseminated the surveys and collected the quantitative and qualitative data involved in that effort.

The target of 100 verified state legislative lobbyists (both physical addresses and email contact information) for each state (N = 5,000) was set; a combination of online and mail follow-up surveys was employed, with a goal of collecting a minimum of 1,000 returns (20 per state). In several states, some scholars known to be active in research on state-level politics were contacted to assess their interest in research collaboration. Several of these scholars expressed the desire to replicate the public events in Washington once the survey data were collected. A target of 30+ returns was established as a minimum for holding such an event, during which the findings for one state legislature would be compared to those for the other 49 states. In 12 states this 30+ threshold was reached—Washington, Arkansas, Oregon, Idaho, Nevada, Kansas, Utah, Iowa, Illinois, Pennsylvania,

North Carolina, and California; in the end, over 1,200 completed surveys (and many extended commentaries and follow-up email and phone calls) were obtained through online and mail surveys fielded in 2018 and 2019.

PUBLIC PRESENTATIONS OF FINDINGS IN SEVERAL STATES AND AN ACADEMIC CONFERENCE

Public events concerning civil discourse in a state legislature such as those held in Olympia, Seattle, and Spokane were subsequently held in several of these "oversample" states. One event was hosted by the J. William Fulbright College at the University of Arkansas in Fayetteville, another in Boise was hosted by the School of Public Service at Boise State University, another held in Corvallis was hosted by the School of Public Policy at Oregon State University, another done in Salt Lake City was hosted by the Hinckley Institute of Politics at the University of Utah, and yet another took place in Reno, hosted by the Department of Political Science at the University of Nevada. These public events all entailed the reaction panel format and were well attended. One or more of the WSU-based research team of Lovrich, Benjamin, and Stehr would make the presentation and interact with the panelists and audiences. The COVID-19 pandemic put a halt to plans to conduct similar public outreach events in Kansas (University of Kansas), Pennsylvania (Shippensburg University), California (Sacramento State University), Texas (Texas A&M International), Indiana (Indiana State University), and North Carolina (Duke University).

Along with these practitioner audience events, there was a plan to present preliminary findings drawn from the survey data at a major academic conference. The annual meeting of the State Politics and Policy Conference, hosted by the Department of Political Science at the University of California, San Diego, was to feature a panel on which four papers derived from the national survey of state legislative lobbyists would be presented. Scholars John Pierce and Burdett Loomis were slated to give a paper on the comparison of rent-seeking and nonrent-seeking lobbyists vis-à-vis sentiments about civil discourse and perceptions of their own state legislature; Nicholas Lovrich and Christopher Simon were to give a paper on the effects of political culture heritage on perceptions of civil discourse phenomena; William Schreckhise and Francis Benjamin were slated to give a paper on the impact of legislative professionalization on these legislative phenomena; and, finally, Luke Fowler, Stephanie Witt, and Jaclyn Kettler were going to test the relative impact of political culture, professionalism, term limits, and additional factors in a multivariate cross-state comparison. Once more, COVID-19 intervened and the conference scheduled for San Diego was cancelled, and each of these academic papers was redirected toward providing chapter contributions to this edited book. As well, three additional research-based chapters that were derived from the national survey of state legislative lobbyists were developed as additional contributions to this book. One chapter presents the comparison of lobbyists with and without prior service as legislators or legislative staff (Benjamin and Huett), one chapter focuses on the effects of the rural/urban divide, and another explores the effects of inequality. The last two chapters were prepared by Leanne Giordono, Claire McMorris, and Brent Steel at Oregon State University. John Pierce and Max Neiman conclude the book with a summary overview of principal findings and a tentative agenda for further research to be undertaken in the coming years.

CHAPTERS NINE AND TEN: THE WORLD OF PRACTICE

Chapters nine and ten will be of interest to both practitioners and social science researchers. Rob Boatright details the types of interventions made by the National Institute for Civil Discourse when that organization is invited into a state legislature to promote the rebuilding of norms supportive of civil discourse. Boatright details the desire to document the favorable impact that the organization has had on state legislatures with legislative leaders who requested help in building the capacity for bipartisan problem-solving. In the last chapter, Karl Kurtz describes the efforts made by the National Conference of State Legislatures to advance the cause of civil discourse. He also speculates on why those efforts have led to such marginal positive results.

In your reading of this book, whether as a researcher, a legislative politics community practitioner, a student, or a concerned citizen, you should find the scholarship presented here to provide considerable insight into how the decline in the civility of our national political discourse has seeped into the 50 state legislatures. The coeditors of this book welcome all inquiries—whether from public affairs educators, state legislators, state legislative staff, lobbyists, public agency legislative liaison officers, media reporters whose beat is the state house and/or state legislature, or academic researchers working in the area of state politics and policy. If you have questions regarding access to the survey data collected or the interpretation of the results noted for any specific state, please contact any of the coeditors.

INVITATION TO BROADENED ACADEMIC AND PUBLIC USE OF DATA COLLECTED

This book is the result of a three-year collaborative effort involving the hard work of numerous scholars from across the country. The editors would very much like this collaborative effort to continue. To maintain this collaboration and broaden its scope, we have developed a website that includes several resources we believe readers will find useful in this regard. The website is housed at Washington State University and can be accessed at https://labs.wsu.edu/outside-looking-in/.

Scholars interested in exploring the topic of legislative civility further will find the survey instrument used by the authors to collect the extensive dataset analyzed in the first eight chapters in this book. They will also find the actual dataset in SPSS, Stata, and Excel formats, along with a search-able database for the written comments submitted by the state legislative lobbyists who participated in our survey. The website also contains information about the contributors to the creation of the National Survey of State Legislative Lobbyists, the core elements of the collaborative project that led to the creation of the dataset and comments archive, a listing of the study's primary findings, and links to research papers and published articles that grew from this collaborative research effort. We also include a discussion of our future research plans related to legislative civility, and opportunities for others to join us in this highly timely work.

Practitioners will find on the website video recordings and PowerPoint slides used for public presentations made by the book's editors and contributing authors in Arkansas, Washington, Idaho, Oregon, Nevada, and Utah. In each of these states, findings were presented with comparisons to neighboring states and to the U.S. as a whole. Plans for similar public presentations to be made in Kansas, Illinois, Pennsylvania,

Indiana, California, North Carolina, Texas, and Washington DC (NICD headquarters) were cancelled due to COVID-19 pandemic conditions and concerns for public health. For those readers interested in hosting a public presentation of their own using survey data collected and the comment archive, the contact information for the editors is also included on the website. We would be happy either to put on a presentation for your state or to help you organize your own event.

CHAPTER ONE

Political Culture, Historical Legacy, and Contemporary Levels of Civil Discourse in U.S. State Legislatures: Evidence on Selective Impact vs. Ubiquitous Penetration of Incivility in U.S. State Legislatures

Nicholas P. Lovrich
Christopher A. Simon

THE NATIONAL SURVEY OF STATE LEGISLATIVE LOBBYISTS: BACKGROUND

The impetus for the study of state legislative lobbyists came from early work undertaken in the state of Washington. The Secretary of State at the time was Sam Reed, a moderate Republican who was among the few members of his party to be successful in competing for a statewide office in a state drifting inexorably in a "blue" direction in the 1980s and 1990s (Long and Ammons, 2018). During his third term of office, Secretary Reed began in earnest to promote across-the-aisle bridge-building, hosting bipartisan conclaves of centrist legislators—the *moderate middle*—who were often able to collaborate on matters of common interest. While his efforts were most often quite successful, they became progressively more difficult both to initiate and then sustain. His successor in the office, Kim Wyman, is likewise a moderate Republican winning office in a blue state seeking to follow the same themes of bipartisanship, across-the-aisle bridge-building, and the maintenance of a broad scope of *nonpartisan* policy legislative work. This was especially true with respect to election practices, where the primary focus for both Sam Reed and Kim Wyman was solidly fixed on broadening voter participation and ensuring security in the state's balloting (vote by mail) process, carried out by locally elected—Democratic and Republican—county auditors (Donovan, 2018).

During his final term of office (2008–2012), Secretary Reed, an alumnus of WSU who earned BA and MA degrees in political science there, requested applied social science research assistance from the Thomas S. Foley Institute for Public Policy and Public Service, the William D. Ruckelshaus Center (colocated at the University of Washington and Washington State University), and the WSU Division of Governmental Studies and Services. He sought to have university-based scholars collect data from among the principal actors in the state's legislative process, and then share the findings of that research in a series of workshops and presentations during legislative sessions and during the interim periods when legislators hold hearings around the state and engage in public forums. Secretary Wyman continued this initiative, and upon retirement Secretary Reed was honored by having an endowed Distinguished Professorship in Civic Education and Public Civility created and housed in the Foley Institute. The inaugural holder of that Distinguished Professorship is Dr. Steven Stehr, the director of the School of Politics, Philosophy, and Public Affairs at Washington State University.

Benefitting from the assistance and support of Secretaries of State Reed and Wyman, field research work was undertaken to develop survey instruments and collect survey data from five major groups: state legislators past and present (going back 20 years); legislative staff (both career professional nonpartisan staff and party caucus staff); mass media professionals covering the state legislature for print and broadcast outlets; legislative interns (present and going back 20 years); and legislative lobbyists (contract, lobby firm-based, nonprofit advocates, and public agency legislative liaison personnel). Blessed with endorsements from the Office of the Secretary of State and the Office of the Governor, and with the blessings of the legislative leadership of both parties in both chambers of the state legislature, substantial survey data and commentaries were collected from all five groups of interested parties. The additional formal endorsements from the Foley Institute and the Ruckelshaus Center, and their coordinated efforts to encourage participation by former and present legislators serving on their respective advisory boards, ensured a reasonably good response rate on surveys undertaken.

Findings derived from the survey data collected over the course of a five-year period were shared with multiple parties in various forums and public settings across Washington. The findings from the survey of college and university (undergraduate and graduate) interns were shared with the House and Senate Intern Coordinators and the legislative internship program coordinators in over 20 colleges and universities active in the state's very well-run legislative internship program (Benjamin and Lovrich, 2011). Findings from the four other groups were shared with legislators and the public (via TVW) during events held Washington's capital, Olympia, during the legislative session, and at events hosted by the Foley Institute and the Ruckelshaus Center in the state's two largest cities, Seattle and Spokane. The Seattle and Spokane events typically involved several experienced legislators providing commentary on the findings reported and responding to questions from citizens and mass media representatives. The Washington State League of Women Voters was a principal resource in generating public interest in the Seattle, Spokane, and Olympia events.

As word of this work reached the National Institute for Civil Discourse (NICD), institute personnel—in particular, political scientist Rob Boatright at Clark University and longtime Ohio politician Ted Celeste of NICD—expressed their interest in working with the Washington state academic and public affairs-involved people engaged in legislative civility as they carried out their own work in various state legislatures across the country. Their initial interest was in the potential for state legislators to use the surveys, which were developed and refined in field use in Washington and in NICD initiatives in some 17 states. In due course their interest turned to the potential to document the impact of their work in the state legislatures where NICD on-site workshops had been conducted.

In discussions regarding a national survey, Francis Benjamin (director of the WSU Department of Psychology's Political Interaction Lab) and Nicholas Lovrich (WSU Regents Professor Emeritus) opined that of all the groups surveyed in Washington the lobbyists were: 1) the *most responsive* to being surveyed; 2) the *most likely to offer informed commentary*; and 3) were the *most interested in discussing results and adding deeper insight* into what the data were saying about state legislative affairs. This was particularly the case with lobbyists who had once served as state legislators. Lobbyists, whose job it is to move legislation through the state legislature and block legislation deemed unwise by interested parties, know perhaps better than anyone whether the legislative process is healthy and vibrant or is being seriously hampered by hyperpolarization and a decline in adherence to legislative norms of fair play and loyal opposition. With that background discussion, the NICD decided to provide a small grant to underwrite the costs associated with an online Qualtrics survey of state legislative lobbyists, and later a mail follow-up to the online survey. That survey work was carried out at WSU with assistance from the Foley Institute and WSU Extension's Division of Governmental Studies and Services.

NATIONAL SURVEY OF STATE LEGISLATIVE LOBBYISTS: RESEARCH TEAM

Effective data collection required active assistance from several people in the numerous U.S. states where access to the names, organizational affiliations, and email and physical addresses of registered lobbyists and state and local government legislative liaison personnel was difficult to obtain. While some U.S. states maintain relatively easy access to such information (often digitized), others make the composition of such survey sample lists very difficult. In many cases, researchers contacted for assistance in compiling the lists of registered lobbyists expressed an interest in having the data collected simultaneously from their own state and all other states to enable the sharing of study results with their colleagues, students, and interested civic audiences.

In due course, a team of 20 scholars from across the country contributed materially to the data collection process, and now each of these research collaborators enjoys access to the data collected from over 1,200 state legislative lobbyists from all 50 U.S. states. Those hardy souls who worked throughout 2018 and early 2019 to refine the survey questionnaire and amass the sample of lobbyists in their states and others, and who helped generate participation in their respective states, are as follows:

William Schreckhise, *University of Arkansas*

John Pierce and Burdett Loomis, *University of Kansas*

Gary Moncrief, Stephanie Witt, Luke Fowler, and Jaclyn Kettle, *Boise State University*

Megan Remmel and R. Craig Curtis, *Bradley University*

Brent Steel, Claire McMorris, and Leanne Giordono, *Oregon State University*

Christopher Simon, *University of Utah*

Daniel Chand, *Kent State University*

John Tennert, *University of Nevada Las Vegas*, and Robert Morin, *University of Nevada Reno*

Michael Moltz, *Shippensburg University*

Leslie Winner and John Hood, *Duke University*

Francis Benjamin, Steven Stehr, and Nicholas Lovrich, *Washington State University*

Gary Moncrief of Boise State University was a critical player among this team of scholars because of his key role (co-principal investigator) in the National Conference for State Legislatures' (NCSL) 2015–2016 national survey of state legislators. That survey focused on issues of civility, adherence to longstanding legislative norms of conduct, and capacity for bipartisan problem-solving. That survey effort resulted in the collection of 1,600+ responses and led to case studies being carried out in ten states varying from low to high levels of partisan polarization. Having Gary Moncrief participate in the drafting and refinement of the lobbyist survey benefitted our study in two extremely important ways. First, it allowed for the application of learning from an assessment of which items worked best in the NCSL study to explore state legislative discourse civility. Second, it permitted the inclusion of questions in our survey that would allow comparisons of the views of state legislators and the lobbyists who work with them to move legislation through the legislative process in their respective states.

NATIONAL SURVEY OF STATE LEGISLATIVE LOBBYISTS: METHODS, DATA COLLECTED, AND PRESENTATIONS

Once the research team achieved agreement on the content of the survey instrument (available upon request), the WSU Institutional Review Board (IRB) approved data collection. The Qualtrics online survey process was used as an initial contact; that process was initiated in mid-2018 and carried through until early 2019. With resources provided by NICD, two rounds of mail survey follow-ups were conducted in 2019, with the following ultimate results.

- Completed surveys = 1,200+
- Returns from all 50 states
- Average responses per state = 25+ [min. 14 (GA), max. 79 (OR)]
- *Oversamples* (30+) for AR, KS, ID, WA, UT, CA, NV, IL, IA, OH, PA, OR, & NC
- Many former state legislators; diverse group of respondents, including agency liaison personnel, nonprofit and public interest group advocates
- Rich collection of comments and extended commentaries; many telephone and email follow-up contacts with survey participants

The survey data, including comments on specific questions and commentaries on the overall survey and topic of legislative civility, were compiled into SPSS files and text documents shared with each member of the research team. In several of the "oversample" states, public events featuring the presentation of findings for that state as compared to the rest of the country were made to promote public education. Such presentations have been coordinated with members of the research team, and have been hosted by the William J. Fulbright College of Arts and Sciences at the University of Arkansas, the Hinckley Institute of Politics at the University of Utah, the School of Public Policy at Oregon State University, the School of Public Service at Boise State University, the Department of Political Science at the University of Nevada, Reno, and the WSU Extension 4-H Teen Know Your Government annual conferences in Olympia, which take place during legislative sessions. In 2021, events are planned as part of presentations hosted by the Dole Institute at the University of Kansas, Department of Political Science at Shippensburg University, Department of Social Sciences at Texas A&M International University, and North Carolina Leadership Forum at Duke University.

POLITICAL CULTURE AND LEGISLATIVE CIVILITY

A rich literature in political science has been generated based on the work of Daniel Elazar, work directed at documenting three hypothesized strains of American political culture that he characterized as *traditionalistic, individualistic,* and *moralistic.* Elazar argued that these three approaches to the conceptualization of the democratic polis were widely present within the original colonies. He argued further that these strains persisted in the earliest years of nationhood on the eastern seaboard. As America's manifest destiny played itself out, the state origins of early settlers in the newer states that later joined the union primarily reflected one of these three hypothesized strains of American political culture, according to Elazar's interpretation of American history (Elazar, 1966; 1970; 1982; 1984; 1987; 1994). Joel Lieske (1993) characterized Elazar's work as follows:

> Twenty-seven years ago, Elazar (1984) advanced a revolutionary new theory of American regional subcultures. This new theory was designed to help explain variations in the political processes, institutional structures, political behavior, and policies and programs of state and local government. In short, Elazar argued that subcultural differences could help us understand: (1) what state and local governments do; (2) how they are organized; (3) what political rules they observe; and (4) who participates in the political process. (p. 888)

According to Elazar, the predictive value of this history-based classification of state political cultures derives from distinct conceptions of democratic governance associated with each of the three cultural strains in question. In the traditionalistic strain, government is viewed as the rightful realm of elites of wealth and social position, people who should be entrusted with the responsibility to guide public affairs in appropriate directions with minimal disruptions from persons of lesser erudition and means. In contrast, the individualistic strain reflected the view that democratic government is best viewed as a neutral forum for open competition for favor and influence, a setting in which self-interested parties engage in the push-and-pull of economic and political life and the institutions of government provide a fair playing field within which the ongoing competition for public offices takes place. In the moralistic strain, the vision of government is quite different from either of these conceptions. Democratic politics is conceived of as an ongoing process of movement toward more noble and just forms of governance, and government provides both a forum for open discussion and civic involvement and a concrete vehicle for doing justice once moral dialogues identify appropriate areas for positive action on behalf of noble ends (Pierce et al., 2011).

In Elazar's telling, all contemporary U.S. states experience the presence of all three strains of the American political culture heritage to some extent, but the relative presence of each varies in such a way that some states are principally of one or another type. His underlying argument is one of *path dependence*—that is, once it is established, the political culture of a state persists over time, and politics in the state continue to reflect established values, norms, and routines of governance long after their initial codification and routinization at the time of admission to statehood. Robert Putnam made the same type of path dependency argument with respect to social capital in his classic *Making Democracy Work* (1993). He argued in that widely read and highly regarded work that patterns of varying social capital in the regions of Italy prevailing prior to *L'Unificazione d'Italia* continued to influence the character of political life in the major regions of the country much later in history. Some recent research has shown that social capital presence or absence in the distant past continues to influence political life in the regions of contemporary Italy, predicting such important things as regional government commitment to environmental sustainability (Pierce et al., 2016) (see Chart 1.1).

In similar manner, many scholars have made use of Elazar's theory of political culture conceived as historical legacy with lasting effects to explain cross-state variation in political life (Jackman and Miller, 1996; Moon et al., 2001), the adequacy of state funding for public schools (Wirt, 1980), the operation of the criminal justice systems of the states (Herzik, 1985; Lovrich et al., 2014), and variations in the enactment of various public policies (Kincaid, 1980 and 1982; Rosenthal and Moakley, 1984; Sharp, 2005; Miller et al., 2006). Connections between political culture and the presence of political reforms (Ritt, 1974), women in state and local government offices (Sigelman, 1976), and passage of state ratifications of the Equal Rights Amendment (Wohlenberg, 1980) have been reported in the research literature. In addition, evidence of a connection between political culture and the attitudes of state senators toward various social, economic welfare, and corruption issues has been reported (Welch and Peters, 1980). While critiques of Elazar are most definitely to be found in the literature

(Sharkansky, 1969; Savage, 1981; Nardulli, 1990; Woodard, 2011), it is also the case that contributions continue to be added to the published research literature showing the potential of measures of political culture to predict such state-level political phenomena as adoption and rejection of capital punishment (Fisher and Pratt, 2006).

For the study of state legislative politics and civil discourse, is it possible to demonstrate that the historical heritage of political culture helps explain variation in what state legislative lobbyists in the 50 states report as their perceptions of the status of civil discourse in their respective states? Can political culture be used to predict: 1) their perceptions of the importance of civil discourse to the quality of legislative deliberations; 2) the erosion of long-standing norms of civil conduct in carrying out the business of legislating on the public's behalf; and 3) the scope of state legislative work that remains in the realm of nonpartisan problem-solving? Those are the questions this chapter seeks to address.

THREE MEASURES OF POLITICAL CULTURE: MAJOR MIGRATION PATTERNS, HYBRID STATE CLASSIFICATIONS, AND PERSONALITY TRAIT CONFIGURATION REGIONS

Fortunately, it is possible to make use of three separate classifications of the 50 U.S. states with respect to their political culture heritage as derived from the work of Daniel Elazar. The first classification reflects a broad interpretation of Elazar's argument stipulating that three predominant patterns of western settlement occurred in the United States. The first primary path of migration flowed from upper New England across the top tier of northern states, and then down the west coast and over to the Rocky Mountain states—all the way to Kansas. This *moralistic* legacy, it is argued, continues to influence the types of politics and public policy enactments occurring in these states. The second primary path of migration and westward settlement is argued to entail major movement westward from the lower New England states through Pennsylvania, Ohio, Indiana, Illinois, Missouri, Nebraska, and Wyoming of the *individualistic* strain of political culture. The third primary path of migration, involving the *traditionalistic* strain of political culture, is argued to entail movement from the eastern seaboard's southern states across the South and Southwest.

The map below displays the classifications of the U.S. states according to this broad general understanding of the deposition of the historical legacy of political culture that took place in the territorial days of our history. This classification has been used by many social science researchers, including Nelson Polsby (1984), Aaron Wildavsky (1982; 1998), and Robert Putnam (2000, pp. 346–347). Polsby used Elazar in exploring the persistence of pluralism, Wildavsky used Elazar to explain the diversity of approaches to common shared problems across the states, and Putnam discussed the connection between political culture and social capital.

This is the classification of states used in the recent analysis of cross-state differences in the proclivity to engage state legislative preemption of local ordinances by Luke Fowler and Stephanie Witt, members of the research team in a 2019 publication in *Publius*. Some of these county and municipal ordinances are directed toward the protection of gay rights in employment and access to public services; others pertain to "living

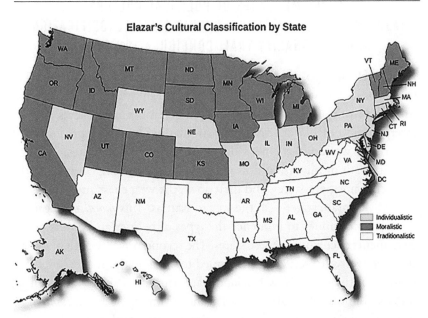

Figure 1.1. Elazar's Cultural Classification by State. Source: Luke Fowler, Department of Political Science, Boise State University.

wage" policies for certain service industry workers; and yet others relate to environmental regulations, housing options for the homeless, and similar social policies.

A second type of classification entails the identification and labeling of hybrid political cultures in many U.S. states. These are states wherein two strains of political culture are present due to secondary waves of substantial westward migration. Hybrid cases entail one predominant political culture, with a second political culture strain also present to a noteworthy extent. In some states, such as Indiana and Illinois, pronounced regional differences are present to such an extent that a Traditionalistic historical legacy obtains in southern counties while an Individualistic legacy obtains in northern counties (see Monroe, 1977; Lovrich et al., 1980). In the case of Washington, the division runs east and west, with the counties on the west side of the Cascade Range being Moralistic and the counties on the eastern side of the state being Individualistic (Lovrich et al., 2018); a similar east/west divide is present in Oregon (Steel et al., 2005). This much more detailed classification of states is possible following Elazar's writings (Elazar, 1982), and this type of classification is detailed in chart 1.1. Each U.S. state has either a single, predominant political culture strain, or has two political culture strains coexisting, with one prominent (first letter) and a second present to a lesser degree (second letter).

The third measure of political culture is derived from the work of a six-member team of social psychologists headed by Peter Rentfrow at the University of Cambridge. Rentfrow and his colleagues make use of a substantial number of surveys conducted on "The Big Five" personality traits, widely agreed to represent the foundation of human personality (John and Srivastava, 1999). It is argued that, in combination, the traits of extraversion (E), agreeableness (A), conscientiousness (C), neuroticism (N), and openness (O) can be used effectively by trained psychologists to classify people into meaningful categories reflecting commonly documented configurations of traits; these configurational classifications are used both for diagnostic and behavior prediction purposes in psychology. By pooling data from a large number of Random Digit Dialing surveys conducted over the course of more than a decade (1999–2010), sufficiently large subsamples of survey respondents for each state are made available to permit the identification of both modal personality traits and

Chart 1.1

Hybrid Political Culture Classifications of the States

T=Traditionalistic; I=Individualistic; M=Moralistic

Alabama	T	Maryland	IM	Pennsylvania	IM
Alaska	TI	Massachusetts	MI	Rhode Island	MI
Arizona	T	Michigan	M	South Carolina	T
California	MI	Minnesota	MI	South Dakota	IM
Colorado	M	Mississippi	T	Tennessee	TM
Connecticut	MI	Missouri	IT	Texas	T
Delaware	TI	Montana	MI	Utah	M
Florida	IT	Nebraska	I	Vermont	MI
Georgia	T	Nevada	IM	Virginia	TI
Hawaii	MI	New Hampshire	M	Washington	MI
Idaho	IM	New Jersey	IM	West Virginia	T
Illinois	IM	New Mexico	TI	Wisconsin	MI
Indiana	TI	New York	MI	Wyoming	I
Iowa	IM	North Carolina	TM		
Kansas	M	North Dakota	MI		
Kentucky	T	Ohio	IT		
Louisiana	T	Oklahoma	TI		
Maine	IM	Oregon	M		

clusters of traits for each of the U.S. states. In total, a rather astonishing 1,596,704 individuals participated in surveys wherein data on the Big Five traits were collected. The sample sizes for each state varied from a minimum of 3,166 in Wyoming to a maximum of 177,085 in California. The demographic variation among survey respondents adequately mirrors the characteristics of the U.S. adult population.

Using these survey-based data, Rentfrow and his colleagues performed psychometrics on the survey data and employed cluster analysis to identify three primary configurations of modal personality types, and assigned values for degree of presence of each modal type in each U.S. state. Using scores for these modal personality types, they applied the Getis-Ord G statistic for geographical clustering analysis (also known as "hotspot analysis" in the GIS research community) to locate geographic concentrations of high and low values on the three modal personality profiles. The three modal personality configurations in question were labelled "Friendly & Conventional," "Relaxed & Creative," and "Temperamental & Uninhibited."

A graph in the Rentfrow et al. (2013) article published in the *Journal of Personality and Social Psychology* provides a detailed representation of the nature of these three modal personality configuration profiles. The set of three U.S. maps showing the continental United States with visible state boundaries was used by Rentfrow and his colleagues to illustrate the differential geographic distribution of these personality types across U.S. states.

The three clusters in question have significance for this chapter in that they tend to mirror variation in the geographic distribution of Elazar's political culture. Rentfrow (2013, p. 1008) and his colleagues note, in this specific regard, the following:

> The present findings have the potential to inform our understanding of theory and research in political science. For example, the psychological regions resemble, to some degree, the political regions identified by Elazar (1994). Specifically, 10 of the 11 (91%) primary states located in the individualistic political region—where government's sole function is to maintain a healthy economy—are located in the Temperamental & Uninhibited region, and seven of the 10 primary states in the traditional political region—where government's sole function is to maintain the status quo—are located in the Friendly & Conventional region. The present findings raise interesting questions about the possible connections between political and psychological regions.

Given this connection between the work of Peter Rentfrow and his fellow social psychologists and the political culture classifications of Daniel Elazar, we make use here of the geographic cluster analysis results. It deserves mention that Peter Rentfrow graciously shared his data with us upon request.

FINDINGS FROM THE NATIONAL SURVEY OF STATE LEGISLATIVE LOBBYISTS

The 2018–19 state legislative lobbyists' survey produced evidence of considerable variance across states on both the weakening of norms supportive of civility and the diminution of the nonpartisan sphere of legislative work. However, near-universal agreement obtains on the questions of the importance of civility norms for the effective operation of state legislatures. It is important that some variation across states exist in the norm weakening and nonpartisan space variables so that there will be some variance to explain in comparisons across categories of political culture and psychological regions. Regarding the weakening of norms, in response to this question posed in the survey, nearly two-thirds of the lobbyists indicated that they felt legislative norms are weakening.

While a clear majority of lobbyists surveyed opine that norm-weakening is occurring in their own states, over a third believe that it is not occurring or that their own state legislatures are recovering after a period of such weakening, or they are uncertain. That does provide sufficient variation for political culture effects to manifest themselves if they are indeed present. The same can be said for the shrinking of the nonpartisan space in state legislative affairs. The survey results on that important question are displayed in graph 1.1.

Graph 1.1

The cover of the June 2017 issue of *Governing: The States and Localities* bears the caption "Checks & Imbalances: With a Constitutional Crisis Consuming Washington, State Lawmakers are Upending Their Own Norms as Well." Alan Greenblatt's article gives several examples of hyper-partisanship putting strains on the observance of long-established norms of proper legislative conduct and processes.

Do you think that norms of fair play are breaking down in the state in which you lobby or advocate for clients?

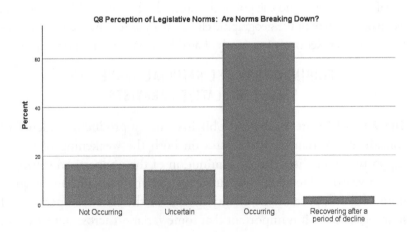

Q8 Perception of Legislative Norms: Are Norms Breaking Down?

While a clear majority (~55%) of lobbyists across the country opine that the nonpartisan space in their states' legislatures is shrinking, many disagree that this is occurring in their own states; some are even of the opinion that there is more such space now than in the past. On this outcome measure, then, there is ample variance for the possible effects of political culture and psychological region to manifest themselves. For specific examples, while the mean score (1–3 scale range) for lobbyists in Indiana (a TI state) is 1.294, the mean for Minnesota (an MI state) is 2.077; the mean for all 1,200+ lobbyists nationwide is 1.612.

With respect to the question of the importance of civility for the effective operation of state legislative bodies, there is evidence of very strong agreement on the importance of civility and the maintenance of civil discourse norms. The question posed in the survey read:

> How important are civility and the maintenance of civil discourse norms in legislative debate to producing good public policy?
>
> Not at all important (1)--------------------------Absolutely essential (10)

The survey results for this question are displayed in the following bar graph. Not only is there strong agreement on the value of civility, and on the importance of norms and traditions supportive of civil discourse, there is virtually no difference in the way state legislative lobbyists feel across the various political culture and psychological regions of the country.

Graph 1.2

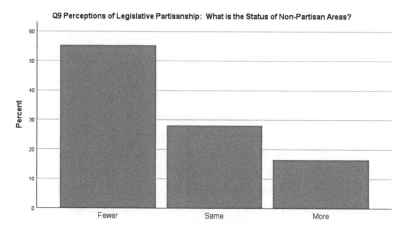

Q9 Perceptions of Legislative Partisanship: What is the Status of Non-Partisan Areas?

Graph 1.3

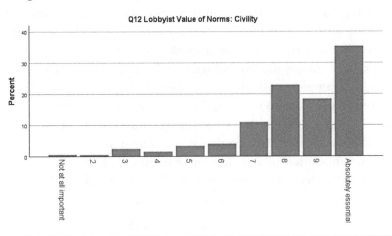

Q12 Lobbyist Value of Norms: Civility

The following table displays results in this regard for both types of Elazar measures and for the Elazar-relevant psychological regions identified by Rentfrow and his associates. For the psychological regions, the two states in each cluster that are the highest-scoring presence of that personality cluster are used to compare results on the question of importance of civility norms to effective state legislative operations.

Regarding the importance of civility and norms supportive of civil discourse in state legislatures across the country, lobbyists working in virtually all political culture settings and all psychological regions express the same high level (mean of 8+ on a 10-point scale) of support for the idea that civility and civility-promoting norms are essential for state legislatures to be effective in their public lawmaking work. Apparently, traditionalistic, individualistic, and moralistic strains of American political culture all find much value in the maintenance of comity, decorum, mutual respect, and civil discourse in their respective state legislatures; state legislative lobbyists virtually everywhere across the country expect to experience civil discourse while lobbying.

What can be said about the question of the weakening of established norms regarding proper conduct and processes noted by Norman Greenblatt? Do the lobbyists working in state legislatures in the various political culture and psychological regional settings differ in the extent

Table 1.1.
Mean Scores (and s.d.) on Importance of Civility for States
in Each Political Culture Category

Simple Elazar

T	I	M
8.28	8.32	8.41
(0.11)	(0.11)	(0.09)

F = 0.46
p = 0.63

Hybrid Elazar

M+MI	I+IM+IT	T+TI
8.35	8.37	8.40
(0.09)	(0.11)	(0.12)

F = 0.06
p = 0.94

Psychological Regions

Cluster 1 Top 2 Friendly/Conventional [MN & IA]	Cluster 2 Top 2 Relaxed/Creative [CA & OR]	Cluster 3 Top 2 Temp/Uninhibited [NY & PA]
8.26	8.31	7.85
(0.31)	(0.21)	(0.33)

F = 0.69
p = 0.50

of their agreement with Greenblatt that state lawmakers are upending their own established norms? Are there signs that one or another political culture strain is more immune to this erosion than others? Likewise, is one of the psychological regions substantially more or less susceptible to this erosion of norms than others? The following table reports findings on this question for the first type of political culture measure, the broad single-strain classification of state political cultures commonly employed in the study of state politics.

This first test of the impact of political culture on state legislative lobbyists' perceptions of norm erosion suggests that there is NO noteworthy connection between political culture strain and the extent of abandonment of established norms of legislative conduct. A substantial majority of state legislative lobbyists (60%+) believe such norm erosion is happening, and they believe this whether they work in states with individualistic,

Table 1.2.
Erosion of Legislative Norms of Proper Conduct—Elazar Single-Strain Political Culture Classification of U.S. States

	Individualistic	Traditionalistic	Moralistic
Not Occurring	17.5%	16.0%	16.4%
Uncertain	17.9%	12.5%	12.4%
Occurring	61.2%	69.4%	67.9%
	Chi-Square = 7.297 (p = 0.294)		

Table 1.3.
Reduction of Legislative Nonpartisan Issue Space—Elazar Single-Strain Political Culture Classification of U.S. States

	Individualistic	Traditionalistic	Moralistic
Occurring	52.4%	62.1%	52.8%
Uncertain	33.9%	20.6%	29.2%
Not Occurring	13.6%	17.3%	18.1%
	Chi-Square = 24.539 (p = 0.006)		

traditionalistic, or moralistic heritages. What can be said of the maintenance of a nonpartisan space in the ongoing due diligence work of the state legislature? Does this same lack of noteworthy effect manifest itself with respect to this frequently used global measure of political culture? The answer to that question is to be found in Table 1.3.

The results displayed in Table 1.3 indicate a statistically significant effect, but that effect is the result of a difference occasioned by the lobbyists working in traditionalistic states. Among that group, there are far fewer lobbyists who opine "uncertain" and substantially more who opine that such a diminution of the nonpartisan space is occurring. Of the six comparisons made, then, only this one regarding traditionalistic states stands out.

Perhaps the impact of political culture, when measured in the hybrid state classification scheme, will prove more salient. In this method of classification, each one of the U.S. states is assigned a score on each of the three political culture strains. For example, on the measure for traditionalistic political culture heritage a particular state can have one of four scores: 0 = trait not present; 1 = trait present as a secondary trait, with another political culture strain in primary presence; 2 = trait present as a primary trait, with another political culture strain in secondary presence; and 3 = trait in exclusive presence. Table 1.4 sets forth findings on the extent to which differing levels of presence of each of the three political subcultures is associated with a perception of the erosion of established legislative norms and customs.

Once more, the extent of presence of the three Elazar political culture strains does not greatly affect the perceptions of state legislative lobbyists with respect to the erosion of norms and customs relating to civility. Pretty much the same proportions of lobbyists sort into not occurring, uncertain, and occurring categories, regardless of the degree of presence of moralistic, individualistic, or traditionalistic political culture legacy. What can be said of lobbyists' perceptions of the shrinkage of nonpartisan space in the work of state legislatures? Perhaps it is in this important area that the effects of political culture are to be discovered. Table 1.5 sets forth those findings.

Once more it appears that political culture effects are minimal. As we move from absence to exclusive presence of each of the three strains of political culture hypothesized by Elazar, there is virtually no change in the perception among lobbyists that the nonpartisan space is shrinking in scope in their respective state legislatures.

What, then, can be concluded from the evidence collected in the survey about the effects of the psychological regions identified by Rentfrow and his associates? Is it perhaps differences in the modal personality types present in the states that might carry over into the operation of the state legislature? Are different scores on the three personality clusters perhaps associated with perceptions of the breaking down of norms and the shrinkage of the nonpartisan space? There is considerable evidence that personality traits are related to economic and political preferences

Table 1.4.
Elazar Hybrid Classifications and Erosion of Legislative Norms

	None	Secondary	Primary	Exclusive
Traditionalistic Political Culture Presence				
Not Occurring	17.1%	14.8%	14.3%	17.4%
Uncertain	14.8%	11.5%	7.1%	18.1%
Occurring	65.0%	70.5%	75.7%	61.8%
	Chi-Square = 10.42 (p = 0.318)			
Individualistic Political Culture Presence				
Not Occurring	14.9%	21.5%	12.8%	15.1%
Uncertain	14.6%	12.5%	15.3%	13.2%
Occurring	67.3%	63.6%	67.7%	71.7%
	Chi-Square = 12.579 (p = 0.183)			
Moralistic Political Culture Presence				
Not Occurring	16.9%	10.8%	22.5%	15.3%
Uncertain	13.8%	13.9%	13.9%	14.8%
Occurring	66.5%	71.7%	61.9%	65.6%
	Chi-Square = 14.711 (p = 0.099)			

(Becker et al., 2012), so our expectations are heightened that personality regions may provide a partial explanation for the cross-state differences documented in our survey of lobbyists' perceptions of civility levels in their respective state legislatures. Table 1.6 presents findings for the top two ranking states in each of the three clusters; if personality regions are a key to our understanding, we should observe differences in how lobbyists working in states differing in personality region location perceive norm weakening and the reduction of nonpartisan space.

Table 1.5.
Elazar Hybrid Classifications and the Reduction of Nonpartisan Space

	None	Secondary	Primary	Exclusive
Traditionalistic Political Culture Presence				
Fewer	52.5%	59.6%	62.3%	59.1%
Same	30.9%	25.0%	20.8%	24.2%
More	16.6%	15.4%	16.9%	16.7%
Chi-Square = 8.502 (p = 0.204)				
Individualistic Political Culture Presence				
Fewer	55.8%	53.2%	57.4%	57.1%
Same	26.5%	31.3%	27.0%	22.4%
More	17.7%	15.5%	15.7%	20.4%
Chi-Square = 3.827 (p = 0.700)				
Moralistic Political Culture Presence				
Fewer	59.0%	59.2%	50.6%	49.4%
Same	23.8%	24.0%	34.5%	31.7%
More	17.2%	15.9%	14.9%	18.9%
Chi-Square = 12.103 (p = 0.060)				

Here we finally see some variation across states; however, that variation is as great within the clusters as across them. The two states that define the clusters as primary archetype cases are, in most comparisons, quite different. Clearly, there are things going on in these six states that are accounting for the large variation in both the norm weakening and the nonpartisan space shrinkage dimensions of interest. What happens when all 48 states for which the three personality cluster scores are available are ranked, and the results of the survey of lobbyists are ranked on the norm weakening and nonpartisan space shrinkage variables, and a rank order correlation for each measure is calculated? Is there any effect of note of any one of the three personality configuration regions on those results? The results of this analysis are displayed in Table 1.7.

When a more detailed analysis of the potential effects of psychological region are explored, it appears evident that this version of a political culture test once more reveals little in the way of predictive power for the effects of political culture.

PRINCIPAL CONCLUSIONS

This preliminary exploration of political culture effects reveals that while Elazar's political culture construct might have proven a useful tool for gaining insight into cross-state differences in political life in many areas,

---

Table 1.6.
Psychological Regions and Lobbyists' Perception of Norm Weakening and Less Nonpartisan Space

	Cluster 1 (MN & IA)		Cluster 2 (CA & OR)		Cluster 3 (NY & PA)	
	Friendly/Conventional		Relaxed/Creative		Temperamental/Uninhibited	
	MN	IA	CA	OR	NY	PA
% Opining Norm Weakening	69.2%	90.0%	29.2%	10.3%	11.1%	4.3%
% Opining Shrinkage of the Nonpartisan Space	30.8%	76.0%	36.7%	62.7%	53.8%	63.6%

that of legislative civil discourse in not one of them. The adverse impact of contemporary hyperpolarization on American political life is present in U.S. state legislatures regardless of the historical legacy of their political culture; states with varying degrees of moralistic, individualistic, and traditionalistic heritages are equally likely to be seen by their respective state legislative lobbyists as experiencing a weakening of norms and customs supportive of civil discourse. Likewise, the states' legislatures are viewed by lobbyists in each type of state political culture setting as experiencing a shrinkage in the nonpartisan space in which active bipartisan problemsolving is taking place.

Groups and organizations such as the National Institute for Civil Discourse, Common Sense America, and the faith community associations collaborating in the *Golden Rule 2020* effort—those being the National Council of Churches, the National Association of Evangelicals, the Presbyterian Church USA, the Evangelical Lutheran Church in America, the American Baptist Churches USA, the Mormon Women for Ethical Government, and the U.S. Conference of Catholic Bishops—are finding that they need to promote civil discourse throughout the country. The problems in getting back to "politics as usual" associated with the current divisive state of political affairs are not relegated to state legislatures alone; they can be witnessed in many aspects of our civic life and civil society. In all sixteen states in which the NICD has been asked to initiate civil

Table 1.7.

Rank Order Correlation[1] Between Rentfrow et al. Clusters and the Norm Weakening and Nonpartisan Space Shrinkage Variables

	Cluster 1	Cluster 2	Cluster 3
	Friendly & Conventional	Relaxed & Creative	Temperamental & Uninhibited
Norms Breaking Down	0.166 (n.s.)	-0.179 (n.s.)	-0.120 (n.s.)
Areas of Nonpartisan Space Shrinking	-0.024 (n.s.)	0.126 (n.s.)	0.026 (n.s.)

[1]States were ranked according to cluster membership for each psychological region in Rentfrow et al. As states were ranked cardinally, the correlation values were multiplied by negative one to reflect correct relationship.

discourse dialogues in state legislatures since 2012, the work undertaken has been challenging, time-consuming, and subject to false starts, as well as to delays occasioned by changes in party leadership, unexpected election outcomes, and changeover in state-based points of contact. These interventions have taken place in virtually each of the different hybrid types of political culture settings depicted in Chart 1.1 (Shaffer, 2019).

In a recent publication in *Science*, a group of researchers report data on the phenomenon of partisan sectarianism whereby people of opposing parties come to view opponents not as honorable adversaries, but rather as enemies whose motives are ill and whose assumptions about reality are corrupted. These attributions are associated with willful distancing and disinclination to listen and engage across partisan lines on the part of citizens. The researchers report that data collected in 12 countries over more than a decade indicate that this phenomenon is the most pronounced in the U.S. and is increasingly characteristic of cross-party attributions (Finkel et al., 2020). It is likely that this deepening of the divide between Democrats and Republicans is taking place in all areas of the country, whether moralistic, individualistic, or traditionalistic in political cultural heritage.

Future analyses of the data collected during the national state legislative lobbyists' survey will be looking at other state-level factors that might predict the extent to which state legislatures are viewed by lobbyists as experiencing a weakening of norms and customs relating to civility in conduct and a diminution of the nonpartisan space within which bipartisan problem-solving normally takes place. Such factors as the level of professionalization of the legislature, the degree of partisan polarization, the presence of term limits affecting legislative leaders' levels of experience, the extent of gerrymandering done in the drawing of district lines, the proportion of women in legislative ranks and in leadership roles, the extent of an urban/rural divide among legislators, the presence of substantial foreign-born and immigrant populations, the extent of inequality in levels of income (GINI index), and the degree of diversity of the state legislature vis-à-vis racial and ethnic subpopulations will be investigated as potential sources of civility and incivility in state legislative life.

Members of the research team will also be looking at different types of lobbyists to determine whether they differ among themselves in their perceptions of their respective state legislatures. For example, do former state legislators who are now lobbyists differ in their assessments from lobbyists who have not had that experience? Does length of time as a lobbyist affect their perceptions? Are public agency legislative liaison personnel viewing the legislative process differently from advocates for private industry and state-regulated commercial interests such as electric power generators and distributors? Are women lobbyists seeing the situation differently from their male counterparts? These and additional topics of research will be forthcoming in due course. In addition to the survey results being analyzed, the comments and often extended commentaries received from lobbyists are being coded for major themes and subthemes for further analysis.

In the case of political culture, it can be safely concluded that none of the three hypothesized strains of political culture heritage is acting to buffer the effects of incivility in our national politics as played out in Congress and in Congressional/Executive branch relations. Rather than having some type of selective impact, it would appear from the findings reported here that Washington DC-based political incivility has achieved ubiquitous penetration into our state legislatures and the political life of our 50 states.

REFERENCES

Becker, A., Deckers, T., Dohmen, T., Falk, A., & Kosse, F. (2012). The relationship between economic preferences and psychological personality measures. *Annual Review of Economics, 4*(1), 453–478.

Benjamin, F., & Lovrich, N. P. (2011). The state legislature. In C. W. Clayton & N. P. Lovrich (Eds.), *Governing Washington: Politics and government in the Evergreen State* (pp. 207–231). Washington State University Press.

Donovan, T. (2018). Elections in Washington. In C. W. Clayton, T. Donovan, & N. P. Lovrich (Eds.), *Governing the Evergreen State: Political life in Washington* (pp. 23–43). Washington State University Press.

Elazar, D. (1966). *American federalism: A view from the states.* Thomas Y. Crowell.

Elazar, D. (1970). *Cities of the prairie: The metropolitan frontier and American politics.* Basic Books.

Elazar, D. (1982). Steps in the study of political culture. In J. Kincaid (Ed.), *Political culture, public policy, and the American states* (pp. 223–232). Institute for the Study of Human Issues.

Elazar, D. (1984). *American federalism.* Third ed. Harper & Row.

Elazar, D. (1987). *Exploring federalism.* University of Alabama Press.

Elazar, D. (1994). *The American mosaic: The impact of space, time, and culture on American politics.* Westview Press.

Erickson, R. S., McIver, J. P., & Wright, G. C. (1987). State political culture and public opinion. *American Political Science Review, 81*(3), 797–813.

Finkel, E. J, Bail, C. A., Ditto, P. H., Iyengar, S., Klar, S., Mason, L., McGrath, M. C., Nyhan, B., Rand, D. G., Sitka, L. J., Tucker, J. A., VanBavel, J. J. Wang, C. S., & Druckman, J. N. (2020). Political sectarianism in America: A poisonous cocktail of othering, aversion, and moralization poses a threat to democracy. *Science, 370*(6516), 533–536.

Fisher, P., & Pratt, T. C. (2006). Political culture and the death penalty. *Criminal Justice Policy Review, 17*(1), 48–60.

Fowler, L., & Witt, S. (2019). State preemption of local authority: Explaining patterns of state adoption of preemption measures. *Publius, 49*(3), 540–559.

Hanson, R. (1980). Political culture, interparty competition and political efficacy in the American states. *Publius, 10*(2), 17–36.

Herzik, E. (1985). The legal-formal structuring of state politics: A cultural explanation. *Western Political Quarterly, 38*(3), 413–423.

Jackman, R. W., & Miller, R. A. (1996). A renaissance of political culture. *American Journal of Political Science, 40*(3), 632–360.

John, O. P., & Srivastava, S. (1999). The Big Five trait taxonomy: History, measurement and theoretical perspective. In L. A. Pervin & O. P. John (Eds.), *Handbook of personality: Theory and research* (2nd ed.) (pp. 102–139). Gilford Press.

Johnson, C. A. (1976). Political culture in American states: Elazar's formulation examined. *American Journal of Political Science, 20*(3), 491–509.

Joslyn, R. A. (1980). Manifestations of Elazar's political subcultures: State opinion and the content of political campaign advertising. *Publius, 10*(2), 37–58.

Kincaid, J. (1980). Political culture and the quality of urban life. *Publius, 10*(2), 89–110.

Kincaid, J. (1982). Introduction. In J. Kincaid (Ed.), *Political culture, public policy, and the American states* (3rd ed.) (pp. 3–15). ISHI Press.

Lieske, J. (1993). Regional subcultures of the United States. *Journal of Politics, 55*(4), 888–913.

Long, C., & Ammons, D. (2018). The governor and other statewide Executive. In C. W. Clayton, T. Donovan, & N. P. Lovrich (Eds.), *Governing the Evergreen State: Political life in Washington* (pp. 171–189). Washington State University Press.

Lovrich, N. P., Lutze, F. E., & Lovrich, N. R. (2014). Criminal justice policy and public safety in the American states: From rehabilitation to retribution. In R. G. Niemi & J. J. Dyck (Eds.), *Guide to state politics and policy* (pp. 355–365). SAGE/CQ Press.

Lovrich, N. P., Daynes, B. W., & Ginger, L. (1980). Public policy and the effects of historical-cultural phenomena: The case of Indiana. *Publius, 10*(2), 111–125.

Lovrich, N. P., Pierce, J. C., & Elway, H. S. (2018). Two Washingtons? Political culture in the Evergreen State. In C. W. Clayton, T. Donovan, & N. P. Lovrich (Eds.), *Governing the Evergreen State: Political life in Washington* (pp. 1–22). Washington State University Press.

Miller, D. Y., Barker, D. C., & Carman, C. J. (2006). Mapping the genome of American political subcultures: A proposed methodology and pilot study. *Publius, 36*(2), 303–315.

Moon, D. C., Pierce J. C., & Lovrich, N. P. (2001). Political culture in the urban West—Is it really different? A research note. *State and Local Government Review, 33*(3), 195–201.

Nardulli, P. F. (1990). Political subcultures in the American states: An empirical examination of Elazar's formulation. *American Politics Research, 18*(3), 287–315.

Pierce, J. C., Lovrich, N. P., & Budd, W. W. (2016). Social capital, institutional performance, and sustainability in Italy's regions: Still evidence of enduring historical effects? *The Social Science Journal, 53*(3), 271–281.

Pierce, J. C., Lovrich, N. P., & Elway, H. S. (2011). Washington's political culture. In C. W. Clayton & N. P. Lovrich (Eds.), *Governing Washington: Politics and Government in the Evergreen State* (pp. 1-19). Washington State University Press.

Polsby, N. (1984). Prospects for pluralism in the American federal system: Trends in unofficial public-sector intermediation. In R. Golembiewski & A. Wildavsky (Eds.), *The costs of federalism* (pp. 212–236). Transaction Publishers.

Putnam, R. D. (1993). *Making democracy work: Civic traditions in modern Italy.* Princeton University Press.

Putnam, R. D. (2000). *Bowling alone: The collapse and revival of American community.* Simon & Schuster.

Rentfrow, P. J., Gosling, S. D., Jokela, M., Stillwell, D. J., Kosinski, M., & Potter, J. (2013). Divided we stand: Three psychological regions of the United States and their political, economic, social and eealth correlates. *Journal of Personality and Social Psychology, 105*(6), 996–1012.

Ritt, L. G. (1974). Political cultures and political reform: A research note. *Publius, 4*(2), 127–133.

Rosenthal, A., & Moakley, M. (1984). *The political life of the American states.* Praeger.

Savage, R. L. (1981). Looking for political subcultures: A critique of the rummage-sale approach. *Political Research Quarterly, 34*(2), 331–336.

Sharkansky, I. (1969). The utility of Elazar's political culture: A research note. *Polity* 2(1): 66–83.

Sharp, E. B. (2005). Cities and subcultures: Exploring validity and predicting connections. *Urban Affairs Review, 41*(2), 132–156.

Sigelman, L. (1976). The curious case of women in state and local government. *Social Science Quarterly, 56*(4), 591–604.

Steel, B. S., Henkels, M., & Clucus, R. A. (Eds.). (2005). *Oregon politics and government: Progressives versus conservative populists.* University of Nebraska Press.

Welch, S., & Peters, J. G. (1980). State political culture and the attitudes of state senators toward social, economic welfare, and corruption issues. *Publius, 10*(1), 59–67.

Wildavsky, A. (1998). *Federalism and political culture.* Transaction Publishers.

Wirt, F. (1980). Does control follow the dollar? School policy, state-local linkages, and political culture. *Publius, 10*(1), 69–88.

Wohlenberb, E. H. (1980). Correlates of equal rights amendment ratification. *Social Science Quarterly, 60*(4), 676–684.

Woodard, C. (2011). *American nations: A history of the eleven rival regional cultures of North America.* Viking.

CHAPTER TWO

The Connection between Legislative Professionalism and Legislative Civility

William D. Schreckhise
Francis A. Benjamin

INTRODUCTION[1]

This chapter examines the link between state legislative civility and legislative professionalism. We do this with an eye to the question of whether the extent to which civility pervades a state legislature can be attributable to legislative careerism, institutionalization, and lawmaking capacity. We posit that more professionalized state legislatures are likely to be more civil than more amateur state legislatures. We suspect this to be the case because one key component of professionalization—the amount of compensation a legislator receives in the form of salary—can either promote or be a roadblock to legislative careerism. Legislators who earn more money while in this role may see their position as a state legislator more as a career than as a secondary avocation. The resulting careerism could promote civility for a couple of reasons. Legislators who are better paid may be less likely to become dependent on interest groups, to be subject to bribery or undue influence, or to seek higher office, and be more likely to stay in the state legislature for longer periods of time and thereby build their own expertise and network of contacts and confidential sources. As a result, they would have less incentive to act uncivilly and risk precluding the opportunity to work with other legislators and interest groups to collaborate on legislation of mutual interest. They may also focus more on policymaking and constituent service out of a sense of wishing to earn their pay rightfully. By contrast, service in an amateur legislature where pay is low is more of a burden for its members, manifesting in shorter stays in office and less of a sense of needing to maintain good relations with a wide range of persons and interests that might be of service over the long term. This, in turn, plausibly leads to less need for the demonstration of civility among the members of the amateur legislative body.

We examine this potential link between professionalism and civility via a survey of over 1,000 lobbyists—a combination of solo practitioners, lobby firm employees, associational representatives, nonprofit group advocates, and public agency legislative liaison officers—who work in each of the 50 U.S. state legislatures. In the online and mail survey questionnaires used to collect data, we asked the lobbyists how civil they believed the legislators in their own state to be. We asked them to compare their own state legislature to legislatures in other states, to the legislature in their own state 10 years ago, and to the U.S. Congress. We surveyed lobbyists because, as a group, they are among the people best positioned to evaluate the civility of their state legislatures. Their frequent contact with individual legislators and their detailed knowledge of the dynamics of state government and the relationship obtaining between and among state legislators provides for the rendering of informed opinions and the recording of insightful comments and commentaries (encouraged in the survey questionnaire).

From these impressions held by the lobbyists, we construct an *index of civility* for each state. We then examine the link between various characteristics that scholars have used in the past to distinguish more professionalized state legislatures from more amateur ones to determine the extent to which legislative professionalization is linked to civility. Importantly, we examine which of the key elements of our professionalization measure—i.e., salary, staffing support, and session length—are related to higher levels of civility as assessed by informed judgments rendered by our lobbyist respondents.

THE PROFESSIONALIZATION OF STATE LEGISLATURES AND ITS CONSEQUENCES

For much of the last five decades, some state legislatures have consciously sought to improve their own institutional capacities for governance (Rosenthal, 1996). These efforts have included increasing compensation for legislators, moving from "old world" citizen legislatures to modern professionalized legislative chambers, the latter meeting annually with longer sessions, and even in some cases meeting year-round. In the years following World War II, legislative committees in many states began to see the addition of more legislative staff support for carrying out their work; individual legislators in some cases could even enjoy the help of personal and district staff in carrying out their legislative duties. The compensation for state legislators was increased in many states, and most state legislatures began to offer other important employment benefits such as per diem pay, travel allocations, retirement benefits, and health insurance.

This movement toward greater professionalization caught the attention of a good number of state politics researchers. As Bowen and Greene (2014) note, "Few concepts in the field have received as much attention as the transformation of some state legislatures from 'horse and buggy, 18th century anachronisms' (Mooney, 1995, p. 47) to institutions of high capacity, equipped with financial resources and staff, full-time sessions, and attractive legislative compensation packages" (Bowen and Greene, 2014, p. 278). Reformers advocated for greater legislative professionalization in the postwar years in order to deal with the heightened demands that arose from the larger role that state governments were coming to play in the maturation of the welfare state and the broadening of the social safety net. These developments included such features as longer sessions, more interim activities, and better pay for legislators (Bowen and Greene, 2014, p. 280). In fact, the very concept of state legislative professionalization has been used as a marker of legislative maturation—with some scholars noting that the term "refers to the development of [a state's] legislative capacity" (Berry et al., 2000, p. 859; see also Hibbing, 1999).

Several researchers have examined the consequences of professionalization with respect to some noteworthy outcomes. Squire (1992), for example, examined whether professionalized legislatures tended to have more diverse memberships in terms of race, sex, and occupational diversity. Fiorina (1994) noted that professionalization in state legislatures is related to the partisan composition of state legislatures; that is, the higher the salary a state pays its legislators, the more Democrats are serving in the state legislature. Gamm and Kousser (2010) found, perhaps relatedly, that states that pay their legislators higher salaries are more likely to see legislation focusing on the routing of benefits to legislators' districts. Some researchers have also reported that legislative professionalization plays a role in rates of incumbent reelection (Berry et al., 2000) and in the success of legislative bodies in their bargainings with state governors (Kousser and Phillips, 2009). Maestas (2000) and Lax and Phillips (2012) have reported that states that have more professionalized legislatures are inclined to be more responsive to public opinion. Other researchers have found levels of legislative professionalization to be related to several other matters of interest, including the enactment of stricter regulations for lobbyists (Opheim, 1991) and the presence of more state laws that preempt local-level ordinances on a number of issues ranging from employment practices and environmental regulations to gun laws (Fowler and Witt, 2019).

Although legislative professionalism has been linked to a variety of legislative outputs and characteristics in prior scholarship, it remains unknown whether legislative professionalization is linked to legislative civility. In the following section we explain why we suspect that such a link might exist.

PROFESSIONALIZATION AND CIVILITY

We posit that more professionalized state legislatures may produce more civility in comparison to less professionalized legislatures for two distinct reasons. First, we strongly anticipate that more professionalized legislatures—those characterized as providing better compensation and other professional benefits—will be more likely to be composed of lower and upper house members who view legislative service as a career, one in which acting in a civil manner brings benefits vis-à-vis continued potential for timely, mutually beneficial collaboration with other legislators to gain passage of legislation of shared interest. Second, a more professionalized legislature features enhanced lawmaking capacity; longer sessions and better staff support lead legislators to craft better-informed policies to be pointed to when seeking reelection. In concentrating on making good policy and being able to point to that accomplishment, there is less need to "make a name for themselves" by demeaning political opponents uncivilly for the sake of attracting public attention.

Careerism

We posit that more professionalized legislatures are composed of legislators who are more career-oriented as professional legislators, which in turns leads to more civil behavior benefitting a seasoned public official. Why is there reason to suspect that there is a link among legislative profes-sionalization, career-mindedness, and legislative civility? To provide an answer to this question, we begin with some assumptions related to the legislators themselves. First, we assume along with Mayhew (1974) that, as is the case with members of Congress, state legislators in our 50 state legislatures desire reelection. What is more, since state legislatures often serve as the "farm team" for higher office, legislators as a group may also desire higher office (Fiorina, 1994, p. 304). Second, we assume legislators use the tools at their disposal that can either facilitate reelection to their current position or help them attain higher office. They use their status as legislators to stake out public positions, claim credit for successful legislation, issue blame for bad legislation, and create policy responsive to expressed needs and preferences (Fenno, 1978).

As Carey et al. (2000, p. 683) note, the concept of professionalization itself can be expressed as "the degree to which service in a state legislative chamber represents a full-time, lucrative, and prestigious career." As such, the more an individual legislator thinks of his or her office as his or her main job, and not merely an interesting hobby or stepping-stone, the less likely that person is to behave in an unprofessional, uncivil manner. Service as an underpaid state legislator is less attractive to politicians over the long term than service as a well-paid legislator. Legislators earning lower pay may engage in more aggressive and hence more uncivil behavior in order to make a name for themselves and become better-known can-didates for Congress or another higher office among their co-partisans. In fact, Berry (2000) and his colleagues found that more professional-ized legislatures do indeed tend to have a greater number of long-serving members. They note in this regard that "professionalization changes both the incentives and capabilities of legislators because it gives them resources (e.g., money, perquisites, staffers, information) that makes a long career in the legislature attractive" (Berry et al., 2000, 860). At the same time, it provides the "electoral resources that members may use to insulate themselves from changing political tides" and make a long career pos-sible.[2] Indeed, past research has found more professionalized legislatures tend to experience less turnover among their members (Rosenthal, 1974; Calvert, 1979). This notion is reinforced by Squire's (1992) finding that more professionalized legislatures tend to have higher concentrations of members who identify their own occupation as that of "legislator" as opposed to attorney, business owner, rancher or farmer, and the like. Along somewhat similar lines, Carey and his colleagues (2000) found that larger legislative salaries, more so than other resources, accounted for higher rates of incumbent reelections in state legislatures.

Institutionalization

We posit that more professionalized legislatures will have stronger norms against uncivil behavior. Nelson Polsby (1968) noted that the U.S. House of Representatives evolved over time from the raucous maelstroms of the early days of the Republic—when fisticuffs were not uncommon—to a legislature that was at the time of his writing in 1968 far more civil in its operations. He notes in this connection that "the history of the House does suggest that there has been a growth in the rather tame virtues of reciprocity, courtesy, and predictability in legislative life since the turn of the [twentieth] century" (Polsby, 1968, p. 167), a change in organizational culture that can be linked to the increasing institutionalization of the chamber. He then goes on to cite a former member of the U.S. House of Representatives who wrote about the degree of courtesy emanating from Congress in 1962 thusly:

> One's overwhelming first impression as a member of Congress is the aura of friendliness that surrounds the life of a congressman. No wonder that "few die and none resign." Almost everyone is unfailingly polite and courteous. Window washers, clerks, senators—it cuts all ways. We live in a cocoon of good feeling.[3]

Moreover, as Polsby notes, this increase in courteous behavior occurred at a time when Congress itself became a career destination. Since the mid-1800s, the average tenure of members of Congress has increased steadily. Unlike previous periods, after 1900 the Speakers of the U.S. House of Representatives typically served in that position until death or retirement, first coming to it only after having served several terms in the House. Additionally, it was not until 1856 that members of Congress began to receive annual salaries, and only in the 1860s did those salaries increase consistently above the inflation-adjusted 2020 amount of $75,000 (see Congressional Research Service, 2020; Sahr, 2020). Of course, these observations involve significant generalizations covering large tracts of time. Nonetheless, it is without a doubt the case that American politicians had come to view both chambers of Congress as potential destinations for a political career in far more favorable terms by the mid-1900s than they did in the mid-1800s. As this transformation occurred, so did the levels of pay and the levels of civility in Congress.

Emphasis on lawmaking

This brings us to the second principal reason why professionalization and civility may be linked. When the resources are available to legislators to reap the benefits of their positions as lawmakers, they will use these resources to gain recognition by working with other legislators to create important policy and serve their constituents' needs effectively in their district "service work" and delivery of benefits to their home districts/states. As Berry and his colleagues (2000, p. 862) note:

> resources enhance [legislators'] ability to achieve the goal of a long career. Large budgets permit extensive constituency service. Strong staff support enhances the governing capacity of legislatures and thus the ability of members to claim credit for policy initiatives. Both effective governance and constituency service heighten the popularity of members and their chances of reelection….These advantages contribute to their public visibility and name recognition, which increase their probability of winning re-election.

This sentiment is reinforced by Maestas (2000) and Lax and Phillips (2012), who found that legislators who serve in more professionalized legislatures tended to be more responsive to the broader public opinion of their states than those serving in less-professionalized legislatures. Gamm and Kousser (2010) found that legislators who serve in more professionalized assemblies were more likely to engage in constituent service, or at least service of a type, in the form of authoring and cosponsoring more locally focused legislation. Holbrook and Tidmarch (1991) found the presence of personal staff likely facilitated such constituency service to the point where it benefited the members when running for reelection. Cox and Morgenstern (1993, 1995) found that members of legislatures with larger state operating budgets were more likely to be reelected.

To be sure, the empirical evidence linking institutionalization, professionalism, and civility in state legislatures is, at best, somewhat mixed and less than fully developed. In their survey work on long-serving state legislators, Thompson and his colleagues (1996) found that veteran legislators from more professionalized state legislatures reported that their colleagues were more likely to run against their own institutions when seeking reelection than was the case in citizen legislatures. They also reported that individuals serving in more professionalized legislatures had less of a commitment to the institutions in which they served than citizen legislators. However, there was no difference in the responses from those veterans serving in the two types of legislatures when asked about their colleagues' commitment to learning and adhering to the mores of the institution, playing by the rules, and getting along civilly with the other members. Thus, at the very least, this useful but indirect evidence suggests that a negative relationship might exist between professionalization and civility. We argue below, however, why we believe this is not the case.

The Components of Professionalization and Civility

We contend there is sufficient evidence to suggest that three components of professionalism—compensation, staff support, and session length—could each have different consequences for behaviors related to civility (Kousser and Phillips, 2009; Gamm and Kousser, 2010; Bowen and Greene, 2014). Woods and Baranowski (2006) found greater resources available to legislators in the form of expenditures and staff provide legislators with greater influence on state agencies, while the careerism associated with higher legislative salaries makes them less influential. As such, we consider it possible that different aspects of professionalization could affect legislative civility in different ways. The first suggests professionalism could have a positive impact on careerism; that is, higher levels of compensation may make the full-time nature of a modern state legislator's job worthwhile for a longer period than would be the case for service in a citizen legislature featuring limited compensation (Rosenthal, 1996). As Squire (2007, pp. 213–214) reasons, better pay for legislators "allows them to focus their energies exclusively on their legislative activities rather than having to juggle them with the demands of their regular occupations." Higher rates of pay for legislators could make staying in the job as a state legislator more attractive for individuals, and, conversely, make the prospects of moving on to a higher office comparably less attractive. As a result, we suspect that legislators in states with higher levels of legislative compensation would be less likely as a group to try to make public names for themselves by engaging in uncivil behavior. We are less sure about the role that staff support can play. On the one hand, more staff support allows legislators to concentrate on earning a reputation as crafters of good legislation, allowing them to gain notice through the good deed of statecraft; on the other hand, it could also allow the legislators to engage in more political infighting with the information they receive from staff. We are similarly unsure about the role that longer legislative sessions play. Longer sessions could facilitate the making of good legislation. They could also provide more opportunities to engage in political infighting simply because legislators' time in the high-visibility political arena is longer. It is commonplace for legislative sessions to begin with proclamations of commitment to bipartisanship and problem solving across the aisle, only to witness bitter divisions toward the ends of sessions as serious disagreements arise, patience runs out, and steadfast stands are proclaimed by opponents.

DATA AND HYPOTHESES

Dependent Variable

It is important to note that we measure civility as *perceived* civility. To obtain the data for our measure we conducted an email and follow-up mail survey of samples of lobbyists registered with the 50 states. Names, email addresses, and physical addresses were obtained from Secretary of State offices, ethics commissions, and the like for all 50 states. Two hundred registered lobbyists selected at random from each state were then invited to participate via email in a Qualtrics online survey, with two waves of printed surveys being sent to the lobbyists surveyed via the U.S. Postal Service. We obtained over 1,200 usable responses with the online survey and two follow-up mailings combined, with many containing extensive comments on individual questions and commentaries on legislative affairs in their own states.

We constructed an indexed dependent variable composed of three measures in our survey. Respondents were asked to state their level of agreement with each of the following statements on a 10-point scale (with 10 being the highest level of agreement):

- My state legislature is more civil than other state legislatures.
- My state legislature is more civil than Congress.
- My state legislature is more civil than it was 10 years ago.

These three measures were then combined into an additive index, and that index serves as our primary dependent variable.[4]

Asking respondents to gauge the level of civility comparatively—with other state legislatures, with Congress, and with how civil the legislature was 10 years ago—provides us with a better measure than simply asking them if they thought their legislature was "civil" or "not civil." To do the latter would not provide the respondent with a measure against which to gauge their responses. To be sure, making comparisons with the past, Congress, or other state legislatures is inherently subjective. This is because there is no absolute measure of each legislature's civility over the ten years past, or of the levels of civility manifesting in Congress or other legislatures currently. However, we contend that by providing respondents with a set of yardsticks against which to compare their own state, the state legislative lobbyists surveyed can give us a good sense of their assessments of civility in their respective states. The mean values of the indexed dependent variable *Civility* are displayed in Figure 2.1.

Independent Variables

Our primary independent variable is the level of legislative professionalization, a measure composed of the three measures mentioned above: the level of compensation legislators in each state receive, the number of staff members per member, and the number of days in a year the state legislature is in session. These are the "three core components" (Squire, 2007; Bowen and Greene, 2014, p. 278; see also Opheim, 1991, p. 410) on which past research has relied to indicate the degree to which state legislatures are professionalized. Unlike some examinations of the role that professionalism can play in legislative dynamics which combine these traits into a single index of professionalization (e.g., Squire, 192; Maestas, 2000; Bowen and Greene, 2014), in this study we employ these measures of professionalization as separate independent variables along with the index. We do this because we suspect each of the three variables may have an independent impact on civility on its own. Serving in a legislative body providing better pay might make the job as a state legislator more attractive, and thus less likely to be viewed as a temporary stepping-stone to higher office or a means to build public recognition for the pursuit of extra-legislative goals and objectives.

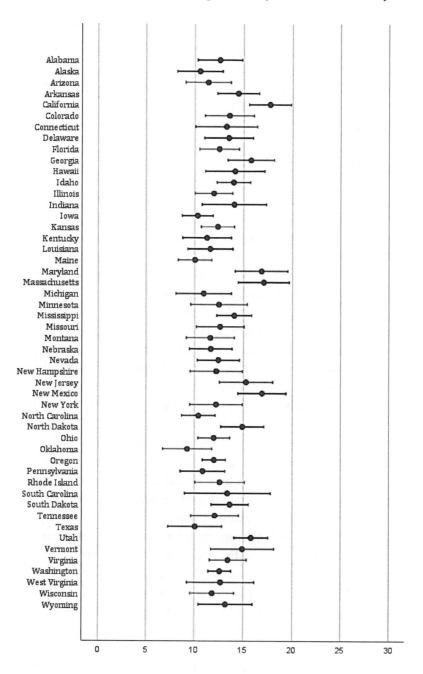

Figure 2.1. State Civility Index Means with 95% Cis.

Although longer sessions and better staff support could enable legislators to deliberate more effectively on important legislation, the longer calendar could invite more conflict and engender lasting enmities.

As was done by Bowen and Greene (2014) and Squire (1992), we include a measure of legislative compensation as reported via a survey published by the National Conference of State Legislature (2018). In some states, legislators receive their pay on a per diem basis only while the legislature is in session. In these cases, we calculated level of compensation by multiplying the per diem rate by the number of days the legislature was in session. For both salaried legislatures and legislatures that pay per diem rates, we calculated their compensation based on the 2017–2018 biennium (and divided by two). We normed these salary figures by dividing the total amount a legislator will earn in a year by the state's median income in 2018 dollars (U.S. Census Bureau, 2020). We report the compensation as a proportion of the median household income for the state to adjust for regional variations in regional living costs and to reflect the relative attractiveness of the legislators' salaries. This variable in our statistical models is labelled *Salary.*

We also include as a separate variable the per diem rates, calculated on the basis of the number of days the legislature was in session for the biennium (NCSL, 2018).[5] It is worth noting here that the National Conference of State Legislatures reports that states pay different per diem rates within some states, determined by the geographical location of legislators' homes; in some cases, those legislators who live in the state capital or in the county in which it is located are excluded from per diem compensation; in some cases, a lower rate is paid to those who live closer to the state capitol. Because this exclusion presumably affects a small portion of the total number of legislators, we include the maximum rate in our measure. Still other states tie their legislative per diem rate to the federal per diem rate. In these cases, we calculated reimbursement for lodging and food based on the location of the state capital, using information from the federal government's General Services Administration website (GSA 2020). In Michigan, legislators receive an allowance for the year as opposed to a daily set rate. In this case, we included the total annual amount allowable. In the states that have different rates for Senate and

House members, we averaged the two numbers. In some cases, legislators are paid per diem in the same way as state employees who are working on state business away from their home offices. Because this money is not paid to legislators at a per-day rate while they are taking part in a legislative session, we report these states has having no per diem. We also adjust this amount to reflect a percentage of the median household income for the state. This resulting variable is labelled *Per Diem.*

We include measures of the extent to which legislators receive fringe benefits. As Squire (2007) notes, some states, such as California, offer comparatively high salaries to their legislators, but since 1990 that state has ceased to provide retirement benefits. At the same time, state legislators in Texas receive little in terms of salary, yet are eligible to receive some rather generous retirement benefits after 12 years of service. We include a measure of whether legislators may participate in an optional retirement benefit program (or are required to do so) (NCSL, 2020). We include a measure that reflects the extent to which various forms of insurance—health, dental, vision, disability, and life insurance—are offered to state legislators. This is a six-point scale, with the value indicating the number of each of the forms of retirement benefits and insurance that are offered and at least partially paid for by the state for the legislators (NCSL, 2020).[6] This variable is labelled *Benefits.*

We also include a measure of session length. Since four states meet only once per biennium, we include in the variable *Length* the total number of days the legislature met for the 2017–2018 biennium as reported by the National Conference of State Legislature's state legislative calendar for the years 2017 and 2018. As Bowen and Greene (2010) did in their work, we include in the variable indicating the session length both the number of regular session days and the number of special session days for the biennium. The measure *Total Staff* includes the total number of staff members employed by the legislature, as either personal, district, or shared staff. We combine these into a single variable simply because the National Conference of State Legislatures reports them this way instead of reporting separately the number of pooled, individual, and district staff. In this measure we include both regular session staff and staff who work when the legislature is out of session.[7]

1. Control variables.

a) OPPORTUNITY. In order to explore the dimension of the opportunities for higher office enjoyed by state legislators in each state, we examined the number of total U.S. House seats available to the legislators as a group, following the example of Maestas (2000). The extent to which an individual legislator views his or her current job as a virtual stepping-stone to higher office will be influenced by the extent to which that person has any potential to reach higher office. It is important to note that this potential varies considerably across the 50 states. In the case of California, for example, the 53 U.S. House seats do not represent a substantially smaller number than the 120 seats in the two chambers of the California State Legislature. Numerically speaking, from the perspective of a California state assembly member, the likelihood of taking the next step to Congress is not particularly daunting. In contrast, for members of New Hampshire's General Court, the numbers are quite a bit more daunting. The state legislators in the 424-person New Hampshire legislature have only two U.S. House seats to serve as their potential desideratum. Accordingly, to consider the different opportunities for federal office we include in our models a measure we label *Opportunity*. This variable is the ratio of U.S. House seats to the total number of legislative seats for each state. A higher value reflects more opportunity to advance to the U.S. House of Representatives.

b) POLARIZATION. Much of the widespread concern regarding declining levels of civility in the U.S. has come with recognition of the ideological polarization of political elites at the national level (Boatright et al., 2019). Shor and McCarty (2011) note that growing ideological differences between the two national political parties have been reflected in similar differences among state legislators over the course of the preceding 15 years. As such, it is possible that states with more ideological polarization could have lower levels of civility. To account for this possibility, we include a measure of the ideological distance between the median ideological score for members of both political parties in each legislative chamber for each state, averaged across the two chambers in the state. These ideological distance scores for state legislators were developed by Shor and McCarty (2011), produced in part from survey data from state legislators, and developed similar to the way in which Poole and Rosenthal (1991, 1997) produced ideological scores for members of the

U.S. Congress. States with a higher score for the variable *Polarization* have more ideological distance between each party in the two chambers of their state legislatures than states with a lower score.

c) PARTY COMPETITION. It is possible a legislature's degree of perceived civility could be a function of the partisan composition of the legislature in which the lobbyists advocate. This can occur in a couple of ways. State legislatures that have a roughly even number of Democrats and Republicans serving in their chambers could see lower levels of civility because of the intensity of competition between the two parties—either to obtain majority party status for the minority, or to retain majority party status for the majority party. As Hinchliffe and Lee (2016, p. 173) note, "close competition for party control fosters partisan contentiousness, as legislators look for opportunities to criticize and embarrass their opponents." From this heightened competition perspective, states that have roughly equal numbers in their chambers might produce more conflict and less civility, as strategy defection is a concern for the leaders of both parties. At the same time, states dominated by a single party may experience less conflict simply because the costs associated with uncivil behavior are not likely to be compensated by potential benefits. Viewed from the perspective of a legislator from a minority party, there is little to gain from being hostile toward the majority party that controls access to the many avenues to enhanced name recognition and public credit for favorable legislative actions.

However, it is possible that the opposite could hold true; that is, legislatures that are dominated by a single party could, in fact, be among the least civil. This might be the case because states with roughly equal proportions of Democrats and Republicans must work together in order to pass legislation and produce a balanced budget. In this case, the majority party cannot count on a ready-made majority able to pass components of the majority party's legislative agenda if any of its members votes with the minority party. Correspondingly, according to this view, majority parties in states that are single-party dominated have no incentive to reach across the aisle to garner minority party support for their legislative goals, and the degree of interparty competition would thus be inversely related to levels of civility.

To examine these possibilities, we include a measure of legislative interparty competition that we label *Competition*. This index is calculated by determining the absolute value of the difference between the number of Democrats and Republicans for each state's legislative chambers, divided by the total number of members in each chamber and averaging the number between the states' two chambers (see Lax and Phillips, 2012, p. 159 for a similar measure). We excluded Nebraska because of its unicameral make-up and officially nonpartisan legislature. The original data for our measure were obtained from the National Conference of State Legislatures (NCSL, 2018). States with a value closer to 1 have more numerical parity between the parties in the states' two chambers; states with values closer to 0 are more single-party dominant.

d) Turnover. The varying levels of civility also could be a product of turnover. Legislatures with a large influx of new members could bring with them a weakened sense of decorum that is, in turn, a product of the newer members' ignorance or lack of genuine appreciation for the courtesy norm described above in our discussion of Nelson Polsby's work on Congress. To account for this, we include the variable *Turnover*, which is a measure of the percentage of the total number of seats occupied by new members in the two years of the 2017–2018 biennium, averaged across the states' two chambers (Council of State Governments, 2018, p. 33; Council of State Governments, 2019, p. 35). Additionally, the diversity of the legislature could also play a role in shaping the extent to which it is perceived to be civil. We include a measure for the percentage of the chambers' members consisting of women and a measure for the percentage consisting of racial or ethnic minorities. The data for the variable *%Women* are from 2018, and the data for *%Minority* are from the most recent year available, 2018.

Finally, we include some measures for the survey respondents themselves as control variables. Their personal characteristics could have an impact on the extent to which they perceive their states' legislatures as civil or lacking in civility. These personal characteristics include the lobbyists' age, sex, race/ethnicity, and the number of years they have served as a lobbyist in that state. The summary values for the variables in our models are included in Table 2.1.

RESULTS

To test the relationship between our independent variable and our indexed dependent variable measuring perceived civility we ran multilevel models, with our respondents, the state legislative lobbyists, being nested in states. The results of our analysis are presented in Tables 2.2 and 2.3. Model 1 includes variables that are specific only to our measures related to professionalization. The results noted are not consistent with some of our expectations. The variables for salary level, session length, benefits, and staff do not produce statistically significant results. The only variable in Model 1 that produces significant results, *Per Diem*, goes in the opposite direction to that predicted, indicating that states that pay their legislators

Table 2.1. Summary Statistics

Variable	Mean	Std. Dev.	Min	Max
Independent variable				
Civility	12.78	4.96	3.00	27.00
Dependent variables				
State level				
Salary	0.49	0.36	0.00	1.52
Length	294.27	192.59	88.00	730.00
Per Diem	0.52	0.41	0.00	2.07
Benefits	4.08	1.84	0.00	6.00
Staff	4.58	3.62	0.35	17.51
Opportunity	0.07	0.08	0.01	0.44
Polarization	3.50	1.04	1.56	6.87
Competition	0.70	0.20	0.27	0.97
Turnover	25.06	9.81	6.00	61.50
%Women	26.43	7.50	11.10	40.00
%Minority	16.32	10.69	1.00	49.00
Moralistic	0.45	0.50	0.00	1.00
Individualistic	0.26	0.44	0.00	1.00
Population	7.13	8.00	0.58	39.56
Diversity	31.05	13.95	6.85	63.17
Per Capita GDP	5.29	0.91	3.44	7.20
Individual level				
Years	15.48	10.89	0.00	55.00
Age	4.69	1.47	1.00	7.00
Woman	0.41	0.55	0.00	7.00
Republican	0.30	0.46	0.00	1.00
Minority	0.09	0.28	0.00	1.00

lower per diem rates have higher rates of civility. Thus far, it appears that professionalism is at best weakly related to civility, and the nature of the relationship goes in the opposite direction to what we expected.

Model 2 includes results from the broader range of measures that are related to the other characteristics of the legislature. When we include these measures, statistically significant results emerge for our professionalization-related measures. Specifically, legislators' salaries are now positively related, indicating that states that pay their legislators higher salaries have

Table 2.2. Models of Perceived Civility

	Model 1		Model 2	
	Coef.	S.E.	Coef.	S.E.
Fixed effects				
Intercept	13.458***	0.739	15.094***	0.924
State				
Salary	2.123	1.287	4.145***	0.927
Per Diem	-1.580*	0.791	-1.433**	0.530
Benefits	-0.079	0.159	-0.236*	0.116
Length	-0.003	0.002	-0.004**	0.001
Staff	0.073	0.096	-0.144	0.109
Opportunity			-0.143	5.744
Polarization			0.749**	0.255
Competition			-5.846***	1.112
Turnover			-0.100***	0.020
%Women			0.074*	0.031
%Minority			0.066**	0.021
Random effects				
Intercept		2.211		0.000
Residual		22.141		22.131
No. of respondents		853		812
No. of states		48		44
LL		-2554.9639		-2409.5533
df		8		14
AIC		5125.928		4847.107
BIC		5163.918		4912.900

Note: The indexed variable Civility is the dependent variable in each model.
*p<.05; **p<.01; ***p<.001.

legislatures rated as more civil. Additionally, legislatures with longer sessions are less civil. Contrary to our expectations, legislatures that provide their members with more generous benefits packages are less civil, as are states that pay their legislators higher per diem rates.

Five additional significant results emerge from the additional legislature-related measures we include in Model 2. Perhaps contrary to popular wisdom, legislatures with higher degrees of ideological polarization between the two main political parties in fact saw *higher* levels of reported civility (we discuss this finding in greater detail in our conclusion). State legislatures with more numerically even party distributions in their chambers, as well as states with lower turnover of their memberships, were also perceived by state legislative lobbyists as more civil. Additionally, states with higher proportions of women and members of racial/ethnic minority groups also received higher civility ratings from state legislative lobbyists.

As we mention above, we were uncertain about our expectations regarding the relationship between a legislature's session length and the degree to which it would be rated as civil. The results presented in Model 2 show that states with legislatures employing longer sessions are rated as less civil. It is important to note that past research has linked longer sessions with lower public ratings of legislatures (Squire, 1993), a finding that could have relevance for perceptions of civility. As Squire points out regarding states with longer sessions:

> [They] tend to be found in larger and more economically and socially diverse states. This means they are likely to be asked to handle more complex issues and to take more initiatives, which can make people less favorable toward them, even without having to pay much attention. Because professionalized legislatures are likely to have more expected of them, they are apt to disappoint people. (Squire, 1993, p. 488)

In order to be able to take into proper account the possibility that lobbyists' ratings of legislative civility could be explained by a similar dynamic, we include in Model 3 measures that reflect the economic size and racial and ethnic diversity of each state. We include in our models 3 and 4 the variable *State GDP,* a measure of the state's per capita gross domestic product. We also include a measure of *Diversity,* which is a measure of the percentage of individuals in the state who identify racially as non-White or ethnically as Hispanic.

We also include two measures for political culture. It is possible a state's political culture could play a role in shaping the degree to which legislatures are civil. As Elazar (1972) noted, residents in states with moralistic political cultures view public service as a higher calling, and thus those who serve may engage in less uncivil behavior. As such, we include one variable if the state has a moralistic political culture, and another if it has traditionalistic political culture.

In Model 3, the coefficients for the variables for salary, per diem, and session length remain significant and in the same direction as they were in Model 2. Regarding the concern we express pertaining to the session length variable, the addition of the state economic and diversity variables (*Per Capita GDP* and *Diversity*) in Model 3 does not alter the relationship between a legislature's session length and the degree of perceived civility. In other words, the expectation of longer sessions in states with more diverse economies and more diverse citizenries does not mitigate the extent to which legislatures with longer sessions are generally rated as being less civil. The variables for party competition and turnover remain significant, as does the variable indicating the racial and ethnic diversity of the legislature (*%Minority*). Neither of the variables reflecting state political culture is shown to be a statistically significant factor in Model 3.

Finally, in Model 4 we present results that include several variables related to the respondents themselves. We do this to take into proper account the possibility that different types of individuals may rate their legislatures differently regarding civility, which in turn could have an impact on our findings from models 1 through 3. In fact, we find that older and female state legislative lobbyists give their legislatures, *ceteris paribus*, lower ratings for their respective state legislatures, while Republicans give higher ratings. The variables for legislative salary and session length remain significant, as do the variables indicating turnover and competition. The value for the coefficient indicating the degree of political polarization is again significant and positive, indicating that the more highly polarized legislatures are rated as having higher degrees of civility. As was the case in the previous three models, the coefficient for the variable indicating the proportion of the legislature composed of racial minorities was significant and positive again in Model 4.

Table 2.3. More Models of Perceived Civility

	Model 3		Model 4	
	Coef.	S.E.	Coef.	S.E.
Fixed effects				
Intercept	14.310***	1.476	15.099	1.571
State				
Salary	3.931***	1.032	4.121***	1.015
Per Diem	-1.195*	0.561	-0.890	0.553
Benefits	-0.185	0.122	-0.222	0.121
Length	-0.004*	0.002	-0.004*	0.002
Staff	-0.111	0.131	-0.177	0.130
Opportunity	8.369	10.328	10.745	10.161
Polarization	0.526	0.290	0.622*	0.284
Competition	-5.465***	1.442	-5.192***	1.434
Turnover	-0.092***	0.024	-0.103***	0.023
%Women	0.043	0.042	0.052	0.042
%Minority	0.125*	0.056	0.128*	0.055
Population	-0.112	0.095	-0.132	0.094
Per Capita GDP	0.225	0.315	0.306	0.311
Diversity	-0.026	0.053	-0.030	0.053
Moralistic	0.926	0.868	0.725	0.857
Individualistic	0.371	0.800	0.392	0.791
Individual				
Years			-0.006	0.018
Age			-0.270*	0.136
Woman			-1.179**	0.304
Republican			1.300**	0.369
Minority			1.104	0.589
Random effects				
Intercept	0.000		0.000	
Residual	21.940		20.874	
No. of respondents	812		803	
No. of states	44		44	
LL	-2406.0354		-2359.3763	
df	19		24	
AIC	4850.071		4766.753	
BIC	4939.361		4879.273	

Note: The indexed variable Civility is the dependent variable in each model.
*p<.05; **p<.01; ***p<.001.

DISCUSSION

As we suspected, there is a relationship between legislative professional-ization and the degree of perceived civility. In each of our models, the amount a legislator earned in the form of salary was positively related to the degree to which respondents rated their legislatures as civil. However, this relationship does not hold for the other traditional components of professionalization. Longer sessions frequently held as an indication of professionalism were shown to be associated with lower civility ratings. The number of staff per legislator does not seem to be related to civility ratings in any systematic way either. Other things that might make service in a legislature attractive, such as the number of benefits (e.g., retirement and higher per diem rates), were significant in Model 2, but these were not related to civility when other factors were taken into consideration in subsequent models. Thus, as we also suspected was the case, the dif-ferent components related to professionalization were related to civility in different ways.

The other state-level variables provided us with additional clues related to civility. One variable that stands out is the one measuring the degree of racial and ethnic diversity of the state legislatures (Hero, 2007). More diverse legislatures were rated consistently more civil than less-diverse bodies. Additionally, in models 2 and 4 we found that states with more polarized legislative parties were also rated as being more civil. Both find-ings suggest that to the extent that the U.S. Congress sees more conflict and less civility, such incivility cannot be blamed on the growing (albeit still anemic) racial and ethnic diversity of the body, nor can the lack of civility in Congress be blamed principally on the ideological polarization of the parties in Congress.

CONCLUSION

This chapter is part of a broader research effort that examines the varying levels of civility in state legislatures and examines some potential explana-tions for the differing levels across states. In focusing here on *institutional professionalization*, we hoped to gain insight into what can account for why some legislatures are noted for being decidedly civil and others far less civil. In particular, in this chapter we explored the role that the separate elements of legislative professionalization could play in setting the levels of civility in state legislatures.

Similar to the results reported by Carey, Niemi, and Powell (2000), we find that compensation holds a highly privileged position among the variables generally noted as constituting the measure of professionalization. In their study of predictors of incumbent reelection success among state legislators, they found that among the variables analyzed–compensation, session length, and operating budget–only the compensation variable demonstrated any predictive power. They point out that "when service in the legislature pays well enough that representatives do not have to hold down a second job and they value greatly the rewards of holding office, they can devote all their career energies to legislative service, fundraising, and campaign work" (Carey et al., 2000, p. 688). We suspect a similar dynamic is in effect with respect to civility. Better compensation makes service in the legislature a genuine "job" with its attendant obligations. More important than that, it makes it a job worth keeping for some legislators. As a result, legislators will want to stay and work on matters legislative. Although in our models we did not predict turnover, we did find that legislative bodies experiencing less turnover were also more civil. It does not require a logical leap to assume that the two things are connected; better paid legislators wish to stay in their legislature, and while there engage more in ways that are civil and engage in fewer behaviors associated with incivility.

It is important to note that our variable *Opportunity* was not significant in any of the models. This suggests that civility (or lack thereof) is not related to the degree to which other career opportunities are available to the state legislator. This variable was expressed in the form of the ratio of U.S. House seats to the number of seats in the state legislature. The results from our models indicate the opportunities afforded California legislators, with the low ratio of the number of U.S. House seats to the number of California legislative seats, does not breed greater incivility. Nor does the very large ratio of House seats to state legislative seats for New Hampshire's legislators foster great civility. Although this suggests that career opportunities and civility are unrelated, we should note that our measure does not capture all post-legislative possibilities for a state legislator. These other career prospects include work as an appointed official in the executive branch, service as a judge, work as a lobbyist, or returning to his or her career prior to becoming a legislator. Thus, we contend it is still possible that those who view their careers as state legislators, first and foremost, may be the most civil, and legislatures having a wealth of these types of legislators will have elevated rates of reported civility.

Despite the connection that is often made between the growing polarization of *national* politics and the decline of civility, our findings suggest that such a connection is inappropriate at the *state* level. Our models show that the ideological distance between political parties in state legislatures in 2018 is not the cause of any decline in the perceived level of civility in state legislatures. In fact, the opposite of this expected phenomenon seems to be in effect: our state legislative lobbyists rated states with greater ideological polarization between legislative parties as being *more civil* than was the case with states with less ideological distance between their parties.

Such a finding is, of course, counterintuitive and demands an explanation. We suspect that the explanation lies in the type of competition obtaining between the two parties. One way in which parties can seek to gain or retain their majority is to offer clear policy alternatives to the electorate through the way their legislators vote. When the parties are ideologically polarized, they are not in competition for the same voters, and thus are less likely to engage in uncivil behavior as a means to capture the attention of the "fence sitters" who might sway the balance. It is possible that the parties in these states with more polarized legislative bodies are acting in a way that comports with the Responsible Party Model of old (Kirkpatrick, 1971). We cannot say this with any degree of certainty, but such a possibility warrants further scholarly attention.

It should be noted that our study is limited by a couple of factors. Our response rate was lower in some states than we had hoped. This opens the door for response bias, as it is possible that those who hold a certain view regarding the degree of civility in state legislatures were more likely to respond to our survey. Moreover, the number of responses in some states are lower than we would prefer. Although there is no agreed-upon minimum number of Level 2 cases required in multilevel modelling in order to conduct analyses, we recognize that this is a genuine concern. It should be noted that we ran our models excluding states with fewer than 14 responses, and compared our results with the ones presented above. In these models that included only the 26 states with the larger number of Level 2 cases, the coefficients listed in the tables above were largely unaffected (the coefficients for the variables for %Minority and Age ceased to reach conventional levels of statistical significance). It should be noted that we ran models that included a variable that reflected the number of respondents from each state. The coefficient for this variable did not reach conventional levels of statistical significance, indicating that state legislative lobbyists in states with more respondents did not differ in their evaluations of their state legislatures' level of civility from counterparts from states with fewer responses.

Finally, we note that our dependent variable was a measure of perceptions of civility from one group—the lobbyists who responded to our survey. These are, of course, perceptions held by one group. We did not survey members of the press who cover legislatures, nor did we survey the individual rank-and-file members of the legislature, the party leaders, or governors or other elected executive branch officials who work with their respective state legislatures. As a result, our findings are limited to merely the impressions held by the lobbyists. To be sure, we contend lobbyists are certainly an important, knowledgeable, and diverse group of individuals among whom to gather informed impressions because of their familiarity with the current operations, politics, and key political personalities in of each of the 50 state legislatures.

NOTES

1. The authors thank Eric Button, Brianna Huett, Creed Tumlison, and Tyler Garrett for their critical assistance with this research.

2. Citations omitted.

3. Clem Miller. 1962. *Member of the House* (John W. Baker, Ed.). New York: Scribner, p. 93. See also pp. 80–81 and 119–122. Cited in Polsby (1968), p. 167.

4. The Cronbach's alpha for the index variable was 0.800.

5. Legislators are also compensated for their travel in the form of mileage. However, like Bowen and Greene (2011), our measure does not include mileage because the amount paid is not reported by the NCSL, and without knowing how much each individual legislature travelled during the year we have no way of determining how much, on average, legislators received through this method of compensation.

6. Insurance programs that require the legislator to pay the full expense of the premium received a value of "0" for that portion of the index. This includes cases in which the state covered the partial expense of the plan for only a part of the legislator's term when he or she first entered office, then required the legislator to cover the full amount for the rest

of the time in office. In some cases, the NCSL survey did not reveal whether the state covered the full amount or a partial amount, but indicated the coverage was the same for legislators as it was for state employees. In these cases, we assumed this indicated the state covered a portion of the amount. In a few cases, legislators elected after a certain date were not eligible for coverage. In these cases, we gave the state a "0." If only the Senate were covered, that state received a "0" for that portion of the index.

7. Past researchers have used legislative expenditures as a measure of resources (e.g., Berry et al., 2000). As Squire (2007) notes, such a measure is confounded by the fact that such numbers may sometimes include the cost of legislative salaries, building maintenance, and similar housekeeping items. For this reason, and due to the fact that the states' legislative expenditures are highly correlated with staffing numbers, in accord with Squire we have opted to include only staffing numbers in our analytical models.

REFERENCES

Berry, W. D., Berkman, M. B., & Schneiderman, S. (2000). Legislative professionalism and incumbent reelection: The development of institutional boundaries. *American Political Science Review, 94*(4), 859–874.

Boatright, R. G., Shaffer, T. J., Sobieraj, S., & Young, D. G. (2019). *A crisis of civility? Political discourse and its discontents*. Routledge.

Bowen, D. C., & Greene, Z. (2014). Should we measure professionalism with an index? A note on theory and practice in state legislative professionalism research. *State Politics & Policy Quarterly, 14*(3), 277–296.

Carey, J. M., Niemi, R. G., & Powell, L. W. (2000). Incumbency and the probability of reelection in state legislative elections. *Journal of Politics, 62*(3), 671–700.

Calvert, J. (1979). Revolving doors: Volunteerism in state legislatures. *State Government, 52*(4), 174–181.

Council of State Governments. (2018). *Book of the states*. Membership turnover in the legislatures: 2017. http://knowledgecenter.csg.org/kc/system/files/3.4.2018_0.pdf.

Council of State Governments. (2019). *Book of the states*. Membership turnover in the legislatures: 2018. http://knowledgecenter.csg.org/kc/system/files/3.4.2019.pdf.

Cox, G. W., & Morgenstern, S. (1993). The increasing advantage of incumbency in the U.S. states. *Legislative Studies Quarterly, 18*(4), 495–514.

Cox, G. W., & Morgenstern, S. (1995). The incumbency advantage in the multimember districts: Evidence from the U.S. states. *Legislative Studies Quarterly, 20*(3), 329–349.

Elazar, D. J. (1972). *American federalism: A view from the states*. Thomas Crowell.

Fenno, R. F., Jr. (1978). *Home style: House members in their districts*. Little, Brown.

Fowler, L., & Witt, S. L. (2019). State preemption of local authority: Explaining patterns of state adoption of preemption measures. *Publius: The Journal of Federalism, 49*(3), 540–559.

Gamm, G., & Kousser, T. (2010). Broad bills or particularistic policy? Historical patterns in American state legislatures. *American Political Science Review, 104*(1), 151–170.

Hero, R. (2007). *Racial diversity and social capital: Equality and community in America.* Cambridge University Press.

Hibbing, J. R. (1999). Legislative careers: Why and how we study them. *Legislative Studies Quarterly, 24*(May), 149–171.

Hinchliffe, K. L., & Lee, F. E. (2016). Party competition and conflict in state legislatures. *State Politics & Policy Quarterly, 16*(2), 172–197.

Holbrook, T. M., & Tidmarch, C. M. (1991). Sophomore surge in state legislative elections, 1968-86. *Legislative Studies Quarterly, 16*(1), 49–63.

Kirkpatrick, E. M. (1971). 'Toward a more responsible two-party system': Political science, policy science, or pseudo-science? *American Political Science Review, 65*(4), 965–990. https://doi.org/10.2307/1953493.

Kousser, T., & Phillips, J. (2009). Who blinks first? Legislative patience and bargaining with governors. *Legislative Studies Quarterly, 34*(1), 55–86.

Lax, J., & Phillips, J. (2012). The democratic deficit in the States. *American Journal of Political Science, 56*(1), 148–166.

Maestas, C. (2000). Professional legislatures and ambitious politicians: Policy responsiveness of state institutions. *Legislative Studies Quarterly, 24*(4), 663–690.

Mayhew, D. R. (1974). *Congress: The electoral connection.* Yale University Press.

Moncrief, G. F., Thompson, J. A., & Kurtz, K. (1996). The old statehouse, it ain't what it used to be. *Legislative Studies Quarterly, 21*(1), 344–362.

Mooney, C. Z. (1995). Citizens, structures, and sister states: Influences on state legislative professionalism. *Legislative Studies Quarterly, 20*(1), 47–67.

National Conference of State Legislatures. (2020). *2016 survey: State legislative retirement benefits.* https://www.ncsl.org/Portals/1/Documents/legismgt/2016_Leg_Comp_Retirement_Benefits.pdf.

National Conference of State Legislatures. (2020). *2016 survey: Legislative compensation: health, dental, vision, disability, and life insurance.* https://www.ncsl.org/Portals/1/Documents/legismgt/2016_Leg_Comp_Insurance.pdf.

Opheim, C. (1991). Explaining the differences in state lobby regulation. *Western Political Quarterly, 44*(2), 405–421.

Poole, K. T., & Rosenthal, H. (1991). Patterns of congressional voting. *American Journal of Political Science, 35*(1), 228–278.

Poole, K. T., & Rosenthal, H. (1997). *Congress: A political-economic history of roll call voting.* Oxford University Press.

Polsby, N. W. (1968). The institutionalization of the U.S. House of Representatives. *American Political Science Review, 62*(1), 144–168.

Rosenthal, A. (1974). Turnover in state legislatures. *American Journal of Political Science, 18*(3), 609–616.

Rosenthal, A. (1996). State legislative development: Observations from three perspectives. *Legislative Studies Quarterly, 21,* 169–198.

Sahr, R. (2020). *Yearly pay of members of Congress 1789 to 2012, in current and constant (2012) dollars*. https://liberalarts.oregonstate.edu/sites/liberalarts.oregonstate.edu/files/polisci/faculty-research/sahr/inflation-conversion/pdf/congress_pay_1789-2012.pdf.

Sarbaugh-Thompson, M. (2010). Measuring 'term limitedness' in U.S. multi-state research. *State Politics & Policy Quarterly, 10*(2), 199–217.

Shipan, C. R., & Volden, C. (2006). Bottom-up federalism: The diffusion of antismoking policies from U.S. cities to states. *American Journal of Political Science, 50*(4), 825–843.

Shor, B., & McCarty, N. (2011). The ideological mapping of American legislatures. *American Political Science Review, 105*(3), 530–551.

Squire, P. (1992). Legislative professionalization and membership diversity in state legislatures. *Legislative Studies Quarterly, 17*(1), 69–79.

Squire, P. (2007). Measuring state legislative professionalism: The squire index revisited. *State Politics & Policy Quarterly, 7*(2), 211–227.

Thompson, J. A., Kurtz, K., & Moncrief, G. F. (1996). We've lost that family feeling: The changing norms of the new breed of state legislators. *Social Science Quarterly, 77*(2), 344–362.

U.S. Census Bureau. (2020). *Historical income tables: Households, table H-8*. https://www.census.gov/data/tables/time-series/demo/income-poverty/historical-income-households.html.

U.S. Congressional Research Service. (2020). *Salaries of members of Congress: Recent actions and historical tables*. https://fas.org/sgp/crs/misc/97-1011.pdf.

U.S. General Services Administration. (2020). *Per diem rates look-up*. https://www.gsa.gov/travel/plan-book/per-diem-rates/per-diem-rates-lookup.

Woods, N. D., & Baranowski, M. (2006). Legislative professionalism and influence on state agencies: The effects of resources and careerism. *Legislative Studies Quarterly, 31*(4), 585–609.

CHAPTER THREE

Nonprofits, Civility, and the Legislative Processes: Does Public Interest Lobbying Make a Difference?

John C. Pierce
Burdett A. Loomis

INTRODUCTION

Hospice leader: We publish a newsletter, but we never tell our people to urge a vote.

Professor Jeff Berry: You don't tell them to contact their legislators on issues of importance to you?

Hospice leader: We tell them to contact their legislators, but we *don't* tell them to urge them to vote a certain way.

Jeffery M. Berry (Berry and Arons, 2003, p. 47)

Nonprofit groups have a long and mixed history with advocacy and lobbying. Historically, many such groups have often avoided many forms of advocacy, especially those easily identified as lobbying of legislatures or executives. Federal tax regulations do limit the extent of such lobbying, but, even so, as Berry (1999) and others (Berry and Arons, 2003; Salamon, Geller, and Lorenz, 2008) have concluded, many nonprofits are quite timid in interpreting allowable activities under these laws. Yet Crutchfield and Grant report, "Almost half the organizations we examined lobby the government—at the federal, state and local levels—for appropriations and contracts," while at the same time "some nonprofits engage in policy advocacy, but do not accept government funding because to do so would represent a conflict of interest" (2012, p. 219). On the other hand, the increased blending and blurring of the lines between both the private and public sectors on one hand and the nonprofit "third sector" on the other (Corry, 2010) have elevated the relevance of lobbying as a nonprofit strategy.

Organizations have been broadly distinguished between a) rent-seeking or b) public interest and non-rent-seeking. Gordon Tulloch has described that difference this way: rent-seeking is when "people use their votes or other political means" to gain benefits exclusively for themselves (2005, 92). On the other hand, "non-rent-seeking" organizations seek benefits that are not held exclusively for members, but rather are available to the public as a whole. In the latter case, the nonprofits obtain "public goods." There also are altruistic rent-seeking organizations, ones that obtain goods specifically for their members but also for others who share their particular interests but do not participate in achieving those benefits. Those non-participating beneficiaries of nonprofit activity are referred to as "free-riders" (see Gradstein, 1993; Baron, 2003; Folbre and Nelson, 2000).

Lobbying state legislators is a significant strategy in attempting to produce both public goods and rent-seeking benefits. In all of this, nonprofits exist in what has been called "a contested space" between the public and private spheres, or, as Frumkin describes it, "the arena between the state and the market where public and private concerns meet and where individual and social efforts are united" (Ott and Dicke, 2016, p. 11). The conventional definition of nonprofit lobbyists would be those who represent interests that seek private goods (rent-seeking) or public goods (non-rent-seeking), but in either case "operate without distributing profits to stakeholders" (Frumkin, 2016, p. 12). In this chapter, we label non-rent-seeking lobbyists as representing *public interest* nonprofits and those who pursue private goods as acting on behalf of *rent-seeking interests*.

Within American politics, nonprofits play an important, even crucial, representational role in speaking for interests with limited voices or no voice at all. Groups representing environmental interests, such as The Friends of the Kaw (the Kansas River) or the Coalition to Restore Coastal Louisiana, can speak for interests that have no voice. Likewise, for the disadvantaged, nonprofits are significant for those whose voices need amplification and dissemination within a complex, multi-faceted political context that often favors powerful and moneyed interests (Nownes and Loomis, 2020). The role of nonprofits in American society is substantial, in terms of both representing interests and implementing policies. In human services, for example, Berry and Arons (2003, p. 15) note that "the growth in employment in social service nonprofits has far outpaced that of government welfare offices.... In the United States, when people need help beyond cash assistance, they go to nonprofits and do not interact directly with the government."

Nonprofits dominate the delivery of many services, especially within the social welfare sector, and especially when government does not provide that service or has diminished that provision substantially. Given this, as government activity in social welfare programs declines, nonprofits have large and growing stakes in affecting the policymaking process. Moreover, as politics become more partisan and polarized, nonprofits must build relationships that transcend partisan politics, regardless of who is in power. In this sense, nonpartisan civic engagement stands as an organizational virtue. In a related vein, maintaining high levels of civility in politics and policymaking, and especially within the legislative process, should be important to nonprofits, which must work with whoever exercises power regardless of party or ideology. This is not always easy—think of educational nonprofits trying to work with Secretary of Education Betsy DeVos—but it is essential. Providing an effective voice to those who need it is central to many nonprofits' missions, and a civil setting offers greater chances for those voices to be heard.

Although there are many advocacy tools available for nonprofits, addressing policy specifics requires lobbying the legislature, the executive, and various administrative agencies. Even so, while voluntary sector scholars do address lobbying to an extent, they find relatively little nonprofit lobbying (Almog-Bar and Schmidt, 2014). Political scientists, on the other hand, identify a considerable amount of such advocacy, even as they argue that nonprofits could easily do more (see, among others, Berry and Arons, 2003; Salamon, Geller, and Lorenz, 2008). Still, the data are mixed, given unrepresentative samples or single-state responses. At the national level, despite no claim of representativeness, Salamon,

Geller, and Lorenz (2008) find that almost three-fourths of nonprofits engage in either advocacy, lobbying, or both; moreover, three-in-five of these groups do so at least monthly and in multiple venues.

State-based nonprofits, represented by studies from California and North Carolina, find less lobbying by nonprofits, especially when the entire universe of these groups is included, per the California study (Suarez and Hwang, 2008; Prentice, 2018). Indeed, in California between 1998 and 2003, the total number of nonprofits rose from 19,213 to 25,740, while the number of those lobbying at the state level grew from just 380 to 544. On average, Suarez and Hwang (2008, p. 97) find that only 2% of all the state's nonprofits lobbied over this five-year span. They argue that misconceptions about restrictions on nonprofit lobbying are so pervasive that many groups simply do not consider lobbying a viable strategy. More importantly, most of the nonprofits deliver services, beyond everything else; these groups usually do not lobby, but that does not mean that their interests go unrepresented in Sacramento, given the 544 nonprofits that did lobby as of 2003. Similar figures exist for North Carolina, where in 2010 412 nonprofits (395 of them exempt under IRS rules) registered to lobby.

In sum, even if many nonprofits do not lobby, a substantial number do; indeed, in North Carolina, they made up approximately one-half of all lobbying entities (Prentice, 2018). This raises a host of questions as to the potential impact of nonprofit lobbying on the policymaking process, and especially how legislatures function. Do public interest nonprofits and their lobbyist agents act differently from other, rent-seeking lobbyists? How many lobbyists represent both public interest nonprofits and other groups, including business, professions/trade associations, or unions? To what extent do public interest nonprofits rely on in-house advocates, contract lobbyists, or both? These are basic questions for this analysis, but we are also interested in how lobbyists perceive overall civility within the legislative process. More specifically, do self-identified public interest nonprofit lobbyists, whether in-house or contractors, prefer a more civil legislative process?

This is no idle question in an era of increasing partisanship and polarization, in both state legislatures and within the U.S. Congress. The literature on the latter is voluminous (Sinclair, 2014; Smith, 2014; Lee, 2009, 2016, among many others), but there is less work and less consensus regarding state legislatures (Shor and McCarty, 2011; Shor, 2015). This lacuna exists partly because partisanship and polarization affect various state legislatures differentially, given the partisan contexts of individual states. Thus, for a deep red or deep blue state, extreme partisanship might well lead to a dominant party that could work its will. Alternatively, such a situation might generate intra-party factional divisions that would lead to bargaining or deadlock on given issues.

To present one state example, for the four years after the 2012 legislative elections Kansas experienced a period of far-right Republican control of both chambers and the governorship (Sam Brownback). Many lobbyists and opposing legislators (both Democrats and moderate Republicans) were frozen out of the policymaking process, which severely reduced deliberation on important issues. When Democrats and moderate Republicans regained a substantial number of seats in the 2016 elections, the 2017–18 legislative sessions returned to a more conventional process of active committee hearings, negotiation, and compromise. Parenthetically, the statehouse attitude of most lobbyists and many legislators improved markedly, with the return of greater civility and respect for the deliberative process.

While the above discussion notes the variety of approaches to and conclusions about the actual practice of nonprofit lobbying, few if any look at how public interest lobbyists may differ from lobbyists for other sectors in their views of the legislative process, especially in terms of civility and conflict.

DATA COLLECTION

The data on which this chapter is based were obtained via a national Qualtrics survey of lobbyists in every state in the United States, organized and managed by researchers at Washington State University (WSU) working with a group of a dozen scholars at ten major U.S. universities across the country. The following brief description is provided by the WSU principal investigators (see chapter one for a more detailed account of the data collection process):

Once the research team achieved agreement on the content of the survey instrument (available upon request), the WSU Institutional Review Board (IRB) approved data collection. The Qualtrics online survey process was used as an initial contact; that process was initiated in mid-2018 and carried through until early 2019. With resources provided by NICD, two rounds of mail survey follow-ups were conducted in 2019, with the following ultimate results being attained.

• Completed surveys = 1,200+
• Returns from all 50 states
• Average responses per state = 25+ [min. 17 (AL), max. 79 (OR)]
• Oversamples (30+) for AR, KS, ID, WA, UT, CA, NV, IL, IA, OH, PA, OR, & NC
• Many former state legislators; diverse group of respondents, including agency liaison personnel, nonprofit and public interest group advocates
• Rich collection of comments and extended commentaries; many telephone and email follow-up contacts with survey participants

The survey results, including comments on specific questions and commentaries on the overall survey and topic of legislative civility, were compiled into SPSS files and text documents shared with each of the members of the research team.

MEASURING LOBBYISTS' REPRESENTATIONAL FOCUS

One baseline question in the survey asked, "How often do you lobby on behalf of each of the interests listed below?" Responses ranged from 1 (very often) to 4 (never). We employ those responses (see Table 3.1) as the criteria for distinguishing public interest lobbyists from rent-seeking lobbyists. The two categories of public interest lobbyists and rent-seeking

Table 3.1. Frequency of Lobbyists' Representational Focus

Frequency	Business or Business Associations	Rent-Seeking Professional Trades or Occupations	Organized Labor or Unions	Public Interest
Very Often	33	35	8	28
Often	9	10	2	11
Occasionally	14	13	9	20
Never	44	42	82	41
Total	100%	100%	101%	100%
N	1069	1070	1035	1062

lobbyists contain 457 and 714 lobbyists, respectively. Our primary interest is in those respondents who self-identify as lobbying on behalf of public interest nonprofits. We do not have independent confirmation of that self-identification via state lobbying registration records. On the other hand, since we are interested in the views of the respondents, we believe that their self-perceptions of their representational roles would be central to their evaluations of the legislative process.

As Table 3.1 shows, the lobbyists in this sample are only slightly less likely to self-identify as lobbying very often or often (39%) for public interest nonprofits as for business (42%) or for professional/trade/ occupational interests (45%). At the same time, compared to the other alternatives, these respondents report much less lobbying activity (10%) for organized labor or unions. But do the nonprofit lobbyists represent *only* public interests, or do they also lobby for those that seek rents? The results in Table 3.2 (below) report the average amount of lobbying for rent-seeking interests by those lobbyists in each frequency category of public interest nonprofit lobbying. Recall that the *lower* average score represents more frequent lobbying effort. Analysis of variance results indicates that the differences among the public interest nonprofit lobbyist categories are all statistically significant. The "very often" nonprofit public interest lobbyists are much less likely than the other three categories to lobby for business and professional interests and for labor interests.

Table 3.2. Average Lobbying Frequency for Business, Professional, and Labor by Frequency of Public Interest Lobbying*

Public Interest Lobbying Frequency

Other lobbying	Very Often	Often	Occasionally	Never	F	Sig.
Business	3.34	2.25	2.26	2.61	36.3	.000
Professional	3.30	2.30	2.15	2.61	21.8	.000
Labor	3.68	3.50	3.50	3.74	5.6	.000
Other	3.30	3.02	2.90	3.13	2.9	.000

*The figures in the table are the average lobbying frequency by nonprofit lobbyists in lobbying for other than nonprofit interests. The frequency scale is 1 = very often, 2 = often, 3 = occasionally, and 4 = never.

The primary distinction is between the "very often" and the other categories, with the latter more likely than the former to lobby also for business and professional interests.

Do high-frequency public interest nonprofit lobbyists bring different backgrounds and beliefs to the legislative process than their rent-seeking lobbyist colleagues? For this analysis, the self-identified public interest nonprofit lobbyist indicator is dichotomized, with 1) "very often" and 2) "often" combined as public interest nonprofit lobbyists, and 3) "occasion-ally" and 4) "never" collapsed into the rent-seeking nonprofit category (see Table 3.3). Nonprofit public interest lobbyists are less likely to be former state legislators (4.2%) than are rent-seeking nonprofit lobbyists (7.2%). On the other hand, by far the biggest difference has to do with 47.8% of the public interest lobbyists having had prior experience with a policy-related nonprofit compared to only 20.4% of the rent-seeking nonprofit lobbyists. There is likely (1) a strong mission-based public interest nonprofit commitment that spans working for the nonprofit itself to representing the nonprofit in the legislative arena and/or (2) a pre-lobbying experience that provided the public interest nonprofit lob-byists with the credentials and knowledge that fit with the requirements for the job of legislative lobbying.

While public interest nonprofit lobbyists differ substantially in their more extensive prior experience in working for nonprofits, Table 3.4 shows that the nature of their current employment resembles those who rarely or

Table 3.3. Lobbyists' Prior Experience by Dichotomized Frequency of Nonprofit Lobbying*

	Public Interest	Rent-Seeking Interests	X^2	DF	Sig.
State Legislator	4.2%	7.2%	4.4	1	.02
State Legislative Aide	21.8%	25.8%	2.4	1	.13
State/Federal Agency Staff	22.4%	21.9%	0.6	1	.43
Local agency/government	16.7%	15.9%	0.1	1	.40
Nonprofit organization	47.8%	20.4%	95.1	1	.000

*The entry in each cell is the percentage of the public interest nonprofit or not-public interest nonprofit respondents who indicated prior service in the position in the respective column.

never lobby for public interest nonprofits. That is, the percentages working as self-employed, in-house, or for a lobbying firm are essentially the same regardless of whether the lobbyist specializes in public interest nonprofit work. Moreover, per Table 3.5, the demographic attributes that public interest nonprofit lobbyists bring to the legislature do differ somewhat from those of rent-seeking lobbyists. While the two groups are similar in race/

Table 3.4. Lobbyist Type and Lobbying Employment Status*

Employment Status	Public Interest	Rent-Seeking Interests	X²	DF	Sig.
Self-employed	21.1%	22.5%	.33	1	.31
In-House	61.2%	62.0%	.07	1	.19
Lobbying Firm	17.7%	18.1%	.53	1	.26

*The entry in each cell is the percentage of the nonprofit or not-nonprofit lobbyists who report being employed in each of the ways listed in the column.

Table 3.5. Demographic Backgrounds of Public Interest Nonprofit and Rent-Seeking Interests Lobbyists

Demographics	Public Interest	Rent-Seeking Interests	X²	DF	Sig.
% White race/ethnic	92%	93%	.25	1	.61
% Under 50 age	45%	40%	9.8	1	.13
% Male	45%	66%	36.2	1	.000

Table 3.6. Political and Party Ideology of Nonprofit and Not-Nonprofit Lobbyists

Party/Ideology	Public Interest	Rent-Seeking Interests
% Democrat*	73%	46%
% Social Liberal**	71%	51%
% Fiscal Liberal**	45%	23%

*Self-identified as Democrat or Independent Leaning Democrat.
**Self-identified at positions 1, 2, 3 on 7-point scale.

ethnicity, the public interest nonprofit lobbyists are slightly younger (45% under 50 years of age compared to 40%) and are substantially *less* likely to be male than are the rent-seeking lobbyists (45% compared to 66%). A further question is whether public interest nonprofit lobbyists have different orientations to their work, such as partisan and ideological identification.

Table 3.6 results show what may be the starkest background differences between the two groups of lobbyists. Public interest nonprofit lobbyists are significantly more likely than rent-seeking lobbyists to self-identify as Democrats (73% v. 46%), social liberals (71% v. 51%), and fiscal liberals (45% v. 23%). There may be a consistent selection process in that many, if not most, of the nonprofit public interest organizations promote priorities that are consistent with those of the Democratic Party, with social liberalism, and, perhaps less so, with fiscal liberalism. Such differences may contribute to other differences in perceptions of and views about the nature of the legislative process.

In summary, then, are the backgrounds of the public interest non-profit lobbyists in our database different from those of the rent-seeking lobbyists? The answer is a qualified yes. When compared to rent-seeking lobbyists, public interest nonprofit lobbyists are less likely to lobby *also* for business and professional interests, more likely to have had prior experience in nonprofit organizations, and less likely to have been state legislators. Public interest nonprofit lobbyists are slightly younger, but substantially more likely to be female and much more likely to self-identify as Democrats, social liberals, and fiscal liberals.

Do these background and political differences relate to their respective orientations to the legislative process? For example, are public interest nonprofit lobbyists likely to focus on different issues than rent-seeking lobbyists, or at least to give greater attention to specific issues? Table 3.7 shows the patterns of responses to the question "On which of the following types of issues have you lobbied?" (Note that the higher the score, the *less* likely the respondent is to have lobbied on that type of issue, where 1 = very often and 4 = never.) The issue areas with bold face for the significance level are those for which a statistically significant difference between the two groups was found. The public interest nonprofit lobbyists are: a) less likely than the rent-seeking lobbyists to have lobbied on labor and employment issues, utilities, or taxation; and b) more likely to have lobbied on criminal justice, pensions and retirement, social regulation, social service, immigration, and K-12 education. Those differences fit consistently with the rent-seeking versus public interest distinctions in the interests that are likely represented in those policy areas. And these patterns are also a type of confirmation for the measure of public interest nonprofits.

Table 3.7. Average Frequency of Lobbying on Specific Issues*

Issue Area	Public Interest	Rent-Seeking Interests	F	Sig.**
Environmental Regulations	2.93	2.89	.27	.60
Agriculture	3.41	3.34	1.4	.24
Labor/Employment	3.00	2.74	16.9	**.00**
Land Use	3.07	3.06	.02	.90
State Lottery	3.75	3.72	.39	.53
Health Care	2.47	2.69	7.9	**.01**
Utilities	3.18	3.01	6.4	**.01**
Transportation	2.95	2.85	2.4	.12
Military/Veterans	3.69	3.68	.05	.83
Taxation	2.62	2.32	18.7	**.00**
Criminal Justice	2.99	3.30	23.9	**.00**
Pensions/Retirement	3.35	3.33	.20	.66
Social Regulation	3.12	3.55	59.1	**.00**
Social Service	2.57	3.27	115.7	**.00**
Immigration	3.46	3.60	7.9	**.00**
K-12 Education	2.74	3.22	47.7	**.00**
Higher Education	3.12	3.20	1.7	.20
Cannabis	3.50	3.57	1.6	.21
Other	2.84	2.65	3.3	.07

*The entries in the cells are the average score wherein 1 = very often, 2 = often, 3 = occasionally, and 4 = never.

**Bold face indicates a statistically significant difference between public interest nonprofit lobbyists and not-public interest nonprofit lobbyists.

Table 3.8 shows how public interest nonprofit lobbyists and rent-seeking lobbyists view the legislature they lobby. While in both groups less than a quarter of respondents indicated that they had had a "poor experience in representing clients," that evaluation was more pronounced among the public interest lobbyists. The public interest lobbyists also are more likely to see legislative norms as "breaking down" and to find "fewer nonpartisan areas" of legislation obtaining. However, there are no differences regarding whether legislators have become more partisan and whether a lobbyist's legislature is seen as more partisan than those in other states.

Table 3.9 shows the lobbyists' responses to questions asking for their perceptions of the level of civility in their respective legislatures. While some of the Chi-Square figures reach near-statistical significance, even in those cases there is relatively little difference between the two lobbyist categories. Thus, public lobbyists are slightly less likely than the rent-seeking lobbyists to indicate that there is a high level of civility in the legislature (33.8% v. 38.6%). More significant than those differences is the overall

Table 3.8. Public Interest and Rent-Seeking Lobbyists' Perceptions of Legislature

	Public Interest	Rent-Seeking Interests	X^2	F	Sig.
% poor experience in representing clients*	24.0%	16.0%	23.27	4	.00
% legislative norms are breaking down**	71.7%	63.7%	7.4	3	.06
% fewer nonpartisan areas***	60.5%	52.7%	7.0	3	.03
% legislators more partisan****	63.9%	60.5%	5.5	6	.49
% legislators are more partisan than in other states*****	34.8%	30.4%	2.0		.37

*1 & 2 on 5-point scale

**% occurring on 5-point scale

***% fewer (1) nonpartisan areas on 3-point scale

****% legislators more partisan (1,2,3) on 7-point scale

*****% legislators more partisan (1) than in other states on 3-point scale view of civility (or lack thereof) shared across lobbyist types. In addition, the nonprofit lobbyists are more likely to indicate that the incivility has a personal effect on them. More generally, public interest lobbyists frequently represent interests that upset the status quo, so they may be more likely to face antagonism. Still, the reactions of all lobbyists are roughly the same here.

Table 3.10 shows the results of questions asking the respondents to reflect on the causes of legislative incivility. There is general agreement among the lobbyists regarding the degree to which various possible reasons are at the root of incivility. Indeed, of all the potential causes listed in Table 3.10, in only one cell do less than 50% indicate that incivility

Table 3.9. Perceptions of Civility in State Legislature

Perception	Public Interest	Rent-Seeking Interests	X^2	F	Sig.
Importance of Civility*	86.9%	88.7%	15.4	9	.08
% High Level of Civility in Legislature**	33.8%	38.6%	13.7	8	.09
Legislators' Civility in contrast to 10 yrs ago***	8.1%	6.8%	5.2	8	.74
Leaders' Civility Compared to 10 Years ago***	9.6%	9.2%	10.8	8	.22
Your Civility****	95.8%	94.3%	7.8	4	.10
Other Lobbyists****	71.9%	75.9%	4.4	4	.36
State Legislators in general****	41.1%	46.25%	5.5	4	.24
State Legislators you deal with****	73%	70.6%	3.6	4	.46
State Legislators in U.S.****	15.1%	19%	2.6	4	.60
Average Citizen in State****	27.2%	26.6%	3.9	4	.42
Effect of Incivility on You*****	36%	30.2	6.5	3	.09

*Scores 8, 9, 10 on 10-point scale
**Scores 7, 8, 9 on 9-point scale
***More = Scores of 7, 8, 9 on 9-point scale
****Very Civil or Civil = 4, 5 on 5-point scale
*****% Large amount or great deal = 3, 4 on 4-point scale

can be attributed to the cause, that cell being public interest lobbyists describing lobbyists in general.

STATE POLITICAL CULTURE EFFECTS

So far, we have looked at nonprofit lobbying through the lens of state lobbyists' perceptions and assessments of their institutions and processes. There is no question that state-level variables of partisanship, economics, and demographics could have an impact on these perceptions, but those considerations lie outside our current analysis. Still, the context of nonprofit lobbying could well matter, especially given differing political cultures among the states. One example: Kansas and Missouri are similar in many ways, but the political cultures surrounding their respective state legislatures could not be more different. In Kansas, there have been few scandals and a general sense

Table 3.10. Public Interest Nonprofit and Rent-Seeking Lobbyist's Perceptions of the Causes of Legislative Incivility

	Public Interest	Rent-Seeking Interests	X^2	DF	P
Hostility when running for office*	89.7%	88.8%	1.2	3	.78
Less inter-partisan communication	73.3%	70.5%	6.0	3	.11
Partisan/Ideological media	90.5%	93.7%	5.3	3	.15
Low respect for legislative norms	67.4	61.1%	1.8	3	.61
Reflecting Congress' polarization	81.3%	79.6%	4.2	3	.24
Members more extreme	81.9%	84.9%	3.0	3	.39
More diverse demands from:					
Constituents	61.6%	64.6%	.78	3	.83
Contributors	79.0%	84.5%	6.9	3	.07
Lobbyists	54.5%	45.0%	19.5	3	.00
Leg. Party Leaders	84.2%	81.8%	.95	3	.81
State Party Leaders	80.1%	79.4%	.08	3	.99

*Entries are the percentage of respondents choosing positions 1 or 2 (strongly agree or agree) on a 4-point scale reflecting the perception as a contributing cause "to the declining levels of civility in American political life in recent years."

of fair play in the state's legislative politics (Loomis, 1994; Harder and Davis, 1979; Flentje and Aistrup, 2010). Missouri, conversely, with no campaign finance regulations, a wide-open capitol, and a series of legislator convictions (including a couple of speakers), exhibits norms that are far more flexible and permissive than in Kansas (Hardy, Dohm, and Leuthold, 1995).

Thus in this section we examine the interplay of state political culture and the public interest or rent-seeking lobbying status of the respondents in forming perceptions of incivility in state legislatures. We employ Daniel Elazar's classification of political cultures in the American states (1972; 1994). Elazar rated each state in terms of the extent to which historically it has reflected either a moralistic, individualistic, or traditionalistic political culture. Elazar defines political culture as "the particular pattern of orientation to political action in which each political system is imbedded" (1994, p. 9).

A *moralistic* political culture is seen as communalistic, imposing "a duty [on] every citizen to participate in the political affairs of his or her commonwealth" (1994, p. 233). Moreover, moralistic culture "tends to channel the interest in government intervention into highly localistic patterns" (1994, p. 234). In contrast, an *individualistic* political culture emphasizes "the conception of the democratic order as a marketplace... [putting] a premium on limiting community intervention" (1994, p. 230), and is characterized by "its overriding commitment to commercialism and acceptance of ethnic, social and religious pluralism" (1994, p. 232). A *traditionalistic* culture, however, has as a priority "the continued maintenance of the existing social order. To do so, it functions to confine real political power to a relatively small and self-perpetuating group drawn from an established elite" (1994, p. 235). Moreover, each state can manifest variations and combinations of those cultures, ranging from the presence of only one culture, to a dominant culture with a minor influence from one of the others, to a dominant culture with a strong strain of one of the others. In the context of Elazar's cultural distinctions, one might expect public interest representatives to be more likely to see incivility in the traditionalistic political cultures, those dominated by elite interests rather than reflecting communal concerns. And public interest lobbyists working outside of moralistic cultures (whether they are traditionalistic or individualistic) might be more likely to perceive incivility in the cultural dissonance with their own goals and interests.

As Table 3.11 illustrates, and as we expected, the greatest perception of incivility is found among the public interest lobbyists in an *exclusive traditionalistic* political culture. These states are followed closely by those in which a *traditionalistic* political culture has a primary presence, with another cultural subtype in a secondary position; both of these political culture settings are identified by Elazar as elite-dominated. In addition, in those states with no presence of either individualistic or moralistic culture, state politics are often dominated by traditionalistic political culture. The largest difference between nonprofit lobbyists and rent-seeking lobbyists

Table 3.11. Elazar State Political Cultures, Lobbying Status, and the Perception of State Legislative Incivility Levels*

Individualistic Culture	Public Interest	Rent-Seeking Interests	Difference
None	45.4%	37.2%	+8.2
Secondary	35.2%	30.7%	+4.5
Primary	41.3%	38.9%	+2.4
Exclusive	45.7%	37.6%	+8.1

Traditionalistic Culture	Public Interest	Rent-Seeking Interests	Difference
None	34.4%	34.8%	-0.8
Secondary	31.7%	36.7%	-5.0
Primary	48.2%	41.9%	+6.3
Exclusive	50.0%	29.5%	+20.5

Moralistic Culture	Public Interest	Rent-seeking Interests	Difference
None	45.4%	31.5%	+13.9
Secondary	34.8%	46.0%	-11.2
Primary	29.1%	31.5%	-2.4
Exclusive	41.0%	34.4%	+6.6

*The entry in each cell is the percentage of that combination of political culture and lobbyist status that chose 1, 2, 3, or 4 on a 9-point where 1 = very uncivil and 9 = very civil.

is also in the traditionalistic culture. Even as most lobbyists recognize and decry the rise of partisanship, the historical state context continues to matter.

Another perspective is the kind of experience the respondents encountered in the legislature's deliberations. Across the board, as Table 3.12 shows, the public interest lobbyists had a less-positive experience, although the differences among them depend a lot on the nature of the political culture in which they operate. In individualistic cultures, that difference is greatest in the primary and exclusive categories, and in traditionalistic political cultures it is greatest in the secondary and exclusive cultures. In terms of the moralistic political

Table 3.12. Elazar State Political Cultures, Public Interest Nonprofit Lobbying, and the Percentage Poor Experience with Legislature's Deliberation*

Individualistic Culture	Public Interest	Rent-Seeking Interests	Difference
None	24.9%	18.3%	+6.6
Secondary	19.0%	13.2%	+5.8
Primary	31.1%	16.3%	+14.8
Exclusive	36.0%	14.8%	+21.2
Traditionalistic Culture	**Public Interest**	**Rent-Seeking Interests**	**Difference**
None	22.8%	15.0%	+7.8
Secondary	33.6%	14.0%	+19.6
Primary	20.3%	19.0%	+1.3
Exclusive	37.9%	7.9%	+20.0
Moralistic Culture	**Public Interest**	**Rent-Seeking Interests**	**Difference**
None	32.5%	15.3%	+17.2
Secondary	26.7%	20.2%	+4.5
Primary	17.2%	13.5%	+3.7
Exclusive	17.8%	15.1%	+2.7

*The entry in each cell is the percentage of that combination of political culture and lobbyist status that chose 1 or 2, on a 5-point scale where 1 = uniformly poor and 5 = uniformly good.

capital dimension, the difference is the greatest in the "none" category, representing those states dominated by either of the other two cultures.

Table 3.13 displays results for evaluations of the degree to which norms of fair play are breaking down in state legislatures. In individualistic state cultures, the results are scattered, with the public interest lobbyists more likely to agree—except for the *exclusively* individualistic states, in which the reverse is the case. In traditionalistic cultures, the public interest nonprofit

Table 3.13. Elazar State Political Cultures, Nonprofit Lobbying, and the Perception that State Legislative Norms of Fair Play are Breaking Down*

Individualistic Culture	Public Interest	Rent-Seeking Interests	Difference
None	76.1%	64.1%	+12.1
Secondary	68.6%	61.5%	+7.1
Primary	72.1%	63.2%	+8.9
Exclusive	64.0%	80.8%	-16.8

Traditionalistic Culture	Public Interest	Rent-Seeking Interests	Difference
None	70.4%	62.2%	+8.2
Secondary	80.0%	62.9%	+17.1
Primary	71.4%	79.5%	-8.1
Exclusive	75.0%	57.0%	+18.0

Moralistic Culture	Public Interest	Rent-Seeking Interests	Difference
None	70.1%	65.5%	+4.6
Secondary	74.4%	69.0%	+5.4
Primary	72.1%	57.0%	+15.1
Exclusive	71.1%	63.4%	+7.7

*The entry in each cell is the percentage of that combination of Lobbying Status and Elazar Culture status that sees Legislative Fair Play Norms "Breaking Down," (3) where 1 = Not Occurring and 3 = Occurring.

lobbyists are again more likely to believe that norms of fair play are breaking down, except for the primary category. But is incivility making a difference, at least in the perceptions of the public interest and non-public interest lobbyists, with respect to the quality of legislative deliberations? Moreover, do those perceptions of civility and quality of legislative deliberations depend on the political culture present in the state?

Table 3.14. Elazar State Political Cultures, State Nonprofit Lobbying, and the Perception that State Legislative Incivility Has Affected Lobbyist's Work a Large Amount or a Great Deal*

Individualistic Culture	Public Interest	Rent-Seeking Interests	Difference
None	43.6%	30.6%	+13.0
Secondary	29.1%	29.1%	0.0
Primary	32.6%	31.1%	+1.5
Exclusive	45.9%	30.4%	+15.4

Traditionalistic Culture	Public Interest	Rent-Seeking Interests	Difference
None	34.2%	29.1%	+5.1
Secondary	42.9%	35.5%	+7.4
Primary	34.5%	33.7%	+0.8
Exclusive	42.9%	29.5%	+13.4

Moralistic Culture	Public Interest	Rent-Seeking Interests	Difference
None	40.4%	31.1%	+9.3
Secondary	32.6%	31.7%	+0.9
Primary	28.9%	28.3%	+0.6
Exclusive	42.6%	29.3%	+13.3

*The entry in each cell is the percentage of that combination of Lobbying Status and Elazar Culture Status that sees Legislative Incivility Affecting Lobbyists Work "a Large Amount" or "a Great Deal" (3 and 4 on a 4-point scale, where 1 = not at all, and 4 = A Great Deal).

The results shown in Tables 3.14 and 3.15 provide some answers to these questions. In all three culture types, the largest differences obtain between the states at the extremes (none v. exclusive), and very little difference is presented among the different exclusive cultures. So, clearly, the pattern for a "none" cultural status may also be reflected in the "exclusive" status in another cultural type.

Table 3.15. Elazar State Political Cultures, Nonprofit Lobbying, and the Percentage Seeing State Legislators in General as Uncivil*

Individualistic Culture	Public Interest	Rent-Seeking Interests	Difference
None	20.6%	17.3%	+3.3
Secondary	18.0%	15.7%	+2.3
Primary	18.2%	18.9%	-0.7
Exclusive	29.2%	4.2 %	+25.0
Traditionalistic Culture	**Public Interest**	**Rent-Seeking Nonprofit**	**Difference**
None	17.0%	16.8%	+.2
Secondary	31.8%	16.1%	+15.7
Primary	25.9%	17.7%	+8.2
Exclusive	20.4%	16.7%	+3.7
Moralistic Culture	**Public Interest**	**Rent-Seeking Interests**	**Difference**
None	25.8%	14.4%	+11.4
Secondary	16.3%	20.5%	-4.2
Primary	14.3%	16.0%	-1.7
Exclusive	19.6%	18.3%	+1.3

*The entry in each cell is the percentage of that combination of political culture and lobbyist status that evaluated "your state legislators in general" as uncivil (1 or 2, on a five-point scale where 1 = very uncivil, and 5 = very civil).

DISCUSSION AND FURTHER RESEARCH

The results from this national survey of state-level lobbyists offer a wide range of possibilities in assessing the nature of state lobbying and lobbyists, as well as how this lobbying contributes (or not) to levels of civility and, perhaps, legislative productivity/responsiveness. The most basic finding here is that many, even most, lobbyists take on a range of clients across the populations of nonprofits and those outside that grouping (businesses, associations, unions, etc.), although labor lobbying is the least associated (Table 3.2). Still, public interest lobbying coexists with other lobbying, and that may well have effects on how advocates perceive their roles and carry out their jobs. At the same time, public interest lobbyists do come from somewhat different backgrounds than do their rent-seeking counterparts. Most notably (Table 3.3), they are less likely to have served in the legislature and far more likely to have a nonprofit background. Indeed, almost half of all those who lobby on behalf of public interest nonprofits have prior experience in this kind of organization. Along with this trend, nonprofit public interest lobbyists are disproportionately female (55%, compared to 34% of their rent-seeking peers). Combining background and gender, a distinct picture of nonprofit public interest lobbyists begins to come into focus—fewer former legislators, more nonprofit veterans, and a majority of women. The subsequent question, and one that awaits future analysis, is: Does this make a difference?

Perhaps even more important than demographic elements are the partisan and ideological leanings of nonprofit public interest lobbyists when contrasted to their rent-seeking counterparts (Table 3.6). Stereotypically, perhaps, far more nonpartisan lobbyists, even among the many who lobby for other entities, express Democratic and liberal identifications (social and economic) than do other legislative advocates. Overall, these findings add to our aggregate picture of public interest lobbyists, and that may help us in assessing their views as to how legislatures operate. Most notably, nonprofit public interest lobbyists report: (a) more poor experiences in representing clients; (b) a greater sense that legislative norms are breaking down; and (c) a sense that fewer nonpartisan areas of policymaking are present (Table 3.8). Still, nonprofit public interest lobbyists and their rent-seeking counterparts differ little in their perceptions and assessments of civility in state legislatures, although there is some tendency for public interest advocates to see more personal effects of incivility (Table 3.9). Finally, and perhaps relatedly, nonprofit public interest lobbyists see lobbyists in general as contributing more to legislative incivility than do their counterparts (Table 3.10); otherwise, their perceptions of the causes of incivility do not differ much from those of other lobbyists.

In the end, while public interest and rent-seeking lobbyists reflect many similarities in their backgrounds, preferences, and reactions to their legislature, there are significant differences, sometimes exacerbated by their states' political cultures. We have just scratched the surface of the data from this study, and the evidence here needs to be combined with other multi-state data sets. Still, our analysis here represents a worthwhile first step in unpacking the relationship between differing types of lobbying and the workings of state legislatures.

REFERENCES

Almog-Bar, M., & Schmidt, H. (2014). Advocacy activities of nonprofit human service organizations: A critical review. *Nonprofit and Voluntary Sector Quarterly, 43*(1), 11–35.

Baron, J. (2003). Value analysis of political behavior: Self-interested: Moralistic: Altruistic: Moral. *University of Pennsylvania Law Review, 151*, 1135–1167.

Berry, J. M. (1999). The rise of citizen groups. In T. Scopol & M. Fiorina (Eds.), *Civic engagement in American democracy* (pp. 367–394). Brookings Institution Press.

Berry, J. M., with Arons, D. (2003). *A voice for nonprofits*. Brookings.

Corry, O. (2010). Defining and theorizing the third sector. In R. Taylor (Ed.), *Third sector research* (pp. 11–20). Springer.

Crutchfield, L. R., & McLeod Grant, H. (2012). *Forces for good: The six practices of high-impact nonprofits, revised and updated*. Jossey-Bass.

Elazar, D. J. (1972). *American federalism: A view from the states*. Thomas Y. Crowell Company.

Elazar, D. J. (1994). *The American mosaic: The impact of space, time, and culture on American politics*. Westview Press.

Flentje, H. E., & Aistrup, J. A. (2010). *Kansas politics and government: The clash of political cultures*. University of Nebraska Press.

Folbre, N., & Nelson, J. (2000). For love or money—or both? *The Journal of Economic Perspectives, 14*(4), 123–140.

Frumkin, P. (2016). The idea of a nonprofit and voluntary sector. In J. S. Ott & L. A. Dicke (Eds.), *The nature of the nonprofit system* (3rd ed.) (pp. 11–21). Westview Press.

Gradstein, M. (1993). Rent seeking and provision of public goods. *The Economic Journal, 103*(September), 1236–1243.

Harder, M. A., & Davis, R. G. (1979). *The legislature as an organization: A study of the Kansas legislature.* University Press of Kansas.

Hardy, R. J., Dohm, R. R., & Leuthold, D. A. (Eds.). (1995). *Missouri government and politics.* University of Missouri Press.

Lee, F. E. (2009). *Beyond ideology: Politics, principles, and partisanship in the U.S. Senate.* University of Chicago Press.

Lee, F. E. (2015). How party polarization affects governance. *Annual Review of Political Science, 18,* 261–282.

Lee, F. E. (2016). *Insecure majorities: Congress and the perpetual campaign.* University of Chicago Press.

Loomis, B. A. (1994). *Time, politics, and policy: A legislative year.* University Press of Kansas.

Nownes, A., with Loomis, B. (2020). Lobbying and the balance of power in American politics. In A. Ciglar, B. Loomis, & A. Nownes (Eds.), *Interest group politics* (10th ed.) (pp. 283–361). New York: Rowman and Littlefield.

Prentice, C. R. (2018). The 'state' of nonprofit lobbying research. *Nonprofit and Voluntary Sector Quarterly, 47*(4S), 204–217.

Prentice, C. R., & Brudney, J. L. (2017). Nonprofit lobbying strategy: Challenging or championing the conventional wisdom? *VOLUNTAS: International Journal of Voluntary and Nonprofit Organizations, 28*(3), 935–957.

Salamon, L. M., Geller, S. L., & Lorentz, S. C. (2008). *Nonprofit America: A force for democracy?* Johns Hopkins University Center for Civil Society Studies.

Shor, B. (2015). Polarization in American state legislatures. In J. Thurber & A. Yoshinaka (Eds.), *American gridlock: The sources, character, and impact of political polarization* (pp. 203–221). Cambridge University Press.

Shor, B., & McCarty, N. (2011). The ideological mapping of American legislatures. *American Political Science Review, 105*(3), 530–551.

Sinclair, B. (2014). *Party wars: Polarization and the politics of national policy making* (Vol. 10). University of Oklahoma Press.

Smith, S. S. (2014). *The Senate syndrome: The evolution of procedural warfare in the modern U.S. Senate* (Vol. 12). University of Oklahoma Press.

Suarez, D. F., & Hwang, H. (2008). Civic engagement and nonprofit lobbying in California, 1998–2003. *Nonprofit and Voluntary Sector Quarterly, 37*(1), 93–112.

Tulloch, G. (2005). *Public goods, redistribution and rent-seeking.* Edward Elgar Publishers.

CHAPTER FOUR

Term Limits:
Presumed and Actual Impact on Civility

William D. Schreckhise
Daniel E. Chand
Francis A. Benjamin

INTRODUCTION

Beginning in the early 1990s, voters in 21 states approved citizen initiatives imposing term limits on their state legislators. At the time of their adoption, "the prevailing view among term limits supporters [was] that term limits offer a guaranteed fix to the problems of legislators being too corrupt, too entrenched, and too beholden to special interests" (Scott and Bell, 1999, p. 8). Presently, 15 states limit the terms of members of their legislative bodies. The other six states' experiments with term limits have since ended, either through legislation or court action (National Conference of State Legislatures, 2015).

States that have term limits have adopted slightly different approaches to *how* legislative terms are limited. Arkansas and California impose a limit on the total number of years any individual can serve in either chamber of the legislature, and once that limit is met, the person can never again seek reelection for a seat in either chamber for the rest of his or her life. Other states have adopted chamber-specific limits without lifetime bans. These impose a set number of years an individual can serve in each chamber. Once the limit is reached in one chamber, the individual is free to run for election for a seat in the other chamber (provided he or she has not reached the limit in the second chamber). Michigan, Missouri, and Nevada prohibit individuals from running for a legislative seat once both chamber-specific limits are reached, while 11 other states allow legislators' clocks to "reset" if they do not serve in the legislature for two or more years. Table 4.1 displays the different approaches adopted by term-limit states.

To what extent might term limits impact civility among legislators? In what follows, we examine whether reported levels of legislative civility

Table 4.1. Term-Limited States, 2020

State	Year	Limit in Each Chamber	Lifetime Ban
Arizona	2000	8H/8S	
Arkansas	1998	16 years total	X
California	1996	12 years total	X
Colorado	1998	8H/8S	
Florida	2000	8H/8S	
Louisiana	2007	12 years total	
Maine	1996	8H/8S	
Michigan	1998	6H/8S	X
Missouri	2000	8H/8S	X
Montana	2000	8H/8S	
Nebraska	2006	8S	
Nevada	2010	12H/12S	X
Ohio	2000	8H/8S	
Oklahoma	2004	12 years total	X
South Dakota	2000	8H/8S	

Notes: "Year" refers to the first year any legislators became ineligible to run for reelection in each state. The values preceding "H" and "S" reflect the number of years members can serve in their states' houses and senates, respectively. State senators in Arkansas and California were affected by term limits in 2000. Michigan's senators were affected in 2002.

Source: National Conference of State Legislatures. 2012. "The Term Limited States." https://www.ncsl.org/research/about-state-legislatures/chart-of-term-limits-states.aspx.

differ between states that have adopted term limits and those that have not. We also explore what other factors might cause—or exacerbate—the potential differences in the degrees of levels of civility that occur between states that impose term limits on their state legislators and those that do not. This is done through an examination of term limits' relationships with legislative turnover, partisanship, political polarization, and legislative professionalization. We then explore empirically the link between term limits and civility via an examination of reported levels of civility in the National Survey of State Legislative Lobbyists, a survey of roughly 1,000 lobbyists in all 50 states who work with state legislators. We also examine the responses lobbyists provide in the several opportunities they were given to provide written comments, along with observations provided by lobbyists and legislators from previous research along these lines.

TERM LIMITS AND CIVILITY

Term limits are a popular topic of study among political scientists, particularly those interested in legislative politics. This is for good reason. As Carey et al. (2006) note, "the imposition of limits on time in office is the most significant innovation in state legislatures since the legislative modernization movement of the 1960s and 1970s" (p. 105). Studies along these lines include examinations of term limits' effects on gender and racial/ethnic diversity in representation in state legislatures (Penning, 2003; Carey et al., 2006), their impact on policy innovation and diffusion (Kousser, 2005), the influence of the state executive branch vis-à-vis the legislature (Moncrief and Thomson, 2001; Peery and Little, 2002; Kousser, 2005; Carey et al., 2006), the influence of party and legislative committee leadership (Moncrief and Thompson, 2001; Carey et al., 2006), and the influence of interest groups (Peery and Little, 2002), to name but a few.

Despite the rich body of research examining the various aspects of term limits, to a certain extent, little of it has focused on the impact term limits have possibly had on civil behavior among legislators. One of the few studies that examines somewhat related questions comes from Moncrief and Thompson's (2011) survey of state legislators in states with term limits. The study itself, however, produces conflicting findings. In their survey they asked the lobbyists whether they thought that term limits were more likely or less likely to make legislators "collegial and courteous." Respondents said that term limits made legislators twice as likely to be less courteous in committee hearings and three times more likely to be less courteous on the floor of the chamber. At the same time, however, Moncrief and Thompson found that, as a group, the lobbyists were largely neutral about term limits' impacts: roughly half of them responded that term limits had no effect on the levels of collegiality in their respective chambers.

Another study by Kurtz and his colleagues (2007) examined term limits' effects on the operations of legislatures, as part of the Joint Project on Term Limits (JPTL), a multi-organization collaboration between researchers with the National Conference of State Legislatures, the Council of State Governments, and State Legislative Leaders Foundation. The JPTL concluded that term limits fundamentally alter how legislative bodies operate by increasing turnover. The resulting dramatic decline in institutional seniority has been highly correlated to declines in institutional memory, legislative expertise, and durable long-term relationships for legislators. Notably, legislators report declines not just in long-term relationships among themselves, but also with bureaucrats and lobbyists (Kurtz et al., 2007, p. 3). Clearly, such a notable disruption to legislatures could have profound effects on institutional culture and civility among members of the bodies.

Other studies have indicated a general decline in camaraderie in term-limited legislative chambers. Berman (2007), in his examination of the relationship between term limits and "legislative climate," concludes that term-limited legislators normally show less respect for traditional processes, such as giving advance notice of arguments or amendments. They also exhibit less adherence to unwritten rules or "norms," which results in less-predictable behavior. With shorter tenures in office, members are less likely to take the time to develop significant relationships with fellow members or lobbyists. They are also generally less willing to compromise, less likely to defer to the institution's leadership, and less willing to show respect for institutional procedures (Berman, 2007, pp. 112–114). In a study of Arkansas, English and Weberg (2004) similarly found that both legislators and lobbyists claimed that "legislators don't seem to care as much about their colleagues' feelings or keep their word with lobbyists about supporting legislation" (p. 29) after term limits go into effect.

From this limited body of evidence, we suspect that civility should be stronger in non-term-limited states than is the case in states with term limits. This is because non-term-limited legislators have a greater incentive to create and maintain long-term working relationships with their fellow members, including those individuals working across the aisle. As one respondent to our survey put it, "Term limits prevent legislators from building relationships that promote bipartisan activity [and] polarized elections cause new elected officials to come into the legislature from a bruising election battle and they continue their partisan approach as a legislator." Another one added, "Term limits [have] killed any goodwill across the aisle."

POLARIZATION AND PARTISANSHIP

In addition to the research mentioned above, an examination of term limits' impacts in other areas would be useful. Along these lines, we explore additional work below that could provide insight into how term limits could, in fact, affect civility among legislators. One area that is worth examining is the relationship between term limits and ideological polarization and partisanship. To what extent might term limits contribute to the ideological differences between the two major political parties, and to what extent could these ideological cleavages hinder (or even help) the degree to which legislators behave civilly toward one another? Such an examination of this research could be fruitful because term-limited legislatures, by the more transient nature of their own legislators, may see less bipartisan cooperation.

The broader political science literature indicates that partisanship has increased nationally within the last couple of decades (Iyengar et al., 2019). Many observers attribute the rise in partisanship to parties becoming more ideologically strict, while ideologically moderate candidates for office in both parties are becoming rarer (Thomsen, 2017). This is due, in part, to the greater frequency of moderate legislators being "primaried," that is, being outflanked on the right by Republican primary challengers in Republican-safe districts, and on the left in Democratic districts (Jewitt and Treul, 2019). Additionally, since the 1990s, Americans have increasingly sorted themselves geographically into strongly liberal or conservative communities (Lang and Pearson-Merkowitz, 2015). Consequently, we see increasing partisanship in Congress, which notably lacks term limits (Andris et al., 2015). Taken as a whole, this suggests that the any increase in the levels of state legislator partisanship may not be unique to term-limited states. Nor is there evidence that term limits contribute to ideological polarization. Carey et al. (2006) found instead that newer members of legislatures in term-limited states were no more ideologically extreme than were new members in states without term limits. Given increasing partisanship nationally, it is difficult to determine whether greater partisanship in term-limit-adopting states is genuinely due to a decline in cross-party relationships or simply part of a broader national trend.

With this in mind, the extent to which term limits contribute to polarization and partisanship is also unclear. As Olson and Rogowski (2020, p. 572) recently noted, "After more than two decades of experience with term limits, strikingly little is known about their effects on partisanship and polarization." What research has been done in this area suggests that greater degrees of ideological polarization exist between the legislators from the two major parties in term-limited state legislatures when compared to legislatures without term limits (Olson and Rogowski, 2020). Additionally, the presence of term limits has been found to increase polarization by incentivizing parties in states to recruit and finance candidates for office in more partisan fashions (Masket and Shor, 2015).

The concern that term limits exacerbate party divisions and limit bipartisan cooperation was verified by Swift and VanderMolen (2015), who found that term limits alter legislators' incentive to behave in a bipartisan fashion. They built their work on that of Carey et al. (2006), who found that term-limited legislators author fewer bills that provide direct benefits for their constituents in their districts. Swift and VanderMolen (2015) assert that because term limits weaken the link between constituent and legislator, countering partisan roll-call votes with bipartisan co-sponsorship behavior becomes less necessary. The weaker connection between legislator and constituency frees them (or even compels them) to place their loyalty with their political party. As a result, the instinct to become more partisan in co-sponsorship in a term-limited legislature is more likely to be the product of a legislator's concern over future campaign contributors and possible challengers than constituents.

Evidence suggests the decline in cross-party relationships not only increases partisanship but also decreases overall institutional civility because new, ideologically rigid legislators are less willing to work with their fellow members across the aisle. In Michigan, for example, Sarbaugh-Thompson and her colleagues (2004) reported a decline in cross-party relationships after term limits were adopted. In another study, a Maine legislator stated that "members elected under term limits do not know each other very well and have not had the time to develop personal relationships with their colleagues.... This is particularly true for members from opposite parties" (Powell and Jones, 2004, pp. 37–40).

TURNOVER AND LIFETIME BANS

We suspect that the higher rate of turnover brought by term limits in the legislature will play a role in shaping the extent to which legislators behave in a civil manner to one another. This is because of the simple fact that legislators can assume they will serve for shorter periods of time, which, in turn, creates legislative bodies collectively composed of individuals who are less able to establish long-term working relationships. Even in Michigan, the state with the least restrictive form of term limits, one can expect to have a legislature composed of *entirely* different individuals every 14 years.[1] Such a frequent reconstruction of completely new occupants to the legislature diminishes the functionality of these bodies. One respondent from Michigan said in our survey when asked whether norms of fair play were breaking down in the person's state's legislature, "There has been a long, slow decline in Michigan since instituting term limits, beginning in 1998. It has somewhat accelerated with each cycle of new, less experienced and less qualified legislators."

Table 4.2 reveals the extent to which term limits have an impact on turnover. Specifically, it displays the rate of turnover in 2017 for states without term limits and states with term limits, both those with and without lifetime bans. States without term limits had in the 2017–2018 biennium a turnover rate of 21.8%. In other words, 21.8% of their legislators were in their freshman term. States with term limits but without lifetime bans on the future service of veteran lawmakers had a turnover rate of 32%. Those with term limits and subsequent lifetime bans had a turnover rate of 37%.[2]

We further suspect this turnover will make newer members less inclined to adhere to the norms and traditions of the institutions. As one respondent to our survey stated:

> Term limits has [sic] had a huge impact on our legislature. First, the really good ones (either party) get termed out so we lose their professionalism, their experience, and their knowledge. Second, there are only so many true "leaders" in a generation. With term limits we are down to about the 3rd or 4th level. The legislating for the "greater good" is very rarely happening and…those who do…are primaried by their own party.

Instead, these new members will be more inclined to engage in less civil behavior. As another respondent to our survey said, "Due to term limits, legislators have been divorced from the unwritten rules and traditions of 'old hands' who espoused civility and adherence to 'The Process.'" Indeed, preliminary analysis suggests this is the case. Figure 4.1 shows that legislatures with higher degrees of turnover see less civility. The measure *Civility* will be discussed in further detail below. For now, it is worth noting that the states with the highest degree of turnover also have the least amount of civility. States with less turnover appear to be more civil.

The actual type of term limits may also play a role in shaping a legislature's turnover as it relates to civility. We suspect the type of term limit

Table 4.2. Term Limits and Mean Membership Turnover, 2017

	Turnover (%)	N
States with no term limits	21.8	36
State with term limits and no lifetime ban	31.7	8
States with term limits and lifetime bans	36.7	5

Sources: Council of State Governments. 2019. Book of the States. "Membership Turnover in the Legislatures: 2017." http://knowledgecenter. csg.org/kc/system/files/3.4.2018_0.pdf. National Conference of State Legislatures. 2015. "The Term Limited States." https://www.ncsl.org/ research/about-state-legislatures/chart-of-term-limits-states.aspx.

Note: "Turnover" presents the percentage of membership changes from the previous year's legislature averaged across both chambers (except unicameral Nebraska), and across each group of states.

will affect civility for two reasons. First, although term-limited states may have higher rates of turnover from year to year, over the long run, states that permit individuals to return will likely see them return. Thus, the real impact of turnover could be weakened. Second, individuals who are term-limited yet face the likelihood they will return in the future will be less likely to act in an uncivil manner to their fellow legislators, simply because they might have to face at least some of their old colleagues when they return.

PROFESSIONALIZATION

It is possible that the extent to which a legislature is professionalized could play a role in shaping civil behavior among legislators. As chapter two of this volume reports, one aspect of a legislature's professionalism is related to higher levels of reported civility—that is, the amount of pay a legislator receives. Additionally, there is evidence to suggest that profes-

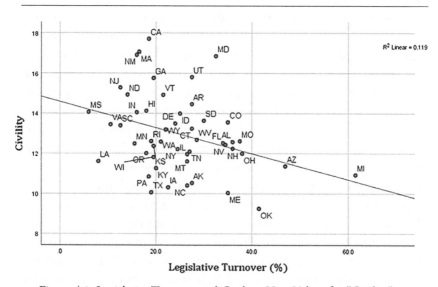

Figure 4.1. Legislative Turnover and Civility. *Note:* Values for "Civility" reflect the mean value for each state on the indexed variable *Civility.* Values for "Legislative Turnover" reflect the percentage of new members starting in each state's legislature at the beginning of the 2017–2018 biennium. *Source:* Council of State Governments. 2019. *Book of the States.* "Membership Turnover in the Legislatures: 2017." http://knowledgecenter.csg.org/kc/system/files/3.4.2018_0.pdf.

sionalism plays a role in assisting legislators in getting what they want. Kousser (2005), in his extensive study of the impact of term limits on state legislatures, found that the effects of term limits as they relate to a legislature's dealings with the state executive branch were muted by the presence of professionalized staff for the legislators. He writes:

> Those in professional houses that meet all year and pay salaries will not suffer greatly from the delays that come when they oppose the executive branch. Members of part-time bodies, though, face high opportunity cost if a governor calls them back into special session to resolve a budget dispute or another major issue. Those members usually hold second jobs, since salaries in citizen bodies are so low (Kousser, 2005, pp. 154–155).

Additionally, Moncrief and Thompson (2011) found that the extent to which a state legislature was professionalized moderated how strongly lobbyists believed that term limits affected the degree to which legislators behaved courteously.

On the other hand, other studies have found that legislators in chambers deemed to be more professionalized behave in ways that seem a bit counterintuitive. While Swift and VanderMolen (2015) found that legislators in term-limited states were less likely to cosponsor bipartisan legislation with legislators across the aisle, legislation that was cosponsored by members from different parties occurred even *less* often in chambers that were more professionalized. Birkhead (2015) provides a similarly counterintuitive finding in his examination of the relationship between how ideologically extreme a candidate for legislative office is and his or her success when seeking election to such an office. He finds that ideologically extreme legislative candidates were generally less successful on election day than were moderates, which is perhaps unsurprising. What is surprising are his findings that this is not the case for candidate seeking seats in more professionalized legislatures. Ideologically extreme candidates running for positions in more professionalized legislatures were instead *more likely* to be successful than moderate ones in their bids for election. In other words, the more professionalized the legislature to which the candidate aspires, the more successful he or she will be by being farther from the ideological center. Together, the work by Swift and VanderMolen (2016) and Birkhead (2015) suggests that more professionalized legislatures seem to breed less bipartisanship and greater ideological polarization, both of which, in turn, could cause less civility among legislators.

PROGRESSIVE AMBITION

Legislators serving in term-limited states, as expected, serve less time in the legislature, which could negatively affect how they behave toward each other. As such, it is possible that individual legislators are less likely to view their positions as long-term. This is for two reasons. First, legislators may view their positions as stepping-stones to other offices. Indeed, Herrick and Thomas (2005) found that legislators in states with term limits hold a higher degree of self-stated progressive ambition (see Schlesinger, 1966). That is, they are more likely to state that they view their political careers as directing them toward higher office. Similarly, Penning (2003), via his surveys of Michigan legislators who were then facing the imposition of term limits for the first time, reported that 70% of respondents agreed with the statement "term limits will force legislators to run for higher office sooner than they would like" (p. 42). Second, the presence of term limits changes the calculus for legislators contemplating a run for higher office. In states without term limits, incumbent legislators face uncertainty if they decide to run for another office. If they choose to seek higher office, this can mean "abandoning a safe legislative seat for an uncertain future," in the words of Powell (2003, p. 134). Term-limited legislators do not have the luxury of remaining in their current seats.

This leaves us with a rough understanding of the relationship between term limits and civility in state government. Based on prior research, term limits appear to have contributed to an erosion of norms in state capitals, which has had some impact on civility. By increasing turnover, term limits fundamentally alter relationships in legislatures, reducing the incentives of members to form long-lasting and cooperative bonds with fellow members, especially those across the aisle. Further, term-limited legislators appear less concerned about institutional norms related to the long-term well-being of the legislative body in which they temporarily serve.

The following section addresses the question of whether term limits have an impact on legislative civility directly. In it, we discuss a measure of civility developed from the responses of lobbyists who participated in the National Survey of State Legislative Lobbyists, a survey conducted of legislative lobbyists serving in all 50 states. In that section, we take into proper account the role that other factors can play in shaping civility, including the extent to which the state legislature is professionalized and/or ideologically polarized, and the degree to which the two parties are numerically competitive, among other things.

DATA

As with the measure employed in chapter two of this volume, we predict in this chapter legislative civility. Thus, the dependent variable examined in the analyses that follow is perceived civility, a variable named *Civility.* The variable is an additive index composed of the lobbyists' responses to three questions, each on a 10-point scale (with 10 being the highest level of agreement for each question) indicating their degree of agreement with the following statements put to them on the survey:[3]

• My state legislature is more civil than other state legislatures.
• My state legislature is more civil than Congress.
• My state legislature is more civil than it was 10 years ago.

Our primary dependent variable of interest is the presence of term limits. This is measured in the models below in two different forms. It is first employed as a dichotomous variable, indicating whether the state has in effect term limits (coded as 1) or not (coded as 0) as the variable *Term Limits.* A subsequent model examines the extent to which form of term limits has the greatest impact on civility, comparing states with term limits with *lifetime bans* with states without term limits. Both variables were derived from NCSL (2018).

We are interested in seeing how term limits and each state legislature's level of professionalization interact to shape the legislature's degree of civility. To do this, we employ in the models an index composed of standardized measures of the "three S's of state professionalization: salary, staff, and session length" (Kousser, 2005, p. 12). Additionally, we include a measure of the number of employment-type benefits legislators receive, including whether they receive state-sponsored health, dental, vision, disability, and life insurance, as well as retirement benefits, all of which are at least partially funded by the state. The values for this measure are reflected in the variable *Professional.*[4] A higher score reflects a more professionalized legislature—that is, one in which legislators receive higher pay, better benefits, and more staff support, and participate in longer sessions. The data for this variable come from the National Conference of State Legislatures (2017; 2018a; 2018b; 2018c; 2020).

Much of the widespread concern with declining levels of civility in the United States has come with a recognition of the ideological polarization of political elites at the national level (Boatright et al., 2019). Shor and McCarty (2011) note that growing ideological differences between the two national political parties is reflected in similar differences emerging among state legislators over the course of the preceding 15 years. However, as chapter two reports, states with higher degrees of political polarization between the two political parties saw higher degrees of reported civility. Because the results for this variable were statistically significant in the models presented in chapter two, we include the same variable, named *Polarization* in the models presented in this chapter.[5] A higher value for this variable reflects greater ideological distance between the parties in each legislature (averaged across the two chambers). Data for this measure come from Shor's (2018) updated dataset.

Legislative civility could also be related to the extent to which the two major parties are in competition with each other in the statehouse. A state legislature that that has two political parties with roughly equal numbers of adherents could see much more intense struggles over just about everything simply because there is no ready-made majority to ensure a measure's success. By contrast, a legislature dominated by a single party does have a more easily obtained majority. It is also possible the opposite is in effect: Parties that control a large majority in the two chambers have less incentive to behave with civility toward members from across the aisle. To take these two possibilities into account, included in the models is a measure of inter-party competition, called *Competition.* It reflects the absolute value of the difference between the number of Democrats and Republicans in each state's legislative chambers, divided by the total number of members in each chamber and averaging the number between the states' two chambers (see Lax and Phillips, 2012, p. 159 for a similar measure).[6] States with a value closer to 1 have more competition and reflect greater numerical parity between the parties in the states' two chambers; states with values closer to 0 are more single-party dominant. The data for this variable are derived from NCSL (2018d).

We include the variable *Opportunity*. It is a measure of the extent to which legislators who desire higher office could expect to win higher office. Specifically, the measure reflects the number of total U.S. House seats available to the legislators as a group. Developed by Maestas (2000), this measure also accounts for the number of state legislators who could reasonably seek higher political legislative office. Thus, this variable is the ratio of U.S. House seats to the total number of legislative seats that exist in each state. A larger value reflects more opportunity to advance to the U.S. House of Representatives. To be sure, there are other higher offices

Table 4.3. Summary Statistics

Variable	Mean	SD	Min	Max	Source
Dependent variables					
Civility	12.823	4.988	3	28	NSSLL
Independent variables					
State (N = 44)					
Term Limits	0.291	0.454	0	1	NCSL (2015)
Term Limit Type	1.438	0.735	1	3	NCSL (2015)
Professional	0.001	0.743	-1.325	2.145	
Opportunity	0.066	0.079	0.005	0.442	
Polarization	3.493	1.035	1.559	6.870	
Competition	0.690	0.204	0.145	0.973	
%Women	26.531	7.492	11.100	40.000	
%Minority	16.993	12.796	1.000	78.000	
Individual (N = 801)					
Years	15.509	10.868	0	55	NSSLL
Age	4.699	1.446	1	7	NSSLL
Woman	0.415	0.493	0	1	NSSLL
Republican	0.287	0.452	0	1	NSSLL
Minority	0.091	0.288	0	1	NSSLL

Note: "NSSLL" refers to the National Survey of State Legislative Lobbyists, the survey referenced throughout this volume.

to which a career-minded legislator could aspire, such as a statewide office or a seat in the U.S. Senate. However, these are roughly equal in number across the 50 states. This variable is included in the model because the long-term career prospects for legislators in term-limited states are different from the prospects obtaining for legislators serving in states without term limits. As mentioned above, term-limited legislators cannot stay in their state legislature positions for a long time. As such, the extent to which they can pursue higher office may have an impact or whether they behave in a civil manner with their colleagues.

Included as additional control variables in the models are two measures related to the demographic composition of the state legislature. These are the percentage of the legislature that is female *(% Women)* and the percentage of the legislature that is not white and non-Hispanic (*% Minority*). We include them because chapter two provides evidence that legislatures with proportionally more women and more racial/ethnic minority members receive higher civility ratings. We also include demographic variables for the lobbyist respondents themselves. They are included because some groups of individuals may respond differently from other groups to questions used to generate the civility index. These personal characteristics include the number of years the lobbyist has worked as such (*Years*), and the lobbyist's age, sex (*Woman*), party affiliation (*Republican*), and race/ethnicity (*Minority*). The summary statistics and mean values of the variables in the analytical models are reported in Table 4.3.

RESULTS

To test whether respondents in states with term limits rate their legislatures' levels of civility lower than their counterparts in non-term-limited states, multilevel OLS models were run, with lobbyist-respondents nested in states. The dependent variable in each of the models is the individual respondent's rating of his or her state legislature on the three-part civility index discussed above—that is, the variable *Civility*. A higher score for the variable *Civility* reflects the respondent rating his or her legislature as more civil; a lower score reflects a less-civil rating for the legislature by the respondent.

Model 1 is presented in Table 4.4. It includes the dichotomous form of the term limits variable, *Term Limits,* as the primary independent variable of interest. Also included are the other variables related to the extent to which the legislature is professionalized, along with the other indicators related to opportunities for higher office, the extent to which the legislature is ideologically polarized, and the extent to which the two parties in the legislature are numerically competitive. The other control variables are also included.

In Model 1, the coefficient for the variable *Term Limits* is negative and statistically significant. As such, it can be said with a degree of certainty that term-limited legislatures have lower degrees of rated civility than legislatures in which there are no such limits imposed on the legislators. The coefficient indicates, *ceteris paribus*, lobbyists from states with term limits score their legislatures one point lower on the *Civility* index than do respondents from states without term limits.

However, not all term limits are the same. As mentioned previously, some states impose a lifetime limit on the amount of time an individual can serve in the legislature, while other term-limited states do not impose such a lifetime ban when a person's limit is reached. To determine whether the presence of such a lifetime ban affects legislative civility, another model is presented in Table 4.4. In Model 2, the independent variable for term limits, *Term Limits Type*, is a factor variable, allowing for the estimation of coefficients that compare the effect of each type of term limits. That is, this comparison will allow for an examination of the link between civility in states without term limits and states with term limits but without lifetime bans, and similarly between states without term limits and those that do impose the ban. The coefficient for either form of the *Term Limits Type* variable is not statistically significant, indicating that the presence of either type of term limit has no impact on civility. As such, although it can be said the *presence* of term limits is related to perceived levels of legislative civility, it is not the case that there is a relationship between the *type* of term limit a state has implemented and a state's level of legislative civility.

The results for the variable *Competition* suggest additional analyses are warranted. It was significant in both of the models examined so far, whereas most of the other variables indicating the natures of the legislatures, such as the variables *Professional, Opportunity,* and *Polarization* were not. It is possible that the extent to which a state's legislative parties are numerically competitive could add to the effect that term limits have on a legislature's levels of civility. Put more simply, states with very

Table 4.4. Term Limits and Perceived Civility

	Model 1 Coef.	S.E.	Model 2 Coef.	S.E.	Model 3 Coef.	S.E.
Fixed effects						
Intercept	14.535***	1.299	14.453***	1.329	14.044***	1.492
State Term Limits	-1.070*	0.529			0.315	2.167
Term Limit Type						
No life ban			-1.178	0.655		
Lifetime ban			-0.925	0.738		
Professional	-0.313	0.488	-0.338	0.495	-0.345	0.487
Opportunity	4.488	5.935	4.393	5.935	4.293	5.905
Polarization	0.384	0.293	0.393	0.294	0.425	0.298
Competition	-4.802**	1.487	-4.722**	1.512	-4.458**	1.568
Term Limits x Competition					-1.993	3.029
%Women	0.031	0.039	0.032	0.039	0.036	0.040
%Minority	0.059*	0.029	0.059*	0.029	0.060*	0.028
Individual						
Years	-0.015	0.019	-0.015	0.019	-0.015	0.019
Age	-0.249	0.137	-0.249	0.137	-0.253	0.137
Woman	-1.338***	0.347	-1.334***	0.347	-1.323***	0.348
Republican	1.193**	0.374	1.199**	0.375	1.200**	0.374
Minority	1.181*	0.594	1.170*	0.596	1.168*	0.595
Random effects						
Intercept	1.193	0.516	1.185	0.515	1.162	0.511
Residual	20.995	1.078	20.997	1.078	20.998	1.078
No. of respondents	801		801		801	
No. of states	44		44		44	
LL	-2,370.887		-2,370.8473		-2,370.672	
df	15		16		16	
AIC	4,771.773		4,773.695		4,773.344	
BIC	4,842.061		4,848.668		4,848.318	

Note: The indexed variable *Civility* is the dependent variable in each model.
*p<.05; **p<.01; ***p<.001.

competitive parties *and* term limits could have even lower levels of civility than is the case in states with only *either* term limits or competitive legislative parties. This is potentially the case because each election puts more stress on the desire of the majority to maintain its majority status in competitive term-limited states, while at the same time providing an opening for the minority party to win majority status. This, in turn, is caused by the fact that in term-limited states, the luxury of remaining incumbent has an expiration date. With presumably more open seats during every legislative election, the fights in competitive states during elections could become more acute, bringing with them the potential for more uncivil behavior in the legislature. To test this possibility, included in Model 3 is a term that intersects the state's *Competition* variable with the *Term Limits* variable. A significant coefficient would indicate that the role term limits play in shaping civility is different in competitive states than in non-competitive ones. However, the variable is not significant, indicating that this is not the case. Thus, there is no evidence that term limits' effects on civility are any greater in competitive states.

DISCUSSION AND CONCLUSION

The models presented above provide some insight into the relationship between term limits and civility. The results for Model 1 indicate that term limits do indeed have a relationship to civility. Legislative lobbyists rate legislators in states without term limits as more civil than those legislators in states that impose term limits on their members. Model 2 indicates that the type of term limit is not important. There is no difference in the levels of perceived civility between states without term limits and those with them without lifetime bans. Nor is there a difference between the levels of civility in states without term limits and those with term limits and lifetime bans.

It is important to note that although Model 1 provides evidence that a difference in civility exists between term-limited states and non-term-limited states, the size of the coefficient is not large. The value of the coefficient indicates that, everything else equal, lobbyist respondents from term-limited states rate their lobbyists only roughly one point lower in the indexed *Civility* variable, a variable that has a standard deviation of 5.0. Hence, although differences exist between the two types of states, the evidence presented here does not paint a picture of term-limited states wallowing in the mire of incivility, while non-term-limited states exist in a condition of perfect utopian civility. Indeed, California is the state with the greatest reported level of perceived civility, yet its term limits come with a lifetime ban imposed after only 12 years of service for its legislators. Oklahoma shares with California the distinction of having the most restrictive form of term limits, and Oklahoma has the lowest level of reported perceived civility. Thus, other explanations are needed to better explain the differences in civility across the different states.

It is important to note that the data included in the analyses are cross-sectional. Because of this, the specific reasons behind the finding that term-limited legislatures are rated as less civil than non-term-limited ones cannot be conclusively determined. In other words, we cannot say for sure what is driving the differences in civility ratings between the term-limited states and those without them. However, our analyses can provide us with some clues. As mentioned above, there are a few ways in which term limits could cause this difference in perceived civility. First, term limits cause greater turnover, as evidenced by the results presented in Table 4.2. States with lifetime bans have a turnover rate that is roughly 70% greater than states without term limits. Even states with term limits and no lifetime bans have a turnover rate of nearly 50% more than states without term limits.

Term limits could cause greater political polarization by discouraging bipartisan collaboration on legislation and other legislative work, which in turn causes greater incivility among legislators. The biennial influx of freshmen lawmakers, and the simultaneous exodus of more experienced ones, could make it difficult to develop the trust and goodwill that come as the result of forming long-term working relationships with others, including those from across the aisle. However, the cross-sectional nature of the analyses here prevents us from making any definitive claims, and as such, we cannot provide evidence that term limits cause greater partisanship, and that growing partisanship makes legislators behave in a less-civil manner. However, we can offer some additional analyses that may shed light on the notion. These can be done via a simple examination of the degree to which the two political parties are distant ideologically and comparing these distances between states with term limits and those without them. While the mean value on the variable indicating ideological distance, *Polarization,* is a bit higher for term-limited states (3.8) than for non-term-limited ones (3.2), a t-test of unequal variances reveals the difference is not statistically significant.[7]

Thus, at the very least, this analysis suggests that state legislatures are not divided into clear camps, that is, one that is term-limited and remarkably polarized, and the other unpolarized and not term-limited. Nor can it be said from the analyses presented above that polarization is causing great incivility. Still, the research mentioned earlier in this chapter that illustrates the difficulties with bipartisan collaboration should not be discounted, and as such, further research that relates state legislative term limits, polarization, bipartisan collaboration, and civility is warranted.

NOTES

1. To be sure, an individual could be elected to a chamber in year one, serve for two years, then sit out of the legislature for the next 11, then return to the legislature in year 13, and serve until year 14. Such a scenario would mean the legislature would not be composed of entirely different individuals in years one and year 14.

2. A t-test between the mean turnover rate for term-limited states and the mean turnover rate for non-term-limited states (assuming unequal variances) was significant: $t = -3.548$; $p = 0.001$; N = 49; df=16.1.

3. The Cronbach's alpha for the indexed *Civility* variable was 0.800.

4. The Cronbach's alpha for the indexed *Professionalization* variable was 0.709. In some states, legislators receive their pay on a per diem basis only while the legislature is in session. For the purpose of creating the indexed variable, in these cases, we calculated level of compensation by multiplying the per diem rate by the number of days the legislature was in session. For both legislators in salaried legislatures and legislatures that pay per diem rates, we calculated their compensation based on the 2017–2018 biennium (and divided by two). We normed these salary figures by dividing the total amount a legislator would earn in a year by the state's median income in 2018 dollars (U.S. Census Bureau, 2020). In some cases, the NCSL survey from which we drew our data did not reveal whether the state covered the full amount or a partial amount of the various forms of benefits, but indicated the coverage was the same for legislators as it was for state employees. In these cases, we assumed this indicated the state covered a portion of the amount. In a few cases, legislators elected after a certain date were not eligible for coverage. In these cases, we gave the state a "0." If only the senate were covered, that state received a "0" for that portion of the index. For the purpose of creating the session length component of the indexed variable, we computed the total number of days the legislature was in session for the 2017–2018 biennium, including days in the count from both the regular session and any special sessions.

5. Ideological scores for state legislators were developed by Shor and McCarty (2011) in a form similar to the way in which Poole and Rosenthal (1991, 1997) calculated ideological scores for members of the U.S. Congress.

6. We excluded Nebraska because of its unicameral make-up and officially nonpartisan legislature.

7. t=-1.345; p=0.099; N=45; df=16.190.

REFERENCES

Andris, C., Marcus, D. L., Hamilton, J., Martino, M., Gunning, C. E., & Selden, J. A. (2015). The rise of partisanship and super-cooperators in the U.S. House of Representatives. *PLoS ONE, 10*(4). https://doi.org/10.1371/journal.pone.0123507.

Berman, D. R. (2007). Legislative climate. In K. T. Kurtz, B. E. Cain, & R. G. Niemi (Eds.), *Institutional change in American politics: The case of term limits* (pp. 107–118). University of Michigan Press.

Birkhead, N. A. (2015). The role of ideology in state legislative elections. *Legislative Studies Quarterly, 40*(1), 55–82.

Boatright, R. G., Shaffer, T. J., Sobieraj, S., & Young, D. G. (2019). *A crisis of civility? Political discourse and its discontents*. Routledge.

Jewitt, C. E., & Treul, S. A. (2019). Ideological primary competition and congressional behavior. *Congress and the Presidency, 46*(3), 471–494. https://doi.org/10.1080/07343469.2019.1600173.

Carey, J. M., Niemi, R. G., Powell, L. W., & Moncrief, G. F. (2006). The effects of term limits on state legislatures: A new survey of the 50 states. *Legislative Studies Quarterly, 31*(1), 105–134.

English, A., & Weberg, B. (2004). *Term limits in the Arkansas general assembly: A citizen legislature responds*. Joint Project on Term Limits. https://www.ncsl.org/Portals/1/documents/jptl/casestudies/Arkansasv2.pdf.

Herrick, R., & Thomas, S. (2005). Do term limits make a difference? Ambition and motivations among U.S. state legislators. *American Politics Research, 33*(5), 726–747.

Iyengar, S., Lelkes, Y., Levendusky, M., Malhotra, N., & Westwood, S. J. (2019). The origins and consequences of affective polarization in the United States. *Annual Review of Political Science, 22*(May), 129–146.

Kousser, T. (2005). *Term limits and the dismantling of state legislative professionalism*. Cambridge University Press.

Kurtz, K. T., Cain, B. E., & Niemi. R. G. (2007). *Institutional change in American politics: The case of term limits*. University of Michigan Press.

Lang, C., & Pearson-Merkowitz, S. (2015). Partisan sorting in the United States, 1972–2012: New evidence from a dynamic analysis. *Political Geography, 48* (September), 119–129.

Lax, J., & Phillips, J. (2012). The democratic deficit in the states. *American Journal of Political Science, 56*(1), 148–166.

Maestas, C. (2000). Professional legislatures and ambitious politicians: Policy responsiveness of state institutions. *Legislative Studies Quarterly, 24*(4), 663–690.

Masket, S., & Shor, B. (2015). Polarization without parties: Term limits and legislative partisanship in Nebraska's unicameral legislature. *State Politics and Policy Quarterly, 15*(1), 7–90.

May, D. A., & Pirch, K. A. (2016). Polarization, inequality, and the state legislatures. *Journal of Politics and Law, 9*(4), 115–123.

Miller, S. M., Nicholson-Crotty, J., & Nicholson-Crotty, S. (2018). The consequences of legislative term limits for policy diffusion. *Political Research Quarterly, 71*(3), 573–585.

Moncrief, G., & Thompson, J. A. (2001). On the outside looking in: Lobbyists' perspectives on the effects of state legislative term limits. *State Politics & Policy Quarterly, 1*(4), 394–411.

National Conference of State Legislatures. (2015, March 13). The term-limited states. https://www.ncsl.org/research/about-state-legislatures/chart-of-term-limits-states.aspx.

National Conference of State Legislatures. (2017). *2017 legislative session calendar.* https://www.ncsl.org/documents/ncsl/2017sessioncalendar.pdf.

National Conference of State Legislatures. (2018a). 2018 legislator compensation information. https://www.ncsl.org/research/about-state-legislatures/legislator-compensation-2018.aspx.

National Conference of State Legislatures. (2018b). *2018 legislative session calendar.* https://www.ncsl.org/documents/ncsl/2018_Session_Calendar.pdf.

National Conference of State Legislatures. (2018c). Legislative staff. https://www.ncsl.org/research/about-state-legislatures/staff-change-chart-1979-1988-1996-2003-2009.aspx.

National Conference of State Legislatures. (2018d). *2018 state & legislative partisan composition.* https://www.ncsl.org/Portals/1/Documents/Elections/Legis_Control_011018_26973.pdf.

National Conference of State Legislatures. (2020). *2016 survey: State legislative retirement benefits.* https://www.ncsl.org/Portals/1/Documents/legismgt/2016_Leg_Comp_Retirement_Benefits.pdf.

Olson, M. P., & Rogowski, J. C. (2020). Legislative term limits and polarization. *Journal of Politics, 82*(2), 572–586.

Peery, G., & Little, T. H. (2002). Views from the bridge: Legislative leaders' perceptions of institutional power in the stormy wake of term limits. In R. Farmer, J. D. Rausch, Jr., & J. C. Green (Eds.), *The test of time: Coping with legislative term limits* (pp. 105–118). Lexington Books.

Penning, J. M. (2003). Michigan: The end is near. In R. Farmer, J. D. Rausch, Jr., & J. C. Green (Eds.), *The test of time: Coping with legislative term limits* (pp. 33–46). Lexington Books.

Powell, R. J. (2003). The unintended effects of term limits on the career paths of state legislators. In R. Farmer, J. D. Rausch, Jr., & J. C. Green (Eds.), *The test of time: Coping with legislative term limits* (pp. 133–146). Lexington Books.

Powell, R. J., & Jones, R. (2004). *First in the nation: Term limits and the Maine legislature.* Joint Project on Term Limits. https://www.ncsl.org/Portals/1/documents/jptl/casestudies/Maine-FinalReportv2.pdf.

Sarbaugh-Thompson, M., Thompson, L., Elder, C. D., Strate, J., & Elling, R. C. (2004). *Political and institutional effects of term limits.* Palgrave Macmillan.

Schlesinger, J. A. (1966). *Ambition and politics.* Rand McNally.

Scott, K., & Bell, L. C. (1999, November). *Modeling mistrust: An event history analysis of term limits for state legislators* [Paper presentation]. Southern Political Science Association Annual Meeting 1999, Savannah, GA.

Shor, B. (2018). *Aggregate state legislator Shor-McCarty ideology data, May 2018 update.* Harvard Dataverse, V2. https://doi.org/10.7910/DVN/BSLEFD.

Shor, B., & McCarty, N. (2011). The ideological mapping of American legislatures. *American Political Science Review, 105*(3), 530–551.

Straayer, J., & Bowser, J. D. (2004). *Colorado's legislative term limits.* Joint Project on Term Limits. https://www.ncsl.org/Portals/1/documents/jptl/casestudies/Coloradov2.pdf.

Swift, C. S., & VanderMolen, K. A. (2015). Term limits and collaboration across the aisle: An analysis of bipartisan co-sponsorship in term limited and non-term limited state legislatures. *State Politics & Policy Quarterly, 16*(2), 198–226.

Thomsen, D. M. (2017). *Opting out of Congress: Partisan polarization and the decline of moderate candidates.* Cambridge University Press.

U.S. Census Bureau. (2020). *Historical income tables: Households*, Table H-8. https://www.census.gov/data/tables/time-series/demo/income-poverty/historical-income-households.html.

CHAPTER FIVE

The Perspectives of Former State Solons: Comparing Revolvers with Other Lobbyists

Francis A. Benjamin
Briana M. Huett

INTRODUCTION

The concept of the "revolving-door" lobbyist was first addressed by the U.S. government through the 1872 Appropriations for the Service of the Post-Office Department Act. That act declared it unlawful for any executive branch official to act as counsel, attorney, or agent for prosecuting claims (or assisting in their prosecution) against the United States during the two years following his or her employment.[1] Since then, revolving-door lobbyists—also referred to as "revolvers"—have consistently represented the subset of lobbyists comprised solely of former legislators. A major focus of research surrounding these individuals has been placed on those who served as members of Congress (MCs) (e.g., Kim, 2013; Lazarus et al., 2016; Makse, 2016; McCrain, 2018; Parker et al., 2012).

Despite the attention paid to those who leave Congress to lobby, little is known about the far more numerous state legislators who have gone on to work as lobbyists. Our focus in this chapter is on these state-level revolvers. We specifically compare state-level revolvers to all state lobbyists. Using data collected from the *National Survey of State Level Lobbyists*, we discuss the characteristics of these state-level lobbyists, focusing on both the traits that define them as well as documenting their perspectives on current operations within their respective state legislatures. This chapter explores whether findings regarding MC revolvers apply to state legislative revolvers in order to understand both the generalizable and state-specific work produced by state legislators-turned-lobbyists—a task that has not been attempted before. The sections that follow examine the responses of roughly 1,200 state-level lobbyists serving in each of the 50 state capitals to questions related to the lobbyists' backgrounds; their respective legislatures' levels of civility and other indicators of successful bipartisan cooperation; how revolvers' perceptions differ from those of other lobbyists; and what this collection of information can reveal about U.S. state legislatures.

PAST RESEARCH ON CONGRESSIONAL REVOLVERS

At the federal level, Lazarus et al. (2016) found that roughly one-quarter of members of Congress made the decision to turn to lobbying after serving their elected terms. Of those former members who become lobbyists, most do so by working in lobbying firms directly; about 79% of former House members and 87% of former U.S. senators, respectively, chose this specific career path. Far fewer in number were former MCs who worked for nonprofits, trade associations, and individual corporations (ibid.).[2] These findings were corroborated more recently by Palmer and Schneer (2019), who reported that slightly higher numbers of former MCs (29% for former House members, 34% for former senators) went on to become lobbyists once leaving Congress. These two groups exhibit the highest rates of turning to lobbying when compared to others, including former congressional staffers and former high-level U.S. executive branch officials.

However, these figures might underreport the actual number of revolvers. An important problem in this line of research is identifying the practice of "shadow lobbying," whereby individuals involved in various forms of interest group advocacy are not reported on official lobbying disclosure reports. Specifically, the self-reporting requirements and loopholes that currently exist in the legal definition of lobbying activities make it difficult to identify precisely the true number of revolving-door lobbyists in active operation at any given time (LaPira and Thomas, 2014). In fact, lobbying activities that do not fit within the technical requirements of lobbying disclosure laws are estimated to comprise a significant portion of the total amount of money spent by lobbying firms. One study estimated that the total number of lobbyists would increase by 30% if more comprehensive and thorough lobbying disclosure rules were enacted (LaPira, 2014).

Even though the true number of revolvers is currently unknown, their relative influence within the lobbying process is unquestionably significant. Baumgartner et al. (2009), for example, found that having a larger number of revolvers within one's lobbying firm significantly improves a firm's rate of success in agency policy campaigns. Lazarus and McKay (2012) have argued that employing these individuals with Congressional experience creates an important advantage in securing earmarks and other budgetary provisions; this same advantage is likely to be present with respect to former state legislators. Perhaps most significantly, a recent study found evidence that the lobbying efforts of former MCs are associated with a greater likelihood of bill advancement toward actual enactment. Makse (2016) found that in the period 2011 to 2014, *19%* of the bills that were later signed into law were lobbied on by at least one former House member. That figure illustrates why many lobbying firms are willing to pay these individuals considerably higher salaries than those awarded to their lobbyist colleagues who lack prior congressional experience (Blanes i Vidal et al., 2012).

WHY REVOLVING-DOOR LOBBYISTS?

Aside from the benefits of employing former legislators as lobbyists, further attention has also been paid to understanding *which* former legislators decide to take this later career path, as well as the specific characteristics of these individuals who are so clearly valued by lobbying firms. The following sections provide a summary of the literature surrounding these two points, discussing in some detail the main determinants of post-congressional lobbying careers and the value that is placed thereupon.

Legislative Connections and Congressional Access

Many researchers have found that former MCs are valued largely for their remaining connections (and thus access) to their former colleagues who are still in office (Blanes i Vidal et al., 2012; Cain, 2014; LaPira and Thomas, 2014). It is here where the literature surrounding the informational role of lobbying is emphasized, with lobbyists being valued for using their expertise and resources to provide information to time- and resource-constrained legislators (Ainsworth, 1993, 1997; Austen-Smith and Wright, 1992; Cotton, 2016; Hall and Deardorff, 2006; Schnaken-berg, 2017). Because of the otherwise high transaction costs associated with becoming knowledgeable about a particular bill and the various subjects covered in it, legislators are much more likely to trust the infor-mation provided by former MCs and former staffers with whom they have worked in the past. This trust is due to their shared experiences, common personal and policy interests, and shared legislative priorities (McCrain, 2018). As a result, many revolving-door lobbyists become especially valuable due to the personal connections made during their previous congressional service, as well as their thorough understanding of the legislative process.

Network Position, Institutional Standing, and Seniority

Other researchers have approached their study of revolvers by focusing on their networks and former networks. This line of research has found that one's network position, institutional standing, and the level of seniority the former MC enjoyed before leaving his or her chamber are all determin-ing factors in whether a legislator becomes a lobbyist after leaving office. In his analysis of members of the U.S. House, Makse (2016) focused specifically on the *centrality* of a legislator's position within the overall congressional network. He used Fowler's (2006) three distinct measures of centrality—closeness centrality, eigenvector centrality, and connected-ness—to determine the relative impact that having a more centralized position within the network had on a potential revolver's likelihood of choosing lobbying as a follow-up career. Specifically, Fowler analyzed the social distance between every given pair of MCs in the network (close-ness centrality), the level of centrality that each supporter of the given MC held (eigenvector centrality), and the average inverse relationship between the number of cosponsors on a bill and the number of times a pair of legislators cosponsored a bill with one another (connectedness) (Makse 2016). Fowler reported that those MCs with more centralized network positions were more likely to become lobbyists.

Outside of this generalized indicator of power, however, Lazarus et al. (2016) determined that one's formal and specific institutional posi-tions were also highly correlated with the decision to embark upon a post-congressional lobbying career. In their analysis of legislators who left

Congress, the same authors found that MCs (and House members specifically) who held certain positions were more likely to become revolvers. They found revolvers were more likely to come from the ranks of members who had served as party leaders, committee chairs, and members of appropriations and taxation committees. Seniority, too, was determined to play an important role; greater seniority in one's specific chamber was associated with a higher likelihood of later serving as a lobbyist.

Legislator's Ideology and Nature of Congressional Exit

Some researchers have reported that a legislator's political ideology also has a significant influence over whether one chooses lobbying as a follow-up career. Lazarus et al. (2016), for example, determined that ideology was influential in determining whether a former U.S. House member would later become a revolver, but only as it related to the level of his or her ideological extremism. They found moderate members were *less* likely to become revolvers, whereas more ideologically extreme members were *more* likely. To be sure, they found that this relationship had limits. Those who held the *most* extreme views on either end of the ideological spectrum were less likely to take this career path.

Kim (2013) similarly examined the career paths of former House members who had served and found that members were more likely to become revolvers if they had more conservative voting records or had held important committee assignments. Kim also found revolvers were more likely to come from the ranks of those with more seniority who retired voluntarily, as well as those who voted less conservatively in their last term compared to their previous records. His findings also reveal the importance of *how* an MC leaves Congress. Specifically, Kim found the probability of receiving a lobbying job was higher for those who retired from Congress voluntarily compared to those who failed to win reelection. He thereby concluded that two types of revolving doors exist between Congress and the lobbying industry. One door is for those who are electorally weak, and thereby need to have served on an important committee and to have been relatively conservative in their voting record; they are attractive to mostly conservative corporate lobbying clients. The second door is for those who retire voluntarily and who possess a record of strong congressional *tenure*—rather than any specific achievements or voting record during their last term in office—that will likely be seen by a lobby firm as desirable for its illustration of inside knowledge gained.

What Issues do Revolving-Door Lobbyists Care About?

Another common focus in the revolving-door literature is determining whether a desire to have lobbying as a career option after one's congressional service shapes how members of Congress behave while still in office. Does the prospect of pursuing such a potential career as a lobbyist affect the specific issues they choose to support while still in office? Does such a prospect influence current members' desire to achieve leadership roles in Congress? Could the promise of eventually becoming a lobbyist shape the behavior of current members of Congress in other ways? Research has provided evidence to suggest that indeed members do engage in such behavior. Ray (2018), for example, found that the legislators who spoke more often to interest group representatives were more likely to later take positions as lobbyists after leaving office. Ray speculated that some legislators make use of the hearings they organized while in office to grant representation to specific elite interests. The respective elites were then found to take this form of representation as proof of the member's commitment to the elites' causes. As a result, the interests involved were then more likely to offer accommodating members of Congress jobs as lobbyists when they left office.

Cotton and Déllis (2016) found that the revolving door can also cause legislators to prioritize the issues of some lobbying firms while ignoring others. Lapira and Thomas (2014) found that revolving-door lobbyists were most likely to specialize in lobbying for appropriations earmarks. In their subsequent analysis of congressional staffers-turned-lobbyists, Shepherd and You (2020) determined that legislator offices that employed staffers who would later become lobbyists were associated with higher levels of legislative productivity. These offices also gave lobbying firms greater access to their members, especially when the members of Congress were in their final terms of office. These same offices also increased their sponsorship of bills in the areas of health, the environment, and domestic commerce, all areas of legislative action that are most frequently addressed by the lobbying industry.[3]

In a relatively recent study, LaPira and Thomas (2017) offer a new means by which to view the relationship between soon-to-be revolvers and the interest groups that often seek to hire them. Unlike previous work, the authors view interest groups as not simply attempting to buy access to policymakers or policy process information, but instead as seeking a form of *insurance* for the health of their individual organizations or realm of public activity. Specifically, the authors argue that these agencies seek lobbyists as a safety monitoring measure for identifying potential future changes in governmental regulations that could adversely affect their operations, along with advocating for policies that promote their immediate success. LaPira and Thomas argue that the demand for lobbyists with specific legislative process-based information in Congress has increased, which gives such people a significant advantage. The need for this type of information would also be the case with state legislatures, where there is an increasing number of areas of policymaking in which federal responsibilities have devolved to state governors and legislatures, such as environmental regulation, marijuana legalization, and public health epidemic management.

HOW STATE-LEVEL REVOLVERS VIEW THE CURRENT LEGISLATURE: A GAP IN THE LITERATURE

Whereas our understanding of the career paths and behavior of Congressional revolvers (and soon-to-be Congressional revolvers) is relatively rich, our understanding of *state* legislative revolvers is less so. More specifically, we know very little about how state legislative lobbyists view their current state legislatures in comparison to those lobbyists who have served in legislatures in the past. Despite this limitation, however, some preliminary research examines the views of state lobbyists more generally. Research on both past and current congressional and legislative members could offer a useful basis for more fruitful analysis of the state legislative lobbyists' survey results and narrative commentaries explored later in this chapter. In this area of pertinent prior research, four specific streams of focus emerge from existing published studies of state legislators: 1) the effect of *term limits* on state legislative power and behavior; 2) the *perceived change in levels of civility* among congressional members; 3) *weakening and shifting norms* of legislative behavior; and 4) *changes needed* to improve legislative deliberative processes vis-à-vis institutional arrangements and forms of legislator interactions.

Term Limits

Moncrief and Thompson (2001) have analyzed the lobbyist perspective on how legislative term limits affect the influence of individual state legislators over the policymaking process. Surveying lobbyists in five states whose legislatures had been affected by the implementation of term limits, Moncrief and Thompson found a strong consensus among respondents that these limits had caused the state political influence structure to shift away from the legislature and toward the governor, administrative agencies, and interest groups. Consequently, interest groups' access to state legislators lost some of its value (as did the lobbying firms which they employed), as they both gained influence in their own right and sought influence within these new state government power structures.

Carey et al. (2006) studied the effect of term limits from the perspective of current state legislators, where their analysis of members from both chambers in every U.S. state determined that these limits had significant effects on the behaviors and priorities of these legislators. Specifically, they found what they deemed a "Burkean shift" taking place among the legislators they studied. This change in the legislators' self-perceptions arises from a weakening of district pressures, since the individual legislators could no longer seek reelection to the same office. This, in turn, caused legislators to show less commitment to their constituents in their individual districts and become more attentive to personal conceptions of the broader concerns of the public good for the state collectively (and for their own personal interest post-elective office service). This movement away from the *delegate* model advocated by Edmund Burke (1774; see also Will, 1992) toward the *trustee* model of representation advocated by Carey and his colleagues was a major consequence of the adoption of term limits in many U.S. states.

Level of Congressional Civility

Benjamin et al. (2011) offer insight into both lobbyist and state-level legislator perceptions of whether and how legislative civility has changed over time. Examining Washington's legislative process, Benjamin et al. (2011) surveyed legislators who served at some point during the period of 1990 to 2009, as well as legislative staff members and registered lobbyists who were active during 2009. Their analyses documented a reduction in mutual trust and inclination to engage in legislative collaboration, as well as an overall decline in bipartisanship.

Specifically, the authors determined that the lobbyists felt more strongly than legislators that the level of legislative civility had decreased in recent years. Legislators opined generally that levels of civility had decreased, but tended to feel it had decreased to a lesser extent than did lobbyists. State legislators who reported a high level of hostility during their election campaigns were also more likely to report the presence of a lower level of civility in the specific chamber in which they served. Further, when asked to compare themselves to other legislators with whom they served, most state legislators felt they as individuals worked to promote bipartisanship to a greater degree than their peers. A form of pluralistic ignorance, or belief that others within one's group have either more or less extreme attitudes or behaviors, was seen in this regard (Allport, 1924; Katz and Allport, 1931).

Changing Norms of Behavior

To gauge the perceptions of legislators' behavioral norms, Thompson et al. (1996) surveyed state legislators in all 50 U.S. states who had served at least 15 years in their respective chambers. In that study, over 75 percent of the respondents agreed that most state legislators had started spending more time raising campaign funds than in the past. Moreover, state legislators had become more concerned with the issues affecting their individual districts rather than with those occurring statewide. The Thompson et al. study also determined that these more seasoned legislators thought newer members were less likely to show customary respect to more senior legislators. The newer members were viewed as not taking sufficient care to learn legislative norms and not staying away from the forefront of issues until their "dues" had been paid. Specifically, the authors found that veteran state legislators tended to feel that newcomers were shirking apprenticeship norms. Instead they were immediately pursuing their own agendas upon entering office. Most usually, the newcomers voted strictly to parrot their districts' sentiments and engaged in other home district public affairs activities meant to improve their odds of reelection. This was the case even if their legislative party caucus was committed to a different position.

Thompson and his colleagues also found some changes to *interpersonal-based* behavioral norms. Just under one-third of their respondents agreed with the statement that current legislators were less likely to compromise and more likely to hide their individual legislative motives than was the case in the past. They also found that cross-state differences reflected the specific format of the legislature in question—whether it took a professional, citizen, or hybrid form along the professionalism continuum. For example, survey respondents from hybrid and professional state legislatures were more likely to agree strongly with the sentiment that newcomers were more inclined to prioritize their reelection than were legislators from citizen legislatures. Members from more professional legislatures tended to agree more fully than did their counterparts from citizen and hybrid legislatures that current legislators had less commitment to the legislature itself. Moreover, current legislators were more likely to campaign *against* "the legislature" than defend its actions to the general public and people in their respective home districts.

Changes and Improvements to Legislative Processes

Perhaps the smallest body of literature analyzing state legislator and lobbyist perceptions is that which examines changes and potential improvements to state legislative deliberative processes. We again look to the Benjamin et al. (2011) study that found a shift in processes due to the inclusion of new forms of technology. Washington state lobbyists felt that televising legislative proceedings on the state's public affairs network (TVW) had led to state legislators dividing their attention between their usual debate contributions and "playing to the camera" for home district folks and other interested parties (p. 19). Further, the lobbyists commonly expressed the view that changes in other forms of technology had significantly affected the work of legislators, often in a negative fashion. Many lobbyists observed that the use of digital information (audio and video) and modern communication technologies (smart cellphones and internet-connected tablets and laptop computers) had visibly reduced state legislators' attention to remarks and testimony offered in public meetings. These forms of technology are believed to have caused legislators to be less willing to engage in bipartisan efforts so as not to be viewed as "cavorting with the enemy" by their respective party bases.

The state legislative lobbyists in Washington indicated there were some clear benefits to the technological advancements witnessed in most contemporary state legislatures. For example, lobbyists tended to agree that legislators gave most of their attention to those present in the meeting itself, despite their apparent distraction with their tablets, laptop computers, and cellphones. Additionally, these state legislative lobbyists saw great benefit in televising and video-recording legislative processes because of technology's ability to increase the public's awareness, knowledge, and perceived openness of these processes. Moreover, to the extent that civility prevails in the legislative proceedings, the technology reveals a powerful modeling of proper conduct that is being aired for people far from the state capitol. And more generally, the lobbyists are inclined to believe that technology has increased legislators' access to bill information and has even provided lobbyists themselves with greater access to individual legislators, specifically through the frequent use of email and text messaging.

OUR FOCUS IN THIS CHAPTER

Further investigation is required in order to gain insight into the perspectives of individuals who fit simultaneously as both lobbyists and legislators. The analysis that follows examines the subset of state lobbyists who are state-level revolvers. We examine who these individuals are and how they view current state legislatures, considering their previous legislative experience. By doing so, we can learn what shapes the perceptions and motivations of lobbyists previously elected to state legislatures. Further, we also include an examination of state-level lobbyists who served in Congress or were employed in the past as congressional staffers, enabling exploration of their views and examination of the influence they hold over state legislative processes. The *National Survey of State Level Lobbyists* allows the curtain around state revolvers to be pulled back and offers a peek into who they are and how they think.

ANALYSIS AND RESULTS

A plurality of lobbyists' (29%) in this survey identified previous careers that included policy-related nonprofit experience. Others identified state legislative staff experiences (23%) and state and federal agency staff positions (21%). An additional 15% had previously worked for a local agency or government. The evaluation of the data, however, will take a deeper look into two other groups: former state legislators or former members of Congress (members of legislative councils, or MLCs), and a second group that includes their staffers (legislative council staff, or LCSs). MLCs and LCSs comprise 6% and 32%, respectively, of the data set. The following data review will first specifically describe what would be considered the "elected official archetype," which includes the general demographics, work schedule, and expertise focus of those who fit into this category. The second and deeper focus of the data, however, examines *what these specific groups of revolvers think*—that is, the nature of their political ideology, what their views are on the current political climate, and what opinions they hold on institutional and procedural changes that have taken place in state legislatures. How they assess the ways in which the deliberations of these institutions could be improved will also be explored.

WHO ARE STATE REVOLVERS?

The lobbyists who participated in this research were more likely to be men (58%) than women (42%), although the number of female lobbyists in this study has slightly increased from an earlier study that identified women federal lobbyists as comprising only 37% of the profession (Lapira et al., 2019). The ages of the lobbyists largely reflected the fact that most had a previous career prior to lobbying, with the largest portion coming from the 60–69 age group (27%), followed by those aged 50–59 (24%), then 40–49 (20%), under 40 (21%), and then over 69 (8%). When comparing this subsample to the rest of the survey respondent pool, former MLCs-turned-lobbyists were older than the average lobbyist (X^2 = 23.952, p = .000).

The race/ethnicity self-identification question, however, revealed that state lobbyists do not reflect the overall population. Caucasians repre-sented 92% of the lobbying workforce, followed much farther behind by those identifying as Hispanic (3.2%), African American (2%), Asian and Pacific Islander (1.5%), and Native American (.2%). MLCs were statistically represented by more Asians and Pacific Islanders (6%), but rather than this being a trend, it is more likely reflective of the initial small sample of non-Caucasians (X^2 = 6.708, p = .010).

Lobbyists participating in the survey had a degree of stability in their current careers. The length of time served as a lobbyist ranged from one year to 55 years, with an average length being 15 years. However, LCSs and MLCs were found to have spent even more time as lobbyists. Specifically,

LCSs represented an average of 16 years of experience, while MLCs averaged 19 years. Additionally, their work schedules were found to be highly dependent on the timing of legislative sessions, as almost 50% of participating lobbyists worked full-time during session. Of the rest, two-thirds worked at least half-time, and almost 25% worked quarter-time or less.

The legislature being outside of session predictably created a sparser lobbyist work schedule. Almost two-thirds of the lobbyists described working quarter-time or less, and only 7% worked full-time when legislatures were out of session. Former state legislators or MLCs, with their recognized status as influential lobbyists, were given the lion's share of the work and were employed as lobbyists for more hours. During legislative sessions, for example, 81% of MLCs were scheduled full-time and 90% at least half-time. Outside of session, 19% of MLCs worked full-time and over 50% at least half-time. Paralleling the MLCs' increased work activities, LCSs, when compared to all lobbyists, also worked more hours both during a given legislative session (X^2 = 42.066, p = .000) and outside of it (X^2 = 61.266, p = .000).

The data indicate that the lobbyists segmented themselves into one of three main employment scenarios; they worked as: 1) an *in-house* lobbyist (62%) as an employee of the organization they represented; 2) a *self-employed* lobbyist (22%); or 3) an employee of a *lobbying firm* (16%). Former elected leaders and staffers tended to eschew in-house positions, with fewer than half (49%) of LCSs working in this type of position (X^2 = 41.136, p = .000), and only 19% of MLCs doing so (X^2 = 60.055, p = .000). MLCs tended to be split in their preference between being self-employed (40%; X^2 = 6.283, p = .000) or part of a lobbying firm (40%; X^2 = 31.346, p = .000). This segmentation was paralleled by the specific policy areas in which they chose to work. Lobbying is a specialized business, and lobbyists typically strive to become subject-matter experts. Lobbyists as a whole were found to focus first in the areas of taxation, health care and hospitals, labor and (un)employment, and transportation, while they lobbied the least in the areas of immigration, cannabis, military and veterans' issues, and the state lottery. MLCs and LCSs mirrored this pattern (see Table 5.1), although they were also more likely to lobby in the areas of taxation, business interests, transportation, and land use, and were even *less* likely to lobby in the area of immigration (X^2 = 12.180, p = .007).

WHAT DO STATE REVOLVERS THINK?

Lobbyists' political leanings influence their approaches to different job assignments, how they relate to legislators, and what they consider an acceptable policy outcome. Within this context, lobbyists in the survey were more likely to identify politically as Democrats (39%) than as Republicans. Lobbyists' partisan identification included Independents, comprising 31%, followed by Republicans with 28%. Interestingly, the

Table 5.1. Background of State Lobbyists: Comparison of Means on Frequency of Lobbying in Varying Areas of State Legislation

Policy Area	*All Lobbyists*	*MLCs*
Taxation	2.42	2.26*
Health care	2.60	2.52
Labor	2.83	2.78
Transportation	2.87	2.76*
Environmental	2.89	2.80
Social services	2.99	3.07
K-12	3.01	2.99
Land use	3.05	2.98*
Utilities	3.07	2.90
Higher education	3.15	3.01*
Criminal Justice	3.16	3.16*
Pensions	3.32	3.22*
Agriculture	3.37	3.33
Social regulations	3.39	3.46
Immigration	3.54	3.61*
Cannabis	3.54	3.47*
Military	3.68	3.64*
Lottery	3.73	3.70

*$p < 0.05$

On which of the following types of issues have you lobbied?
1. Very often   2. Often   3. Occasionally.   4. Never

LCSs did not follow the full group's configuration pattern, but instead reflected a shifted political alignment that balanced the two major parties more fully. Specifically, compared to all lobbyists, they were statistically less likely to be Democrats (34%; X^2 = 3.996, p = .046) and more likely to be Republicans (34%; X^2 = 5.491, p = .019).

Lobbyists positioned themselves along the ideological spectrum on social issues[4] and fiscal issues[5] as slightly more liberal on social issues and slightly more conservative on fiscal issues. However, LCSs, when compared to all lobbyists, were found to be somewhat more conservative on both social issues, moving toward center from 3.15 on a 7-point, liberal-to-conservative scale (the value for all surveyed lobbyists) to 3.42 (X^2 = 22.477, p = .000), and on fiscal issues, moving from 4.25 (all lobbyists) to 4.52 (X^2 = 15.106, p = .019). Both these political positions reveal that it is the moderate former legislators and members of Congress and the staff they influenced (who are more centrist and willing to reach across the aisle) who tend to migrate to lobbying. Theoretically, then, this process creates an expectation that these more moderate individuals would desire and work toward moving the current crop of legislators to operate in a similarly more collaborative and civil manner.

The concept of civility, while not a new theme, continues to be viewed as a virtue facilitating legislative deliberations and public policymaking among lobbyists. Civility is the process of valuing individuals and making an honest effort to understand the views of those with whom one disagrees. It is having an understanding that no one person holds all the answers, and that collaboration generally leads to the discovery of common interests and agreeable solutions to disputes over the proper course for government action. Civility is realized when disagreement or conflict is identified, and an honest effort is made to discern root understandings and seek out agreeable solutions to resolve the conflict—at least in the short run. Civility entails separating the personal from the professional. It involves communicating to others and is reflected in the statement "I care about and value you as a person, and I want to understand why you feel the way you do." Civility is not the same as tolerance; civility involves striving to improve understanding and reduce misunderstandings and enhancing the prospects of effective collaboration over the long run. Civility is also not the same thing as compromise, although compromise is often an outcome among parties that adhere to civility norms. Just because one understands the other person's point of view does not mean that one *conforms* to it. Individual personal views are paramount, as are personal and professional relationships.

As part of this survey, state lobbyists provided their views pertaining to civility, emerging legislative dynamics, and the importance of civility for legislative deliberation and effective operation. The lobbyists resoundingly emphasized civility's importance and acknowledged the value of civil discourse norms in legislative debate on public policy (see Figure 5.1). Further, while lobbyists taking part in the national survey placed great value on civil discourse norms (8.34 on 10-point scale), former MLCs held civility and civil discourse in even higher regard (9.11, X^2 = 8.174, p = .017).

When rating current legislative civility levels for various actors in the legislative process, lobbyists assigned the highest ranking (3.87 on 5-point scale) to the state legislators with whom they worked. State legislators as a group were likewise seen to be a civil group (3.32). This civility ranking of the various groups parallels research that has shown individuals

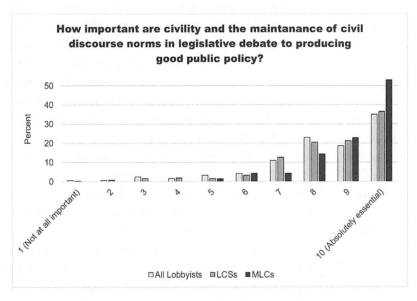

Figure 5.1. The need for civil discourse and good public policy.

relate more positively to those they hold in higher regard than they do to individuals with whom they have had little to no contact. When asked to evaluate legislative civility changes, the lobbyists indicated that, while civility over the last two years had not been at a high level (see Figure 5.2), rating it on average only 5.43 on 9-point scale (with 1 being very uncivil and 9 being very civil), they had also seen a decline over the last ten years (at 3.57 on the same scale) (Figure 5.3).

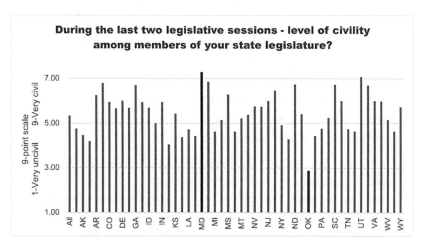

Figure 5.2. Perceptions of civility today compared to the past, by state.

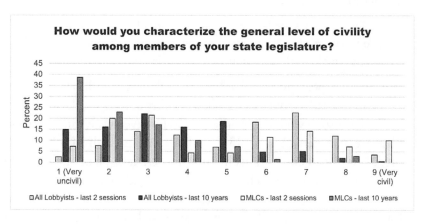

Figure 5.3. Perceptions of changes in civility across time.

Comparing the civility levels of individual state legislatures, lobbyists from Maryland gave their state legislators the highest civility ratings, while lobbyists in Oklahoma gave their legislators the lowest ratings. When asked to rate the civility levels today in their respective legislatures compared to ten years ago, New Mexico lobbyists gave their legislators the highest civility rating and Maine's lobbyists gave their legislators the lowest ratings.

In the national survey, lobbyists expressed marked disappointment in the erosion of legislative civility. Some respondents expressed grave concern that the lowest point had yet to be reached and had low expectations for any significant upward swing. Former MLCs, with their experience as elected officials, were even more critical of the current legislative civility trajectory. In their view, the last two years' change (4.66) represented an even greater decline in civility ($X^2 = 45.409$, p = .000), and the last ten years had been dismal (2.43; $X^2 = 42.585$, p = .000). Expressing this sentiment, one lobbyist commented:

> It was incredibly disheartening as a public interest advocate in another state where legislators and leadership were shockingly uncivil. Had I stayed in that state, I would have stopped lobbying because the Legislature was so retaliatory and uncivil, to the point of doing real harm to the community and degrading the state's ability to govern.

Others found incivility particularly high in some specific policy areas. Another lobbyist stated:

> Members of our state legislature are comfortable being outright hostile on matters of race and racial equity, creating a deeply uncivil and uncomfortable work environment for lobbyists of color.

While the perceptions of lobbyists collectively indicate a serious decline in legislative civility, as a whole, civility among legislative *leadership* is seen as somewhat better. The MLCs, however, were harsher judges of legislative leaders ($X^2 = 38.951$, p =.000). As one such MLC lobbyist noted, "Nearly all contentious discussions here take place among three or four legislative leaders behind closed doors, and we hear tales of some pretty uncivil behavior there." When comparing lobbyists' perceptions of state legislative leaders, California legislative leaders were deemed the most civil and Texas legislative leaders the least civil.

Even with this more critical view of state legislative civility, however, the state legislative lobbyists surveyed still felt they were experiencing a more civil process in their own state legislatures than what was occurring on Capitol Hill in Washington, DC. State legislators often take great pride in separating themselves from their congressional counterparts and the associated gridlock that has come to characterize the U.S. Congress. They often observed, "We are not like Washington," or, for legislators in Washington state, "We are not like the *other* Washington." The *National Survey of State Lobbyists* asked for a comparison of the lobbyists' perceptions of their state's legislative decline in civility against the backdrop of the polarized environment of the U.S. Congress. Although the survey respondents stated their own legislature was more civil than Congress, they nonetheless expressed the view that the decline in civility among their individual state's legislators was rather reflective of the situation they witnessed at the federal level. One respondent commented that "the complete lack of civility and respect in Congress and the executive branch of the federal government sets a tone that prevents bipartisanship at [the] state level."

MLCs expressed this concern that declining civility in American political life was causing legislators to reflect the polarized environment of the U.S. Congress ($X^2 = 6.681$, p =.035) even more so than the other lobbyists. One respondent stated that "on [the matter of] the state legislature reflecting Congress, I believe that it is more of the parties reflecting more of the **national party** [emphasis added]." Another emphasized a "pack mentality that legislators...fall into every day, [whereas] as a lobbyist, we just work with the party in power and keep the other party informed, knowing that partisan winds will change."

This said, while they were inclined to believe that their state legislators were going the way of Congress, the lobbyists in all of the states nonetheless were wont to note that their own states were less polarized than the U.S. Congress (2.28 on 5-point scale, with 1 being much less polarized than Congress and 5 far more polarized). While MLCs held a slightly more concerned view (2.38; $X^2 = 11.414$, p = .022), they still viewed the situation in their respective state legislatures as being better than that of Congress (see Figure 5.4). In fact, the only lobbyists, as a state-level cluster, who viewed their state as being *more* polarized than Congress were those from North Carolina and Oklahoma (Figure 5.5).

In addition to assessing changes in civility and polarization, the survey also explored changes in partisanship and the inclination for legislators to work across party lines. Nevada and Tennessee legislators see the greatest change toward operating in the least bipartisan fashion, and Maryland and Missouri legislators see the greatest movement toward working in the greatest bipartisan fashion. Overall, these state lobbyists viewed legislators as becoming more partisan; the former MLCs continued in their inclination to be the harshest critics of current state legislators, seeing them as becoming increasingly partisan. The MLCs clearly viewed their

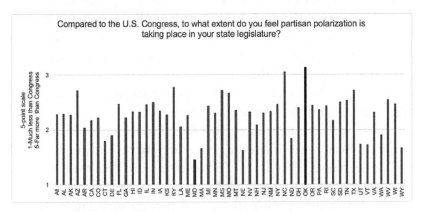

Figure 5.4. State legislative civility compared to congressional civility.

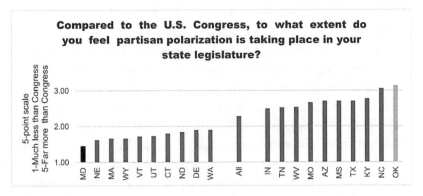

Figure 5.5. Top 10 states rated least and most civil compared to U.S. Congress.

own state legislators as more partisan compared to the lobbyists on the whole (X^2 = 16.038, p = .000). In this regard, from the perspective of lobbyists, state legislators in Oklahoma and North Carolina were viewed as the most partisan and state legislators in Delaware and Nebraska as the most bipartisan.

Just as lobbyists hold civility in high regard, they also place high importance (8.48 on 10-point scale) on effective cross-party communi-cation among legislators. MLCs place even higher importance on this condition than do lobbyists generally (9.33; X^2 = 19.951, p = .000). Further, even as lobbyists generally accorded paramount importance to individual legislator cross-party communications, they accorded even greater importance (8.77 on a ten-point scale) to the necessity of legislative leaders communicating effectively across party lines. MLCs continued their inclination to be distinctive from other lobbyists by indicating an even higher (9.41) level of importance for this form of cross-party com-munication (X^2 = 14.599, p = .002). One lobbyist noted in this regard:

> It is really interesting to see, as a lobbyist who has to work with everyone across party lines, that many members of legislative leadership don't communicate well with leaders of the other party in their chamber. Also, leaders in each chamber don't often have robust lines of communication with leaders in the other chamber *even when they are in the same party*. There tends to be Senate vs. House politics involved even when they are of the same party. [emphasis added]

Another survey respondent indicated the negative effect of a large increase in city and county participation, stating:

> State level politics typically have kept to proper due process and proce-dures [requiring everyone] to hear from both opponents and proponents. With more cities and counties entering the legislative arena on larger issues, I see a decline in this process. They move quickly, don't always allow for testimony from all parties, and don't always seem to really take the time to digest what each side is saying.

Another survey respondent lamented a decline in the tradition of genuine deliberative processes, formerly a part of legislative business in their state. The lobbyist noted, "Initially, legislative proposals were roughly drafted and then through the committee and legislative process would be refined and reformed. Now, it is far more of a predetermined outcome without a lot of substantive deliberation." This lobbyist went on to note that in his/her state (and many others),

> policy is now lumped into [categories as] "controversial"—i.e., one political party agrees with the policy and the other does not—or "non-controversial"—i.e., it is not a partisan issue and a lot of work has been done before a bill is proposed to get buy-in from a diverse set of stakeholders and legislators [and typically] non-controversial bills move through the process with little debate and are generally completely unanimous.

Finally, other survey respondents emphasized important process violations that negatively affected communication and effective legislative deliberations on issues of public policy. One respondent observed the following regarding his/her own state senate:

> The biggest problem is the constant violation of the Legislature open meetings requirements in law. They take the committee into a back room to resolve issues with the Commissioner...outside public view, contrary to legal requirements. No opposition to this process is made by the Attorney General's office, who has used this process to kill bills supported by impacted members of the public seeking amendments to practices supported by the State regulators. This violation of process breeds suspicion and a lack of trust in the process. Also, inadequate notice is provided for meetings the closer to the end of the session it is, and often bills are radically changed in "work sessions" after a public hearing without any ability of impacted groups to offer testimony in opposition or to even review the bill changes and submit comments prior to a vote on the bill.

Lobbyists were in substantial accord on several approaches intended to *improve* legislative civility and develop better working relationships within the state legislature. Respondents assessed the likely *effectiveness* of specific across-the-aisle bridge-building ideas and the difficulty of implementation associated with each. State legislative lobbyists, including the MC subgroup, were in substantial accord regarding several measures under discussion in some state legislatures. Their most highlighted action in this regard was having legislators of opposing parties work together on specific legislative projects featuring issues of high public interest. One lobbyist highlighted the need for state legislative lobbyists to take the initiative to "request more bi-partisan activity and support legislators who are active in working on a bipartisan basis." The state legislative lobbyists also agreed upon the easiest ameliorative action to implement vis-à-vis legislative civility—namely, to have legislators from opposing parties regularly eat meals together. Along these same lines, numerous lobbyists highlighted the importance of creating a variety of social opportunities for members of opposing parties to intermingle. A number of the lobbyists surveyed expressed concern that restrictions on lobbyists' activities in a number of states that did not "allow lobbyists to host social events with both parties present" kept them from doing their part to "facilitate socialization among legislators." One lobbyist working in a state with such restrictions noted a "severe drop in socializing with legislators of both parties" once a citizen initiative prohibiting social events with lobbyists' financial support was passed. The least effective, and the thing perceived as hardest to implement, was actually intermixing party offices and/or changing seating assignments, with one lobbyist commenting that "legislative leadership would be unlikely to go for it" and that "changing offices wouldn't matter much because a lot of work is done outside of [them]."

CONCLUSION

This exploration of the perceptions of state legislative lobbyists provides a productive avenue through which civil discourse issues can be more fully understood. These key actors in the political process place a high importance on norms associated with civil discourse for the quality of legislative deliberations and they express concern about the current incivility levels they encounter within their respective state legislatures. Revolvers see signs of the partisan gridlock and hyperpolarization in Congress having deleterious effects at the state level. Perceiving current state legislators to be more partisan than in previous sessions, state revolvers continually expressed harsher judgments than the rest of the surveyed group of lobbyists; they also more acutely highlighted the need for enhanced cross-party legislator communication among both rank-and-file members and legislative leadership.

These findings provide insight into a sphere of American political life that both affects citizens' lives in major ways and has largely been shrouded in mystery. By understanding state revolvers' experiences and perceptions specifically, one is able to inform more fully the efforts of the National Conference of State Legislatures and organizations such as the National Institute for Civil Discourse to build firmer foundations for the future. This would be a future wherein state legislative politics feature the presence of greater capacity for both bipartisan problem-solving and the inclusive engagement of citizens in an open and effective deliberative process wherein the norms of civil discourse are respected and reinforced.

NOTES

1. 256 U.S.C 5 (1872).

2. Lazarus et al. (2016) found that roughly 5% of congressional revolvers worked for non-profits and trade associations. A slightly higher number (9%) worked for individual corporations.

3. It is important to note that though their findings do not center on legislators who later become lobbyists, Shepherd and You (2020) gauge the effort and incentives of the congressional staffers they study specifically through their associated MCs' legislative activities and votes. This provides a valuable insight into how knowledge of lobbying interests can affect the behavior of congressional offices (and in turn their members).

4. For example, same-sex marriage, abortion, prayer in schools, gun control, medical marijuana, and DREAMer policies.

5. Such as taxes, social security eligibility, the minimum wage, right-to-work laws, and reducing government regulations.

REFERENCES

Ainsworth, S. (1993). Regulating lobbyists and interest group influence. *The Journal of Politics, 55*(1), 41–56. https://doi.org/10.2307/2132227.

Ainsworth, S. (1997). The role of legislators in the determination of interest group influence. *Legislative Studies Quarterly, 22*(4), 517–533.

Allport, F. (1924). *Social psychology*. Houghton Mifflin.

Austen-Smith, D., & Wright, J. R. (1992). Competitive lobbying for a legislator's vote. *Social Choice and Welfare, 9*(3), 229–257.

Baumgartner, F., Berry, J., Hojnacki, M., Leech, B., & Kimball, D. (2009). *Lobbying and policy change: Who wins, who loses, and why*. University of Chicago Press.

Benjamin, F., Lovrich, N., & Parks, C. (2011, April). *Civility in the Washington state legislature: Documentation of decline over time* [Paper presentation]. Western Political Science Association Conference 2011, San Antonio, TX.

Blanes i Vidal, J., Draca, M., & Fons-Rosen, C. (2012). Revolving door lobbyists. *The American Economic Review, 102*(7), 3731–3748.

Burke, E. (1774). *The works of the honourable Edmund Burke.* Henry G. Bohn.

Cain, B. E. (2014). Congressional staff and the revolving door: The impact of regulatory change. *Election Law Journal: Rules, Politics, and Policy, 13*(1), 27–44.

Carey, J. M., Niemi, R. G., Powell, L. W., & Moncrief, G. F. (2006). The effects of term limits on state legislatures: A new survey of the 50 states. *Legislative Studies Quarterly, 31*(1), 105–134.

Cotton, C. (2016). Competing for attention: Lobbying time-constrained politicians. *Journal of Public Economic Theory, 18*(4), 642–665. https://doi.org/10.1111/jpet.12202.

Cotton, C. S., & Déllis, A. (2016). Informational lobbying and agenda distortion. *The Journal of Law, Economics, and Organization, 32*(4), 762–793. https://doi.org/10.1093/jleo/eww005.

Fowler, J. H. (2006). Connecting the Congress: A study of co-sponsorship networks. *Political Analysis, 14*(4), 456–487. http://dx.doi.org/10.1093/pan/mpl002.

Hall, R. L., & Deardorff, A. V. (2006). Lobbying as legislative subsidy. *American Political Science Review, 100*(1), 69–84. https://doi.org/10.1017/S0003055406062010.

Katz, D., & Allport, F. H. (1931). Introduction. In D. Katz & F. H. Allport (Eds.), *Students' attitudes: A report of the Syracuse University Reaction Study* (pp. 1–8). Craftsman Press.

Kim, J. H. (2013). Determinants of post-congressional lobbying employment. *Economic Governance, 14*(2), 107–126.

Klarner, C., Berry, W. B., Carsey, T. M., Jewell, M., Niemi, R. G., Powell, L. W., & Snyder, J. M. (2013). *State legislative election returns (1967–2010).* Inter-University Consortium for Political and Social Research (ICPSR), University of Michigan.

LaPira, T. (2014). Lobbying in the shadows: How private interests hide from public scrutiny, and why that matters. In A. J. Cigler, B. A. Loomis, & A. J. Nownes (Eds.), *Interest group politics* (9th ed.) (pp. 224–248). CQ Press.

LaPira, T. M., Marchetti, K., & Thomas, H. F. (2019). Gender politics in the lobbying profession. *Politics & Gender, 16*(3), 1–29. https://doi.org/10.1017/S1743923X19000229.

LaPira, T. M., & Thomas, H. F. (2014). Revolving door lobbyists and interest representation. *Interest Groups & Advocacy, 3*(January), 4–29. http://dx.doi.org/10.1057/iga.2013.16.

LaPira, T. M., & Thomas, H. F. (2017). *Revolving door lobbying: Public service, private influence, and the unequal representation of interests.* University Press of Kansas.

Lazarus, J., McKay, A., & Herbel, L. (2016). Who walks through the revolving door? Examining the lobbying activity of former members of Congress. *Interest Groups & Advocacy, 5*(January), 82–100. http://dx.doi.org/10.1057/iga.2015.16.

Lazarus, J., & McKay, A. M. (2012). *Consequences of the revolving door: Evaluating the lobbying success of former congressional members and staff* [Paper presentation]. Midwest Political Science Association Annual Meeting 2012, Rochester, NY. https://doi.org/10.2139/ssrn.2141416.

Makse, T. (2017). A very particular set of skills: Former legislator traits and revolving door lobbying in Congress. *American Politics Research, 45*(5), 866–886. https://doi.org/10.1177/1532673X16677274.

McCrain, J. (2018). Revolving door lobbyists and the value of congressional staff connections. *The Journal of Politics, 80*(4), 1369–1383. https://doi.org/10.1086/698931.

Moncrief, G., & Thompson, J. A. (2001). On the outside looking in: Lobbyists' perspectives on the effects of state legislative term limits. *State Politics & Policy Quarterly, 1*(4), 394–411.

Palmer, M., & Schneer, B. (2019). Post-political careers: How politicians capitalize on public office. *The Journal of Politics, 81*(2), 670–675. https://doi.org/10.1086/701762.

Parker, G., Parker, S., & Dabros, M. (2012). The labor market for politicians: Why ex-legislators gravitate to lobbying. *Business and Society, 52*(3), 427–450.

Ray, J. (2018). Walk this way, talk this way: Legislator speech and lobbying. *Interest Groups & Advocacy, 7*(June), 150–172. http://dx.doi.org/10.1057/s41309-018-0033-5.

Schnakenberg, K. E. (2017). Informational lobbying and legislative voting. *American Journal of Political Science, 61*(1), 129–145.

Shepherd, M. E., & You, H. Y. (2020). Exit strategy: Career concerns and revolving doors in Congress. *American Political Science Review, 114*(1), 270–284. https://doi.org/10.1017/S0003055419000510.

Strickland, J. M. (2020). The declining value of revolving-door lobbyists: Evidence from the American states. *American Journal of Political Science, 64*(1), 67–81. https://doi.org/10.1111/ajps.12485.

Thompson, J. A., Kurtz, K., & Moncrief, G. F. (1996). We've lost that family feeling: The changing norms of the new breed of state legislators. *Social Science Quarterly, 77*(2), 344–362.

Will, G. F. (1992). *Restoration: Congress, term limits, and the recovery of deliberative democracy*. Free Press.

CHAPTER SIX

State Income Inequality and Incivility

Leanne S. Giordono
Brent S. Steel
Claire McMorris

WHY WOULD WE EXPECT A RELATIONSHIP BETWEEN INCOME INEQUALITY AND CIVILITY?

Growing income inequality in the world's wealthy countries has been noted as a key trend of the late twentieth and early twenty-first century by researchers, journalists, and politicians alike. Major events and social movements in the United States during the last decade, including the Great Recession of 2008–09, the opioid crisis, and skyrocketing COVID-19 unemployment claims highlight the growing economic divide between low- and high-income groups. Strong evidence confirms that income inequality has grown since the 1970s in the United States, both in the aggregate (Piketty, 2014; Saez and Zucman, 2016) and within individual U.S. states (Kopczuk et al., 2010).[1] Scholars attribute these trends to a combination of structural labor market forces associated with technological changes and increasing demand for high-skill workers, changes in key labor market institutions (e.g., unionization), and shifts in redistributive policy (e.g., minimum wage laws, tax policy) (Giordono et al., 2019).

Research in the economics tradition has often focused on the causes of income inequality and related changes (i.e., inequality as the outcome of interest). More recently, a growing body of literature examines the influence of income inequality on other outcomes, including policy decisions, political institutions, and political behavior (e.g., Boix, 2010; Hacker and Pierson, 2010; Jacobs and Soss, 2010a; Piketty, 2018; Putnam, 2016).

139

Indeed, political polarization and partisanship have risen since the mid-to-late 1970s in tandem with growing income inequality (McCarty et al., 2008; McCarty et al., 1997; Shor and McCarty, 2011). Accordingly, recent scholarship yields evidence of a closer relationship between income inequality and political polarization, although results are sensitive to measurement and specification choices. At the national level, Garand (2010) shows that U.S. senators from states with high levels of income inequality tend to be more polarized than other senators, and that relationship also holds true for the beliefs of their respective constituents. Duca and Saving (2016), in turn, explore the relationship at the level of state legislatures, finding evidence of positive associations between levels of income inequality and polarization. They also note that their findings are sensitive to the particular inequality measure employed for analysis. More recently, Voorheis, McCarty, and Shor (2015) provide more robust evidence of a positive relationship between changes in income inequality and political polarization, and posit specific mechanisms for the relationship. They find that income inequality causes state Democratic parties to become more liberal, leading to the election of more conservative state legislators and the advent of more conservative state legislative chambers when moderate Democrats are replaced by conservative Republicans (Voorheis et al., 2015).

Polarization is often associated with the distinct but closely related concept of *political gridlock*, or failure to act on a key issue in a timely manner (National Conference of State Legislatures, 2018). Rigby and Wright (2015) find that party polarization is associated with gridlock in social policy, suggesting that the combined forces of polarization and gridlock impede timely changes to policies for which the real value tends to erode over time (e.g., minimum wage policy). A 10-case study of state legislatures suggests that the vast majority of policies are passed unanimously or with bipartisan majorities. Nonetheless, an important minority of bills are extremely contentious, in some cases yielding stalemates, walkouts, and/or unilateral partisan action by the dominant majority (National Conference of State Legislatures, 2018). Recent evidence also suggests that legislative gridlock associated with political polarization can yield indirect effects in bureaucratic policymaking; these effects appear in the concrete form of increased rulemaking by governors and administrative agencies (Boushey and McGrath, 2020).

Polarization and gridlock are themselves closely intertwined with the concept of civility, or behaving with politeness, courtesy, and mutual respect in political discourse. There is a broad perception among the general public that incivility is widespread and has increased over time (Kenski et al., 2019). An annual survey conducted by Weber Shandwick (2019) has consistently found that most Americans have described incivility as a "major" problem since the survey was launched in 2010. Almost half of the group surveyed attribute the erosion of civility to the uncivil behavior of politicians. There is also evidence of incivility in political discourse among the electorate and in portrayals of the policy process by the media (Young et al., 2019). However, there is less scholarship about trends in civility among state legislators, and related associations with inequality, partisan polarization, and gridlock. The National Conference of State Legislatures (2018) found that formal institutions (e.g., committees and rules) and informal traditions of civility contribute to the ability of state legislatures to pass important legislation. At the same time, legislators in more-polarized states view compromise more favorably than do those from less-polarized states.

We suspect that there are important connections among inequality, polarization, and, ultimately, civility in state legislatures. The observations about trends in American states and state legislatures motivate the two main questions addressed by this chapter, those being: 1) What is the relationship between state-level inequality and lobbyists' perceptions of civility in state legislatures? and 2) How does partisan polarization influence the relationship between inequality and perceptions of civility? We propose three hypotheses directly related to these two core questions:

H1: Inequality levels and/or rises in inequality are negatively associated with perceptions of civility. As inequality increases (or changes in inequality increase), lobbyist perceptions of legislative civility decreases.

H2: Partisan polarization and/or rises in polarization are negatively associated with perceptions of civility. As polarization increases (or changes in polarization increase), lobbyist perceptions of civility decrease.

H3: Partisan polarization plays a mediating role (i.e., has an indirect effect) on the association between inequality and perceptions of civility. Increases in partisan polarization act as a mediator between inequality and perceptions of civility.

We find a negative association between changes in state-level inequality from 2000 to 2015 and selected indicators of lobbyists' perceptions of legislator civility. Moreover, we find preliminary evidence that lobbyists' perceptions of polarization mediate the effects of changes in inequality. However, the findings are sensitive to how we measure inequality, civility, and polarization. The remainder of this chapter describes this study's approach, sets forth the main findings, and discusses the principal implications of the results.

ANALYTIC APPROACH: HOW DID WE TEST THE HYPOTHESIZED RELATIONSHIPS?

The survey of legislative lobbyists conducted by a collaborative team of researchers and supported by the National Institute for Civil Discourse serves as the primary source of civility data for this study.[2] We selected six items from three questions most closely focused on legislative civility norms as our dependent variables of interest. These include one item about the perceived general level of civility among members of the state's legislature, two items pertaining to perceived changes in civility among individual legislators and legislative leaders over the last ten years, and three items rating perceived behavioral civility among various legislative stakeholder groups. The survey also served as the primary source for respondent (i.e., lobbyist) demographic and political information about the survey respondents (i.e., registered lobbyists and public agency legislative liaison officers), including age, sex, race/ethnicity, political affiliation, and views on social and economic policy issues.

For the purpose of this study, we chose to focus on two main measures of income inequality, the Gini coefficient and the 80/20 ratio, both of which are commonly used measures (Giordono et al., 2019; Glassman, 2016). The Gini coefficient is a measure of statistical dispersion wherein a value of 1 represents perfect inequality and a value of 0 represents perfect equality.[3] The 80/20 ratio represents the ratio of the income at the top of the income distribution (eightieth percentile) to the income at the bottom (twentieth percentile). While the Gini coefficient offers a summary measure of inequality and is sensitive to changes in the middle of the income distribution, it lacks sensitivity to changes at the top or bottom of the distribution. Hypothetically, states could exhibit the same Gini coefficient but differ considerably in their top and bottom distributions, or vice versa (Glassman, 2016). In contrast, the 80/20 ratio is more sensitive to the income shares at the top and bottom of the income distribution, while showing less sensitivity to changes in the middle-income ranges. We do not, *a priori*, have a theory about which type of change is most likely to influence perceptions of civility, so we elected to use both measures.[4] State-level inequality is the study's primary independent variable of interest. We turned to two sources of state-level inequality data. We relied upon the Frank-Sommeiller-Price Series as the source of state-level Gini coefficient data, data assembled using individual tax filing data from the U.S. Internal Revenue Service and that are available for the period of 1917–2015 (Frank, n.d.; Frank et al., 2015). The state-level 80/20 ratio data, available for the 1985–2012 period, were assembled by Voorheis (2016) using Current Population Survey data and made available in the Franko's (2020) replication data set. We also generated indicators of both short-term changes (Gini, 2000–15; 80/20, 2000–12) and long-term changes (Gini, 1970–2015; 80/20, 1985–2012).[5]

Finally, polarization data are employed to test the hypotheses regarding the potential mediation role played by state-level polarization. Two sources of polarization data are included, measured both as individual perceptions and as an objective measure. First, we used two items in the survey indicating lobbyists' own perceptions of polarization, specifically their impressions of how much partisan polarization is occurring in their state 1) compared to the U.S. Congress, and 2) compared to other state legislatures. Second, we used the Shor and McCarty state legislative aggregate ideology data (Shor and McCarty, 2018), which uses state-level roll-call voting patterns of legislators to formulate annual measures of polarization over the period 1993–2016. For simplicity, we created a single index from two variables representing the distance between party medians for each chamber at each of three timepoints (1993, 2000, and 2016); the resulting indices yielded scale reliability coefficients greater than 0.90.[6]

The analysis of these data proceeded in three stages. First, we produced descriptive statistics for each variable (or index) of interest. Second, we tested the relationship between the primary independent variable of interest (state-level inequality, absolute levels, and changes over time) and the dependent variable of interest (perceptions of civility levels only). To do so, we conducted both bivariate and multivariate OLS regression analysis, controlling for lobbyist characteristics and using clustered robust standard errors to take into account the likely heteroscedasticity stemming from the state-level inequality data (Rogers, 1994). Finally, we conducted a two-level mediation analysis to test for an indirect effect of partisanship on norms of civility.

Baron and Kenny (1986) distinguish between the role of a *moderating* variable, which affects the direction and/or strength of a relationship and is functionally similar to interaction, and that of a *mediating* variable, which acts as an intervening variable between the independent variable (state-level inequality) and the dependent variable (perceptions of civility norms). Conceptually, mediation analysis tests the presence of a causal chain. Tests of mediation require evidence of statistically significant relationships between: 1) independent variable (IV) and dependent variable (DV); 2) IV and mediating variable (MV); and 3) MV and DV (Baron and Kenny, 1986; MacKinnon et al., 2007). Figure 6.1 shows the hypothesized linkages in the generic mediation model and related pathways.

Because inequality is measured at the state level, we conducted multi-level mediation analysis (Preacher et al., 2010, 2011; Zhang et al., 2009); in the case of the state-level partisanship measure we conducted a 2-2-1 analysis, while in the case of perceptions of partisanship we proceeded with a 2-1-1 analysis.[7] Where relevant, we included selected lobbyist demographics as covariates and used robust standard errors. All data preparation and analyses were conducted using Stata 15.1.[8,9]

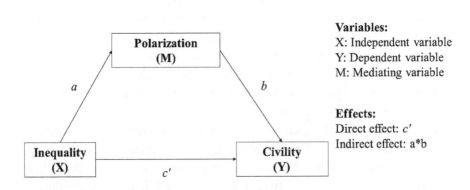

Figure 6.1. Mediation Model (generic)

RESULTS: WHAT DID WE FIND?

In broad terms, the statistical analysis produced evidence supporting the hypotheses, including that of a negative association between changes in inequality and perceptions of legislative civility. Likewise, evidence was produced indicating a mediating effect of lobbyists' perceptions of polarization relative to other institutions. The findings, however, are sensitive to the selection of both inequality indices and polarization measures. This section describes the results of our analyses.

DESCRIPTIVE STATISTICS

The descriptive statistics presented here are limited to levels and changes in the variables of interest identified in earlier sections, namely: 1) respondent characteristics; 2) perceptions of the norms of civility; and 3) measures of state-level inequality and partisanship.

A substantial proportion of data about respondent characteristics is missing from the lobbyist dataset, making it challenging to assess lobbyist characteristics accurately. Among respondents who provided demographic information, the largest share is somewhat older, more often male, and predominantly white/non-Hispanic. The largest shares of respondents indicated affiliation with the Democratic party and have liberal views on social issues but hold more conservative views on fiscal issues. Again, however, missing data may affect these results.

As shown in Table 6.1, we find that on average lobbyists lean slightly toward a perception of civility among state legislators during the two most recent legislative sessions (mean 5.4 out of 10). Moreover, lobbyists describe their state's legislators and legislators with whom they deal as being slightly over the midpoint of a 5-point civility scale (3.3 and 3.9, respectively), on average, while describing their own behavior as being fairly civil (4.6 out of 5). However, they describe both individual legislators and legislative leaders as being somewhat less civil today (3.9 and 3.6, out of 5, respectively) than ten years ago. On average, state legislators in general received the lowest score for civility among the stakeholders listed (2.8 out of 5).

Lobbyists in the sample represent all 50 states, although they are not distributed equally; the number of respondents in each state range from a minimum of 14 respondents from Georgia to a maximum of 79 from

Table 6.1. Descriptive Statistics—Lobbyist Characteristics

Characteristic	Percent (n = 1,240)
Age	
<50	15.4
50+	44.0
Missing	25.3
Sex	
Male	43.0
Female	30.8
Missing	26.2
Race	
White/Not Hispanic	66.0
Non-white	5.7
Missing	28.4
Political party	
Democrat	29.0
Republican	21.1
Independent or other	24.3
Missing	25.7
Views on social issues	
Slightly to very liberal	43.55
Moderate; middle of the road	14.76
Slightly to very conservative	15.64
Missing	26.05
Views on fiscal issues	
Slightly to very liberal	23.87
Moderate; middle of the road	13.71
Slightly to very conservative	36.12
Missing	26.29

Oregon. Table 6.2 displays descriptive statistics for attitudes on civility and Table 6.3 sets forth descriptive statistics for measures of inequality and partisanship, across all observations and collapsed by state.[10]

As measured by the 2015 Gini coefficient, inequality ranges from a low of 55 in West Virginia to a high of 71 in New York, and the average Gini coefficient across all states is 60.8.[11] For reference, the 2015 Gini coefficient across the United States population is 63.9 (Franko, 2020). On average, states have experienced increases in inequality in both the short- and long-term, consistent with referenced inequality scholarship. Only two states, Alaska and New Hampshire, experienced a decrease in the Gini coefficient between 2000 and 2015, and no states experienced a

Table 6.2. Descriptive Statistics—Perceptions of Civility

Concept	Variable	N	Mean	Sd	Min	Max
General level of civility[1]	State Legislators	977	5.4	2.1	1	9
Changes in civility[2]	Individual legislators	971	3.9	1.9	1	5
	Legislative leaders	971	3.6	1.8	1	5
Norms of civility[3]	You	980	4.6	0.6	1	5
	Other lobbyists	975	3.9	0.8	1	5
	Your state's legislators	979	3.3	0.9	1	5
	State legislators with whom you deal	979	3.9	0.9	1	5
	State legislators in general in U.S.	924	2.8	0.8	1	5
	Average citizen in state	979	2.9	0.9	1	5

[1] Scale: 1 = Very uncivil, 9 = Very civil
[2] Scale: 1 = Less civil, 5 = More civil
[3] Scale: 1 = Very uncivil, 5 = Very civil

Table 6.3. Descriptive Statistics—Inequality and Partisanship

		All observations					State-level statistic				
		N	Mean	Sd	Min	Max	N	Mean	Sd	Min	Max
Inequality (Levels and Changes)	Gini 2015	1240	60.8	3.4	54.8	70.7	50	60.8	3.6	54.8	70.7
	Δ Gini 2000-15	1240	2.6	1.6	-1.3	7.0	50	2.7	1.6	-1.3	7.0
	Δ Gini 1970-2015	1240	15.1	3.6	8.6	25.4	50	15.0	3.7	8.6	25.4
	80:20 Ratio	1240	5.3	0.7	4.0	6.8	50	5.3	0.7	4.0	6.8
	Δ 80:20 Ratio 2000-12	1240	0.4	0.5	-1.0	1.4	50	0.4	0.5	-1.0	1.4
	Δ 80:20 Ratio 1985-2015	1240	1.0	0.5	-0.1	2.3	50	1.0	0.6	-0.1	2.3
Partisanship (Levels and Changes)	Part Index 2016	1165	1.7	0.5	0.8	3.4	46	1.7	0.5	0.8	3.4
	Δ Part Index 2000-16	1165	0.4	0.3	0.0	1.4	46	0.4	0.3	0.0	1.4
Perceptions of Partisan Polarization (Levels)	vs. U.S. Congress[1]	891	2.3	0.9	1	5	n/a	n/a	n/a	n/a	n/a
	vs. other state legislatures[2]	887	5.6	2.2	1	10	n/a	n/a	n/a	n/a	n/a

[1]Scale: 1 = Much less polarized, 5 = Much more polarized

[2]Scale: 1 = Among the least polarized, 10 = Among most polarized

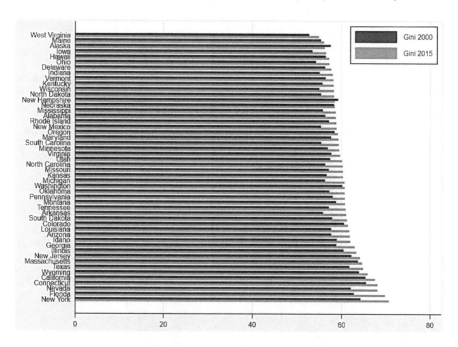

Figure 6.2. Gini Coefficients for All U.S. States, 2000 and 2015.
SOURCE: Franko, W. (2020). *Replication Data for: How State Responses to Economic Crisis Shape Income Inequality and Financial Well-Being* [Data set]. https://doi.org/10.15139/S3/OKCXPZ.

decrease between 1970 and 2015. Figure 6.2 shows both the presence of wide variation among U.S. states and underscores the trend of increased inequality occurring among most states.

Returning to Table 6.3, the 80:20 ratio also demonstrates high levels of inequality. On average, states' income for the top 20% of the population is over five times higher than the bottom 20% of the population; the 80:20 ratio experienced by states in 2012 ranged from 4 to 7. Only ten states experienced short-term decreases in the 80:20 ratio over the period 2000 to 2012, while only one state experienced a longer-term decrease (1985–2012).

Shor and McCarty's (2011, 2018) preferred measures of partisanship are based on differences in roll-call voting between the parties in state legislatures' two chambers (i.e., House and Senate). For simplicity, we combine the measures for the two chambers into simple summative indices

Table 6.4. Bivariate relationships between inequality and perceptions of civility.

| | General level of civility[1] | | Changes in civility[2] | | | | Norms of civility[3] | | | | | |
| | State Legislators (n = 977) | | Individual legislators (n = 971) | | Legislative leaders (n = 971) | | Your state's legislators (n = 979) | | State legislators with whom you deal (n = 979) | | State legislators in general in U.S. (n = 924) | |
	Coeff	Se	Coeff	Se	Coeff	Se	Coeff	Se	Coeff	Se	Coeff	Se
Gini (2015)	0.05*	0.03	0.05	0.03	0.03	0.04	0.01	0.01	0	0.01	0.01	0.01
80/20 ratio (2012)	0.01	0.23	0.25	0.17	0.32*	0.17	-0.03	0.07	0.02	0.06	0.06	0.04
Δ Gini (2000-15)	-0.03	0.27	0.01	0.04	-0.02	0.05	-0.05**	0.02	-0.03**	0.01	0.01	0.01
Δ 80/20 ratio (2000-12)	0.09	0.27	0.23	0.15	0.28	0.2	-0.1	0.09	-0.02	0.08	0.08	0.05

[1]Scale: 1 = Very uncivil, 9 = Very civil

[2]Scale: 1 = Less civil, 5 = More civil

[3]Scale: 1 = Very uncivil, 5 = Very civil

Test of Statistical Significance: *** p<0.01, ** p<0.05, * p<0.10

Robust clustered s.e.'s

for two time points, 2000 and 2016.[12] The Cronbach's alpha statistics associated with these indices were 0.90 and 0.95, respectively, suggesting a high level of reliability. These indices indicate that partisan levels vary substantially among the states, and that partisanship has increased since 2000; these findings are aligned with Shor and McCarty (2011). On average, lobbyists perceive that their state legislatures are slightly less polarized than the U.S. Congress, but slightly more polarized than other state legislatures, as shown in Table 6.3.

BIVARIATE AND MULTIVARIATE RELATIONSHIPS

The analysis begins by testing the bivariate relationships between inequality and perceptions of state legislators' civility. Because inequality indicators are measured at the state level, while perceptions of civility are measured at the respondent level, we used robust standard errors clustered at the state level. As shown in Table 6.4, the findings were somewhat mixed. We found evidence of a negative and statistically significant (p<.05) relationship between changes in inequality (Gini) and lobbyists' perceptions of change in the norms of civility among both state legislators in general and the state legislators with whom the lobbyists work regularly. In other words, lobbyists in states that have exhibited increased inequality over time report lower civil behavior scores for their respective state legislators. However, little evidence of significant associations between levels of inequality (measured either as the Gini or the 80/20 ratio) and predominantly positive coefficients run counter to our expectations of a negative relationship. In addition, the results are sensitive to our choice of inequality measure; while these items yield the same (negative) sign for the 80/20 ratio, the coefficients are not significant. Tests of bivariate relationships with the longer-term changes in inequality did not yield significant results.[13]

Multivariate regressions were conducted for the two norms of civility variables that produced a bivariate relationship above, as shown in Table 6.5, to control for the effects of lobbyist characteristics.[14] Similar to our bivariate approach, we used robust standard errors clustered by state. Importantly, the results indicate that the (negative) associations between changes in inequality (Gini) and perceptions of civility are robust with the addition of other lobbyist characteristics. While the multivariate regression also suggests significant effects of selected lobbyist characteristics, namely that White lobbyists are less likely to perceive uncivil behavior among legislators than non-White lobbyists, and that Republicans are more likely to perceive uncivil behavior than Democrats, the results may be confounded by the degree of missing data.[15]

Table 6.5. Multivariate Relationships between Changes in Inequality and Perceptions of Civility

	Norms of Civility: Your State Legislators in General[1] (n = 979)		Norms of Civility: State Legislators with Whom You Deal[1] (n = 979)	
	Coefficients	Standard Errors	Coefficients	Standard Errors
Δ Gini (2000-15)	-0.06***	0.02	-0.03**	0.01
Age (Older)	0.00	0.06	0.05	0.06
Age (Missing)	0.29	0.46	0.53	0.46
Sex (Male)	0.1	0.07	0.02	0.06
Sex (Missing)	0.08	0.31	-0.28	0.28
Race (White)	-0.36***	0.10	-0.34***	0.11
Race (Missing)	-0.35	0.18	-0.32	0.16
Party (Republican)	0.23**	0.11	0.14	0.09
Party (Ind/Oth)	0.01	0.09	0	0.08
Party (Missing)	-0.23	0.37	-0.17	0.32
Cons	3.68***	0.13	4.21***	0.13

[1]Scale: 1 = Very Uncivil, 5 = Very Civil

[2]Scale: 1 = Much Less Polarized, 5 = Much More Polarized

[3]Scale: 1 = Among the Least Polarized, 5 = Among Most Polarized

Omitted categories include: Age (Younger), Sex (Female), Race (Nonwhite), and Party (Democrat)

Test of Statistical Significance: *** $p<0.01$, ** $p<0.05$, * $p<0.10$

Robust clustered (state) s.e.'s

MEDIATION ANALYSIS

Finally, the mediation analyses explore the indirect effects of polarization on perceptions of civility. Mediation models analyze the causal pathway between two variables, hypothesizing that a third variable provides an indirect pathway between two variables, showing evidence of association with both variables. We began by examining two distinct multi-level mediation models: a 2-2-1 model and a 2-1-1 model, wherein the "1" reflects data collected at the individual (i.e., lobbyist) level and the "2" reflects state-level data, as shown in Figure 6.3. Testing of a mediation effect typically proceeds by first gathering evidence of three conditions, including relationships among: 1) the main independent variable

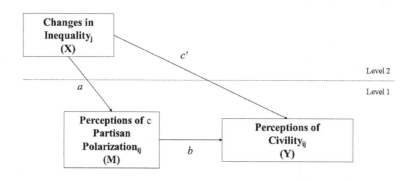

Figure 6.3a. 2-1-1 Mediation Model

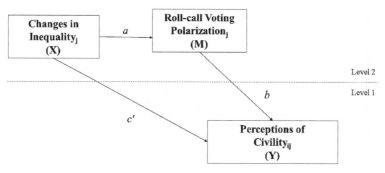

Figure 6.3b. 2-2-1 Mediation Model

Table 6.6. Bivariate Relationship between Inequality and Polarization Measures

	Roll-call Voting Polarization Measure (2016)		Δ in Roll-call Voting Polarization Measure (2000–16)		Perception of Polarization (vs U.S. Congress)[1]		Perception of Partisan Polarization (vs other states)[2]	
	Coeff	Se	Coeff	Se	Coeff	Se	Coeff	Se
Gini (2015)	0.85	0.96	0.06	0.95	-0.05	0.13	-0.01	0.07
Δ Gini (2000–15)	-0.74**	0.36	0.19	0.87	0.22**	0.08	0.11***	0.04
80/20 ratio (2012)	0.15	0.22	0.17	0.29	0.07*	0.03	0.02	0.02
Δ 80/20 ratio (2000–12)	-0.04	0.16	0.56***	0.19	0.03	0.02	0.01	0.01

[1]Scale: 1 = Much less polarized, 5 = Much more polarized

[2]Scale: 1 = Among the least polarized, 10 = Among most polarized

Sample sizes (n) vary from 887 to 1,165.

Tests of Statistical Significance: *** p<0.01, ** p<0.05, * p<0.10

(inequality) and the dependent variable (perceptions of civility); 2) the independent variable and the mediating, or intervening, variable (polarization); and 3) the mediating variable (polarization) and the dependent variable (perceptions of civility) (Baron and Kenny, 1986). Only after these three conditions are met do we proceed to testing the full mediation model, using the Sobel test (Baron and Kenny, 1986; Sobel, 1982).

In this study, we use the product method with delta method standard errors to produce estimates of indirect, direct, and total effects (UCLA Institute for Digital Research and Education, n.d.; VanderWeele, 2016). To accommodate the two-level nature of the data related to changes in inequality, we use multilevel mediation models, which include a latent state-level variable in all paths to account for the possibility of group-level effects (Krull and MacKinnon, 2001; Preacher et al., 2011). Figures 6.3a and 6.3b display the multi-level mediation models and hypothesized pathways.

The previous section offers evidence of a robust relationship between changes in inequality and perceptions of civility, although it is admittedly sensitive to the choice of indicators for both variables. We conducted bivariate regressions among various measures of inequality (levels and changes) and polarization (objective state-level measures and lobbyist perceptions of partisan polarization), expecting to find positive associations. As shown in Table 6.6, the bivariate analyses yielded strong positive relationships between changes in inequality (Gini) and perceptions of partisan polarization, as well as between changes in the 80/20 ratio and changes in state-level polarization based on the Shor-McCarty roll-call voting polarization measure. That said, the findings were again sensitive to the inequality measure, and our directional expectations were not upheld by all the results, especially with respect to the roll-call voting measure.

We then proceeded to examine the bivariate associations between the measures of polarization and perceptions of civility, as shown in Table 6.7. As expected, we find evidence of strong negative relationships between perceptions of polarization (relative to other institutions) and perceptions of civility; it is clear that as perceptions of polarization increase, perceptions of civility decrease. In contrast, we find no statistically significant relationships between the objective measure of polarization (e.g., Shor-McCarty roll-call measure) and perceptions of civility. As such, it is unlikely that state-level polarization (measured objectively)

Table 6.7. Bivariate relationship between polarization and civility measures.

| | General level of civility[1] | | Changes in civility[2] | | | | | | Norms of civility[3] | | | |
| | State Legislators (n = 977) | | Individual legislators (n = 971) | | Legislative leaders (n = 971) | | Your state's legislators (n = 979) | | State legislators with whom you deal (n = 979) | | State legislators in general in U.S. (n = 924) | |
	Coeff	Se	Coeff	Se	Coeff	Se	coeff	Se	Coeff	Se	Coeff	Se
Roll-call Voting Polarization Measure (2016)	0.22	0.26	0.24	0.23	0.28	0.28	0.04	0.08	0.01	0.06	0	0.05
Δ in Roll-call Voting Polarization Measure (2000-16)	0.29	0.45	0.2	0.24	0.37	0.29	-0.07	0.13	-0.02	0.15	0.01	0.11
Perception of Polarization (vs U.S. Congress)[4]	-0.86***	0.09	-0.44***	0.08	-0.54***	0.07	-0.3***	0.03	-0.21***	0.03	-0.07**	0.03
Perception of Partisan Polarization (vs other states)[5]	-0.41***	0.04	-0.25***	0.04	-0.26***	0.04	-0.16***	0.02	-0.11***	0.02	-0.01	0.02

[1]Scale: 1 = Very uncivil, 9 = Very civil
[2]Scale: 1 = Less civil, 5 = More civil
[3]Scale: 1 = Very uncivil, 5 = Very civil
[4]Scale: 1 = Much less polarized, 5 = Much more polarized
[5]Scale: 1 = Among the least polarized, 5 = Among most polarized
Test of Statistical Significance: *** $p<0.01$, ** $p<0.05$, * $p<0.10$
Robust clustered (state) s.e.'s

has an indirect effect on lobbyist perceptions of civility. Moreover, the survey's polarization measure is a relative measure, and respondents from less-polarized states (based on the objective roll-call voting measure) may nonetheless perceive their own legislature as relatively polarized.[16] In combination with the previous results, which showed significant relationships for the other two pathways, these findings suggest that there may be an indirect (i.e., mediating) effect of lobbyists' perceptions of polarization on perceptions of civility.

Based on the preceding evidence, we proceeded to calculate the indirect and direct effects for only the 2-1-1 mediation model with inequality (change in Gini) entered as the independent variable, perceptions of relative polarization entered as mediating variables, and perceptions of civility entered as the dependent variable.[17] The indirect effect of the mediating variable is calculated by multiplying the coefficients from the paths to and from the mediating variable. The total effect can then be decomposed into an indirect effect and a direct effect (VanderWeele, 2016). If the indirect effect causes the direct effect to drop to zero, then there is evidence of complete mediation; evidence of both a direct and indirect effect is considered partial mediation (MacKinnon et al., 2007).

The four mediation models include lobbyist characteristics as covariates in all relevant pathways and use robust standard errors clustered at the state level. As shown in Table 6.8, all models continue to show negative and significant total effects of inequality on perceptions of civility.[18] The results also offer evidence of at least partial mediation through perceptions of relative partisanship, with significant indirect effects present in all models generated. Moreover, in three of the models, the effects of inequality on perceptions of civility are transmitted predominantly through the indirect effects of perceptions of partisanship, indicated by the combination of a significant indirect effect and an insignificant direct effect. In each of these three models there is evidence that perceptions of the relative polarization of lobbyists' state legislatures in comparison to other state legislatures provide a pathway by which changes in inequality are transmitted to perceptions of civility. A direct effect of inequality remains in only one model, which tests the pathways among changes in inequality, perceptions of partisanship compared to the U.S. Congress, and the perceptions of civility for lobbyists' state legislators in general.

Table 6.8. Indirect, direct, and total effects.

Independent Variable: Δ Gini (2000-15)	Norms of Civility: Your State's Legislators in General (n = 891)						Norms of Civility: State Legislators with Whom You Deal (n = 887)					
	Indirect Effect		Direct Effect		Total Effect		Indirect Effect		Direct Effect		Total Effect	
Mediating Variable	Coeff	Se	Coeff	Se	Coeff	Se	Coeff	Se	Coeff	Se	Coeff	Se
Perceptions of Partisan Polarization (vs. U.S. Congress)[1]	-0.02***	0.01	-0.05**	0.02	-0.07***	0.02	-0.04***	0.01	-0.02	0.02	-0.06***	0.02
Perceptions of Partisan Polarization (vs. Other State Legislatures)[2]	-0.01**	0.01	-0.02*	0.01	-0.04***	0.01	-0.03***	0.01	-0.01	0.01	-0.03**	0.01

[1] Scale: 1 = Much less polarized, 5 = Much more polarized

[2] Scale: 1 = Among the least polarized, 5 = Among most polarized

All models estimated with robust clustered (state) s.e.'s

Individual characteristics (age 50+, age missing, male, white, race missing, Repub, ind/other, party missing) included as covariates in all pathways

Tests of Statistical Significance: *** $p<0.01$, ** $p<0.05$, * $p<0.10$

DISCUSSION: WHAT ARE THE IMPLICATIONS AND LIMITATIONS OF THESE FINDINGS?

The findings are rather intriguing. They suggest, first and foremost, that the adverse effects of changes in state-level income inequality extend beyond the narrow changes in relative income experienced by individuals and families. Indeed, shifts in income inequality at the state level appear to generate a widespread influence on the political process, ranging from polarization (as shown by previous scholars) to perceptions of the legislative conduct of state-level legislators. These observations both substantiate and extend the findings reported by other scholars.

While the findings appear to support the hypotheses in most respects, several limitations of the analysis should be noted. First and foremost, the findings represent associations, with causality implied primarily by theory, and to some degree by the use of chronologically sequential data, as in the case of the direct effects of changes in inequality on perceptions of civility. Relatedly, the mediation analysis, which includes two items from the chronologically simultaneous survey, does not conform to usual mediation protocols which more typically draw on parallel longitudinal data for evidence of mediation. This limitation is particularly important inasmuch as it introduces the possibility that civility is the main mediating variable.[19] Moreover, omission of other individual- and/or state-level variables may result in biased estimates of the effects of changes in inequality on perceptions in civility. Finally, the survey itself measures the viewpoints of lobbyists, as opposed to the behavior of state legislators or the perceptions of a broader group of observers. Indeed, this study notes that lobbyist perceptions of relative polarization are not well-correlated with the selected (objective) measure of polarization. Despite these limitations, our findings align with previous literature focused on the relationship between inequality and polarization; perhaps more importantly, they also point to an association between a broad economic shift and the daily experience in state legislatures throughout the country.

Why are these findings important? Longstanding welfare-state theories and related empirical evidence suggest that higher income inequality (Meltzer and Richard, 1981) and/or the structure of inequality (Pontusson and Weisstanner, 2018) have positive effects on support for redistributive policy, potentially dampening the feedback effects of current inequality on future inequality. In contrast, other scholars express concern that income inequality may itself alter the structure of political conflict, thus explaining "the lack of democratic response" to markedly rising inequality (Piketty 2018, p. 61). Moreover, research suggests that polarization may shift policymaking into the hands of bureaucrats (Boushey and McGrath, 2020), with unknown impacts on redistributive decisions. If income inequality and perceptions of relative polarization exist in a positive feedback loop, legislator civility may act as a signal of that loop—or perhaps even a mechanism by which the feedback manifests. While our findings do not fully resolve these questions, they suggest that the broader shifts in inequality are intimately connected to the behaviors of state legislatures. From the perspective of lobbyists, as outsiders looking in, the behavior of state legislators clearly echoes these broader trends.

NOTES

1. While there is also evidence of growing wealth inequality, as well as health, education, and technology inequities and social stratification, this chapter focuses primarily on income inequality for both theoretical and practical reasons.

2. Detailed information about the methods used to conduct the survey is included in the editors' introduction.

3. In this study, we multiply the Gini coefficient by 100 to ease the interpretation of bivariate and multivariate regressions. As such, Gini scores of 0 and 100 represent perfect inequality and equality, respectively.

4. There are several other statistical measures of overall inequality (e.g., Theil Index, Atkinson) and other ratio-based choices (e.g., 90/10; 99/90). We elected to use these two measures due to the combination of their wide use and the straightforward explanation of related results associated with both measures.

5. The Voorheis 80/20 ratio data are only available starting in 1985.

6. Scale reliability coefficients were 0.96 for both 1993 and 2016. In 2000, the scale reliability coefficient was 0.91, suggesting some amount of variation between the roll call voting patterns in the two chambers.

7. In multi-level mediation modeling, this notation specifies the level at which data are collected. The "1" reflects data collected at the individual (i.e., lobbyist) level and the "2" reflects state-level data.

8. The Stata "gsem" command was used to conduct all mediation analyses.

9. Data, syntax, and log file are available at https://osf.io/tnf7q/?view_only=6ebd62e070 ef464f91c3547c545bef63.

10. While Table 6.2 displays all six items associated with the norms of civility question, our analysis ultimately focuses on the norms of civility for "your state legislators" and "state legislators with whom you deal."

11. Recall that in this study we have multiplied the Gini coefficient by 100 for ease of interpretation.

12. Although the Shor-McCarty data include partisanship statistics to 1993, longer-term partisanship statistics are only available for a selection of states.

13. Results are not shown here but can be made available upon request.

14. Characteristics are entered as categorical variables, and coefficients should be interpreted relative to the omitted category. Due to the extent of missing data, we also included categorical variables representing missing data to avoid having to drop observations.

15. Since the main covariate of interest is the change in inequality, Table 5 includes dummy variables for missing data to retain overall sample size. When missing data are dropped from the regression (n=874), the results are comparable with respect to direction and magnitude, and statistical significance.

16. Indeed, bivariate analyses yield consistently negative relationships (p<0.01) between the objective measures of polarization and lobbyist perceptions of relative polarization.

17. We do not proceed with testing the full 2-2-1 mediation model given that the conditions were not met.

18. For simplicity, we provide only the effects in Table 6.8. Results from the full model are available upon request.

19. Indeed, when the mediation models are tested with perceptions of civility as the mediating variable(s) and perceptions of partisanship as the dependent variable(s), we see similarly significant indirect and total effects, with positive coefficients as expected. Results are not shown here, but they can be made available upon request.

REFERENCES

Baron, R. M., & Kenny, D. A. (1986). The moderator–mediator variable distinction in social psychological research: Conceptual, strategic, and statistical considerations. *Journal of Personality and Social Psychology, 51*(6), 1173–1182. https://doi.org/10.1037/0022-3514.51.6.1173.

Boix, C. (2010). Origins and persistence of economic inequality. *Annual Review of Political Science, 13*(June), 489–516. https://doi.org/10.1146/annurev.polisci.12.031607.094915.

Boushey, G. T., & McGrath, R. J. (2020). Does partisan conflict lead to increased bureaucratic policymaking? Evidence from the American states. *Journal of Public Administration Research and Theory, 30*(3), 432–447. https://doi.org/10.1093/jopart/muz030.

Duca, J. V., & Saving, J. L. (2016). Income inequality and political polarization: Time series evidence over nine decades. *Review of Income and Wealth, 62*(3), 445–466. https://doi.org/10.1111/roiw.12162.

Frank, M. W. (n.d.) *The U.S. income inequality page of Mark W. Frank.* https://www.shsu.edu/eco_mwf/inequality.html.

Frank, M. W., Sommeiller, E., Price, M., & Saez, E. (2015). *Frank-Sommeiller-Price Series for Top Income Shares by U.S. States since 1917* [WID.world Technical Notes Series No. 2015/7] (p. 4). https://wid.world/document/wid_methodology_notes_2015_7_us/.

Franko, W. (2020). *Replication data for: How state responses to economic crisis shape income inequality and financial well-being* [Data set]. https://doi.org/10.15139/S3/OKCXPZ.

Garand, J. C. (2010). Income inequality, party polarization, and roll-call voting in the U.S. Senate. *The Journal of Politics, 72*(4), 1109–1128. https://doi.org/10.1017/S0022381610000563.

Giordono, L. S., Jones, M. D., & Rothwell, D. W. (2019). Social policy perspectives on economic inequality in wealthy countries. *Policy Studies Journal, 47*(S1), S96–S118. https://doi.org/10.1111/psj.12315.

Glassman, B. (2016). *Income inequality metrics and economic well-being* [SEHSD Working Paper Number 2016-19]. U.S. Census Bureau. https://www.census.gov/library/working-papers/2016/demo/SEHSD-WP2016-19.html.

Hacker, J. S., & Pierson, P. (2010). Winner-take-all politics: Public policy, political organization, and the precipitous rise of top incomes in the United States. *Politics & Society, 38*(2), 152–204. https://doi.org/10.1177/0032329210365042.

Jacobs, L. R., & Soss, J. (2010a). The politics of inequality in America: A political economy framework. *Annual Review of Political Science, 13*(June), 341–364. https://doi.org/10.1146/annurev.polisci.041608.140134.

Kenski, K., Coe, K., & Rains, S. A. (2019). Perceptions of incivility in public discourse. In R. G. Boatright, T. J. Shaffer, S. Sobieraj, & D. G. Young (Eds.), *A crisis of civility? Political discourse and its discontents* (pp. 45–58). Taylor and Francis Group. http://ebookcentral.proquest.com/lib/osu/detail.action?docID=5709725.

Kopczuk, W., Saez, E., & Song, J. (2010). Earnings inequality and mobility in the United States: Evidence from social security data since 1937. *The Quarterly Journal of Economics, 125*(1), 91–128. https://doi.org/10.1162/qjec.2010.125.1.91.

Krull, J. L., & MacKinnon, D. P. (2001). Multilevel modeling of individual and group level mediated effects. *Multivariate Behavioral Research, 36*(2), 249–277. https://doi.org/10.1207/S15327906MBR3602_06.

MacKinnon, D. P., Fairchild, A. J., & Fritz, M. S. (2007). Mediation analysis. *Annual Review of Psychology, 58*(January), 593–614. https://doi.org/10.1146/annurev.psych.58.110405.085542.

McCarty, N. M., Poole, K. T., & Rosenthal, H. 1997. *Income redistribution and the realignment of American politics.* AEI Press.

McCarty, N., Poole, K. T., & Rosenthal, H. 2008. *Polarized America: The dance of ideology and unequal riches.* The MIT Press.

Meltzer, A. H., & Richard, S. F. (1981). A rational theory of the size of government. *Journal of Political Economy, 89*(5), 914–927.

National Conference of State Legislatures. (2018). *State legislative policymaking in an age of political polarization.* http://www.ncsl.org/Portals/1/Documents/About_State_Legislatures/Partisanship_030818.pdf.

Piketty, T. (2014). *Capital in the twenty-first century.* Harvard University Press.

Piketty, T. (2018). *Brahmin left vs merchant right: Rising inequality and the changing structure of political conflict* [WID.world Working Paper Series No. 2018/7]. http://piketty.pse.ens.fr/files/Piketty2018.pdf.

Pontusson, J., & Weisstanner, D. (2018). Macroeconomic conditions, inequality shocks and the politics of redistribution, 1990–2013. *Journal of European Public Policy, 25*(1), 31–58. https://doi.org/10.1080/13501763.2017.1310280.

Preacher, K. J., Zhang, Z., & Zyphur, M. J. (2011). Alternative methods for assessing mediation in multilevel data: The advantages of multilevel SEM. *Structural Equation Modeling: A Multidisciplinary Journal, 18,* 161–182. https://doi.org/10.1080/10705511.2011.557329.

Preacher, K. J., Zyphur, M. J., & Zhang, Z. (2010). A general multilevel SEM framework for assessing multilevel mediation. *Psychological Methods, 15*(3), 209–233. https://doi.org/10.1037/a0020141.

Putnam, R. D. (2016). *Our kids: The American dream in crisis* (Reprint edition). Simon & Schuster. (Original work published 2015)

Rigby, E., & Wright, G. C. (2015). The policy consequences of party polarization: Evidence from the American states. In J. A. Thurber & A. Yoshinaka (Eds.), *American gridlock* (pp. 236–256). Cambridge University Press. https://doi.org/10.1017/CBO9781316287002.013.

Rogers, W. (1994). Regression standard errors in clustered samples. *Stata Technical Bulletin, 3*(13). https://econpapers.repec.org/article/tsjstbull/y_3a1994_3av_3a3_3ai_3a13_3asg17.htm.

Saez, E., & Zucman, G. (2016). Wealth inequality in the United States since 1913: Evidence from capitalized income tax data. *Quarterly Journal of Economics, 131*(2), 519–578. https://doi.org/10.1093/qje/qjw004.

Shor, B., & McCarty, N. (2011). The ideological mapping of American legislatures. *American Political Science Review, 105*(3), 530–551.

Shor, B., & McCarty, N. (2018). *Aggregate State Legislator Shor-McCarty Ideology Data, May 2018 update.* Harvard Dataverse, V2. https://doi.org/10.7910/DVN/BSLEFD.

Sobel, M. E. (1982). Asymptotic confidence intervals for indirect effects in structural equation models. *Sociological Methodology, 13,* 290–312. https://doi.org/10.2307/270723.

UCLA Institute for Digital Research and Education. (n.d.). *How can I compare indirect effects in a multiple group model? Stata FAQ.* https://stats.idre.ucla.edu/stata/faq/how-can-i-compare-indirect-effects-in-a-multiple-group-model/.

VanderWeele, T. J. (2016). Mediation analysis: A practitioner's guide. *Annual Review of Public Health, 37,* 17–32. https://doi.org/10.1146/annurev-publhealth-032315-021402.

Voorheis, J. (2016). *Essays on income inequality and the environment* [Doctoral Thesis, University of Oregon]. https://scholarsbank.uoregon.edu/xmlui/handle/1794/20478.

Voorheis, J., McCarty, N., & Shor, B. (2015, August 21). Unequal incomes, ideology and gridlock: How rising inequality increases political polarization. *SSRN Electronic Journal.* https://doi.org/10.2139/ssrn.2649215.

Weber Shandwick. (2019, June 26). *Civility in America 2019: Solutions for tomorrow.* https://www.webershandwick.com/news/civility-in-america-2019-solutions-for-tomorrow/.

Young, D. G., Hoffman, L. H., & Roth, D. (2019). "Showdowns," "duels," and "nail-biters": How aggressive strategic game frames in campaign coverage fuel public perceptions of incivility. In R. G. Boatright, T. J. Shaffer, S. Sobieraj, & D. G. Young (Eds.), *A crisis of civility? Political discourse and its discontents* (pp. 45–58). Taylor and Francis Group. http://ebookcentral.proquest.com/lib/osu/detail.action?docID=5709725.

Zhang, Z., Zyphur, M. J., & Preacher, K. J. (2009). Testing multilevel mediation using hierarchical linear models: Problems and solutions. *Organizational Research Methods, 12*(4), 695–719. https://doi.org/10.1177/1094428108327450.

CHAPTER SEVEN

Rural and Urban Polarization and Civility in State Legislatures

Claire McMorris
Brent S. Steel
Leanne S. Giordono

THE RURAL-URBAN DIVIDE

With the election of President Donald Trump in the 2016 presidential election, many political commentators argued that his victory was the result, in part, of the mobilization of angry rural and rust-belt voters who felt disenfranchised, disconnected, and threatened by the current socioeconomic and political systems (Kurtzleben, 2016; Monnat, 2016; Monnat and Brown, 2017). Trump won over 2,500 mostly rural counties compared to Hilary Clinton's wins in 500 mostly urban counties and 88 of the 100 most highly populated counties in the United States. This led David Graham, in an article titled "Red State, Blue City" in *The Atlantic,* to comment that "the United States is coming to resemble two separate countries, one rural and one urban" (2017). Others also suggest that rural communities especially feel threatened by the policy domination of urban "establishment" political and media elites who often belittle more "traditional" and conservative beliefs and values. Hochschild's *Strangers in Their Own Land: Anger and Mourning on the American Right* (2016) and Cramer's *The Politics of Resentment: Rural Consciousness in Wisconsin and the Rise of Scott Walker* (2016a) both document the resentment and anger of rural communities directed toward urban governmental and media elites. As Cramer comments after some follow-up qualitative research for her book (2016b):

> Since 2007, I have been inviting myself into conversations in rural Wisconsin to try to understand how people in such communities are making sense of politics. I have been listening in during early morning coffee klatches in gas stations that serve coffee, in diners, and in churches. The resentment I uncovered predates Trump, but it set the stage for his ascendance…. What I found was resentment of an intensity and specificity that surprised me. The pervasiveness of resentment toward the cities and urban elites, as well as urban institutions like government and the media, was inescapable after several visits to these groups.

Cramer found that the politics of resentment in rural communities is "fueled by political strategy…more casually called notions of **"us"** and **"them"** (2016a, p. 8; emphasis added). Smith and Hanley (2018) further argue that Trump received support from voters "because they share his prejudices" concerning race and gender issues, which are found in some rural communities as well (p. 195).

Much of the polarization of rural-urban politics stems from the migration of people from rural to metropolitan areas, which is typically driven by the departure of highly educated workers and skilled younger residents who seek employment and/or further education (Weber et al., 2017). This migration has caused rural populations to decline in many areas as metropolitan areas grow both in size and diversity. The continuing growth of metropolitan areas has boosted employment in the service sector, which accounts for the overwhelming numbers of jobs in U.S. metropolitan areas in the health, education, financial, and technology industries. Concomitantly, employment in the agricultural and natural resource sectors, which historically has been important in rural communities, has declined to a small portion of the contemporary labor force as automation expands and demands have changed, exacerbating rural migration to urban areas for economic reasons (Alexander et al., 2017; Lichter and Ziliak, 2017; Weber et al., 2017). Without the same diverse economic base that urban areas enjoy, many rural communities in general have found themselves facing higher unemployment and poverty rates (Goetz, Partridge, and Stephens, 2018; Ulrich-Schad and Duncan, 2018).

Increased urbanization has had an important impact on politics by shifting political power (e.g., the number of politicians representing urban areas and the number of urban individuals voting) toward metropolitan areas and away from rural areas (Simon et al., 2018). This has led many rural residents to feel their voices on policy matters are too often drowned out by the interests of metropolitan areas (Cramer, 2016a and 2016b; Hochschild, 2016). Urbanization has led to increasingly different policy priorities for rural and urban residents and their legislative representatives. While rural areas must grapple with economic decline and shrinking populations, metropolitan areas confront a variety of their own public policy challenges, including increasing land and housing prices, persistent traffic congestion, and greater demands for a variety of inner-city services ranging from expanded social services to enhanced public safety to better transportation systems (Alexander et al., 2017; Lichter and Ziliak, 2017; Weber et al., 2017). In short, the continued expansion of urbanization generally means residents of rural and urban areas tend to confront considerably different problems and therefore have different expectations about public policy outcomes (McKee, 2008; Scala and Johnson, 2017). Alan Greenblatt has described the situation in an article in *Governing* (2014):

> There are certainly states in which rural residents feel forlorn. The traditional geographic fights over money for roads and schools have been joined by cultural divides over issues such as same-sex marriage, environmental regulations and guns. In a number of states, particularly those dominated by Democratic majorities based in metropolitan areas, it's become fashionable in rural quarters to talk about secession. Last November, 11 Colorado counties voted on whether to split and form a 51st state. Five of those counties voted in favor of the idea. "We're rarely listened to when it comes to legislation," complains Ault Mayor Butch White.

CASE STUDY: OREGON

The State of Oregon serves as an excellent example of the state-level rural-urban political divide in the United States (Buylova, Warner, and Steel, 2018; Clucas, Henkels, and Steel, 2011). As the 2019 Oregon legislative session opened, Democrats were optimistic about their ability to pass a progressive policy agenda with a Democratic governor and the attainment of legislative supermajorities during the 2018 election,

18–12 in the state senate and 38–22 in the house. This meant Democrats could meet the state requirement of the three-fifths majority required to approve often-controversial revenue increases directly. However, Oregon's two-thirds quorum requirement for legislative business quickly became a hurdle, with a significant number of rural legislators (most of whom were Republican) on high defense in both houses (Buylova et al., 2018).

Democrats, primarily from urban and suburban districts, immediately pursued an ambitious agenda and successfully passed bills that promoted affordable housing and paid family leave, banned disposable plastic bags, limited mandatory sentencing laws, raised tobacco taxes, and referred a measure to the public vote that could allow limits on political contributions. The most visible and contentious moments of the 2019 session occurred when Republican senators "walked out" of the legislature, leaving Democrats paralyzed for the lack of a quorum. There were two Senate walkouts in 2019, the second one concerning a bill to establish a California-style cap-and-trade policy that would incentivize Oregon businesses and industry to reduce carbon use in an effort to mitigate the adverse impact of greenhouse gasses and fight climate change. This piece of legislation had been a Democrat priority for many years, but because of the supermajorities it never got as close to the legislative finish line as it did in 2019. The walk-out occurred late in the legislative session after hours of deliberation and public comment, over one hundred proposed amendments to the lengthy legislation, and multiple close calls in passing it out of committee and the Oregon House.

After days of adjournment in absence of a quorum in the Senate, it was clear that something needed to change if the legislature were to return to functionality and finish up important legislative business, such as passing the state biennial budget before *sine die.* Soon after opponents' "Timber Unity" log truck protests began making national news, it was announced by the Senate president that the bill would move off the floor and back into committee to die. In retrospect, it was speculated that the bill may not have passed a vote of the Senate anyway due to the reservations of some more conservative Democratic senators, who notably happen to be the only rural Democrats, representing a majority of the Oregon coast. However, the acrimony of this moment never dissipated and continued into the 2020 session when Democrats continued to consider a reformed "cap and trade" bill, prompting yet another walk-out of Republicans in both the House and the Senate in February 2020, abruptly ending the legislative session and further consideration of all proposed legislation.

The first 2019 walk out by Republican senators sought to derail the Democrats' HB 3427 *Student Success Act*, which would impose a Commercial Activities Tax (CAT) on corporations and businesses to raise approximately $1 billion per year for K–12 and early childhood education. The Republican senators walked out for four days, but ultimately came back after they agreed to allow a vote on HB 3427. Democrats, in parry, halted efforts to pass gun regulations and a bill that "would have ended families' ability to opt-out of school vaccination requirements for personal, philosophical or religious reasons, both of which state actions are extremely unpopular in rural Oregon" (Zimmerman, 2019). So the Democrats achieved the increased taxes by allowing continued parental control over vaccinations and inaction on gun control, essential policy issues for many rural communities in the state.

The lobbyist's role in the progression and deterioration of the 2019 and 2020 Oregon legislative sessions was parallel, yet also essential, to formal and public political actions. As is discussed in earlier chapters, lobbyists have an inside and influential perspective on how legislative decision-making and strategy is developed and executed. There is no doubt that the breaking down of negotiations and incivility of deliberations in the Oregon legislature was perceived and perhaps perpetrated by "the Lobby" itself.

METHODS

The definition of "rural" has been the source of much discussion and disagreement among researchers and practitioners, as it is a multidimensional concept with various social and cultural associations. Rural, for our purposes, has been defined geographically, by population density, and by population size by the U.S. federal government (USDA, 2020). Therefore, in the analyses presented here we employ six different indicators of ruralness at the state level. These include the percent rural population in a state, the percent of the state landmass that is rural, rural population density, the percent of seats in the upper legislative house that represent rural districts, the percent of seats in the lower legislative house that represent rural districts, and a combined average of rural legislative districts for the entire state. The U.S. Census provides a detailed analysis of many different geographic and population indicators of states, including urban and rural characteristics. The Census defines "Urbanized Areas" as geographic areas of 50,000 people or more. Any area less populated is considered rural (U.S. Census, 2020). The indicators of the percent rural population in a state, the percent of the state landmass that is rural, and the rural population density are sourced directly from U.S. Census data. Because we are specifically interested in state legislative interactions with urban and rural indices, it is also important to measure the rurality of distinct state legislative districts in both of the (typically) bicameral state legislatures' chambers. The U.S. Census provides data on state legislative districts and the rurality of those geographies, but it does not aggregate the percentage of rural and urban legislative seats on a state level. For these variables, we rely on a dataset compiled by the Education Commission of the States (2018).

In general, we expect more rural states to exhibit higher levels of perceived incivility due to their critical mass of rural populations and land and a larger number of rural seats in the legislature, making it more likely that they would have more leverage in divisive legislative processes as was discussed in the opening case study of Oregon. We argue that states such as Oregon, which have a critical mass of rural land, substantial rural populations, and rural seats in the legislature would be most likely to experience incivility in comparison to states with dominant urban populations. In the latter, dominant coalitions in the legislature may mean policymaking processes are less affected by rural minority interests and possibly more civil. Our rurality indicators thus are *proxy* measures for rural-urban polarization.

In terms of the characteristics of lobbyists working in more rural versus more urbanized states, Table 7.1 provides demographic and political orientation information for the percent of state rural population. Three categories of percent rural population were created that roughly represent low (5.0% to 16.0%), medium (16.1% to 30.0%), and high (30.1%+) rural population. Many lobbyists did not provide demographic and political orientation data and so the full picture of who participated in the survey is difficult to document. Mean scores for the ages of lobbyists for all three rural categories is relatively similar, as are the mean number of years working as a lobbyist. The gender of lobbyists in all three rural categories is also similar, ranging from 56.2 to 59.6 percent male. However, for subjective political ideology and party affiliation there are significant differences among the three rurality categories. Lobbyists working in states with the lowest percent of rural population (5.0% to 16.0%) are more liberal than those in the medium rural category (16.1% to 30.0%). However, lobbyists in the third and most rural category (30.1%+) are also more liberal than the medium category and not much different from the least-rural states.

Regarding party affiliation, lobbyists in the low and medium categories are more likely to be Democrats when compared to the high rural population category. Lobbyists in the medium and high rural population categories are more likely to be Republicans than those in the low rural population category. Overall, the demographic and political differences among lobbyists in the three categories of percent rural population are not all that vast and should not affect the following bivariate analyses. Even so, we will present some multivariate models later in the chapter that control for these characteristics.

ANALYSES

We will analyze three sets of questions from the lobbyist survey to determine whether lobbyists perceive incivility in the state legislatures where they work, using the six indicators of ruralness discussed above. The three areas include legislative processes, the causes of incivility, and recommendations to increase civility.

Legislative Processes and Civility

To assess the potential impact of the rural-urban divide on legislative processes and civility, we examine seven questions that are displayed in Table 7.2's coding information. These questions concern norms of fair play, general perceptions of legislative civility, two questions comparing current legislative behaviors to legislative behaviors ten years ago, two questions concerning their own civility and that of other lobbyists in their state, and a question concerning the impact of incivility on their ability to carry out their lobbying work.

Table 7.1. Characteristics of Lobbyists by State Rural Population

	Percent State Rural Population			
	5.0% to 16.0%	16.1% to 30.0%	30.1%+	
	Mean (s.d.)	Mean (s.d.)	Mean (s.d.)	F-test
Age (years) (n = 926)	4.68 (1.47)	4.63 (1.52)	4.69 (1.47)	.621 p = .537
[1 = 29 or less 2 = 30 to 34, 3 = 35 to 39, 4 = 40 to 49, 5 = 50 to 59, 6 = 60 to 69, 7 = 70 or more]				
Years as lobbyist (n = 1,234)	15.63 (11.03)	14.52 (10.98)	14.81 (10.94)	1.846 p =.158
Ideology (n = 917)	3.04 (1.48)	3.41 (1.69)	3.15 (1.61)	5.866 p = .003
[1 = Very Liberal to 7 = Very conservative]				
	Percent	Percent	Percent	Chi-square
Gender:				
Percent male (n = 533)	56.2	59.6	59.0	.816 p = .665
Percent female (n = 382)	43.8	40.4	41.0	
Political Party:				
Percent Democrat (n = 359)	44.4	41.1	32.8	
Percent Republican (n = 261)	23.2	32.7	30.7	15.944 p = .003
Percent Independent (n = 287)	32.5	26.2	36.6	

Table 7.2. Legislative Process and Civility Indicators

a. The cover of the June 2017 issue of *Governing: The States and Localities* bears the caption "Checks & Imbalances: With a Constitutional Crisis Consuming Washington, state lawmakers are upending their own norms as well." Alan Greenblatt's article gives several examples of hyper-partisan-ship putting strains on the observance of long-established norms of proper legislative conduct and processes. Do you think that norms of fair play are breaking down in the state(s) in which you lobby or advocate for clients? (1 = Not occurring to 3 = Occurring)

b. Overall, how would you characterize the *general level of civility* among members of your state's legislature during the two most recent legislative sessions? (1 = Very uncivil to 10 = Very civil)

c. Compared to ten years ago, are individual legislators more or less civil today? (1 = Less civil to 10 = More civil)

d. Compared to ten years ago, are legislative leaders more or less civil today? (1 = Less civil to 10 = More civil)

e. Based on your understanding of norms of civility, how civil in behavior do you feel each of the following legislative process actors tend to be in your state: You as legislative advocate? (1 = Very uncivil to 5 = Very civil)

f. Based on your understanding of norms of civility, how civil in behavior do you feel each of the following legislative process actors tend to be in your state: Other lobbyists in your state? (1 = Very uncivil to 5 = Very civil)

g. How has the experience of incivility on the part of state legislators in your state affected you in your own work in legislative advocacy? (1 = Not at all to 4 = A great deal)

Correlation coefficients (Tau b) between the rural indicators and the seven legislative process and civility questions are presented in Table 7.3. All six of the rural indicators have a statistically significant relationship with lobbyists' perceptions of "norms of fair play" breaking down in the states in which they lobby. For five of the coefficients the relationship is positive, and for the rural population density it is a weak negative relationship. Lobbyists in states with higher percentages of rural population, with larger percentages of rural lands, and with higher percentages of lower and upper house rural seats are more likely to respond that "norms of fair play are breaking down" when compared to lobbyists in states that are less rural. Interestingly, lobbyists in states with lower rural population densities—as is the case in Oregon, with large rural expanses populated by relatively few people—are less likely to say that norms of fair play are breaking down.

For lobbyist perceptions of the general level of legislative civility, there are five statistically significant correlation coefficients, each of which is negative. Similar to the findings for norms of fair play, lobbyists in more rural states as operationalized by percent rural population and land area, percent of rural seats in the lower and upper houses, and the average

Table 7.3. Impact of Rural Variables on Legislative Process and Civility

	% Rural Population	% Rural Area of State	Rural Pop Density	% Upper House Rural Seats	% Lower House Rural Seats	% Total Average Rural Seats
Norms of fair play	.149**	.119**	-.069*	.119**	.132**	.141**
General civility	-.097**	-.075*	.021	-.084**	-.102**	-.117**
Compared to 10 years ago: legislators	-.111**	-.088**	.022	-.095**	-.099**	-.099**
Compared to 10 years ago: leaders	-.066*	-.047	.005	-.053	-.048	-.040
Civility-you	-.056*	-.012	-.020	-.051	-.054	-.055
Civility other lobbyists	-.021	.046	.062	-.004	-.001	.002
Affected you	.019	.094**	-.095**	.022	.024	.025

*Correlation is significant at the 0.05 level.

**Correlation is significant at the 0.01 level.

number of rural seats in the entire legislature are significantly more likely than lobbyists in less-rural states to perceive the presence of legislative incivility. Once again, it should be noted that the coefficients in question are not large, but all five are significant at the .01 level.

When asked to compare current individual legislators to those ten years ago in terms of civility, those lobbyists in states with higher percentages of rural population, with higher percentages of rural land area, with higher percentages of rural seats in lower and upper houses, and with a higher average number of rural seats in the entire legislature are significantly more likely than lobbyists in states with lower rurality percentages to perceive that individual legislators are less civil. All coefficients are statistically significant at the .01 level. There is less evidence of robust relationships between rurality and lobbyists' assessments of legislative leaders' civility compared to ten years ago, with only percent rural population producing a statistically significant result at the .05 level. Those lobbyists in states with larger percentages of rural population were slightly more likely to view legislative leaders as less civil when compared to lobbyists in less-rural states.

For the question concerning the impact of incivility on the responding lobbyists, only percent rural population has a significant impact, with lobbyists from high percentage rural population states being more likely to perceive an uncivil impact on themselves. When asked about the possible impact of incivility on their legislative advocacy work, lobbyists from lower rural density states were significantly more likely to answer that it has affected their work, as were lobbyists from states with larger percentages of rural territory.

Causes of Incivility

Lobbyists were asked their perceptions of the causes of incivility in state legislatures. We examine ten different possible reasons for incivility, which are presented in Table 7.4. The indicators include hostility in political campaigns, the lack of communication between opposing parties, exposure to more partisan media, polarization in the U.S. Congress, and the growing ideological nature of political parties. In addition, lobbyists were asked about a list of "divisive demands" being imposed on state legislators by others outside the legislature, including constituents, campaign contributors, other lobbyists, and state party leaders.

Table 7.5 presents correlation coefficients between the rural indicators and the causes of incivility indicators. Both percent rural area of the state and rural population density had statistically significant results for hostility when running for office and less ability to communicate with legislators from opposing parties. Lobbyists from large percentage rural states were more likely to agree that running for office and less ability to communicate with opposing parties are causes of incivility. However, lobbyists from lower rural population density states were less likely to agree that running for office and less ability to communicate with opposing parties are causes of incivility.

Table 7.4. Causes of Incivility Indicators

---

a. Please indicate your level of agreement with each of the following hypothesized *contributing causes* to the declining levels of civility in American political life in recent years. How does each hypothesized cause tend to play out in your state legislature?
    (1 = Strongly agree to 4 = Strongly disagree)

b. Higher levels of hostility experienced when *running for office*

c. Less ability for legislators from opposing political parties to *communicate effectively*

d. Legislators' increasing exposure to *partisan and ideological media*

e. Legislators *reflecting the polarized environment of the U.S. Congress*

f. The tendency today for legislators to be more liberal or more conservative (*less moderate*) than in the past

g. More divisive demands imposed on state legislators by: Constituents

h. More divisive demands imposed on state legislators by: Campaign contributors

i. More divisive demands imposed on state legislators by: Lobbyists

j. More divisive demands imposed on state legislators by: Legislative party leaders

k. More divisive demands imposed on state legislators by: State party leaders

---

In terms of the impact of increasing exposure to partisan and ideological media, lobbyists from states with higher percentages of rural seats in both lower and upper houses are significantly more likely to identify partisan and ideological media as a cause of incivility. Similarly, lobbyists from states with higher percentages of rural legislative seats in the upper house are significantly more likely to perceive that the polarization of the U.S. Congress is also a contributing factor to state legislative incivility. Lobbyists from states with a higher average number of rural seats are also more likely to identify the U.S. Congress as contributing to incivility. For

Table 7.5. Impact of Rural Variables on Causes of Incivility

	% Rural Population	% Rural Area of State	Rural Pop Density	% Upper House Rural Seats	% Lower House Rural Seats	% Total Average Rural Seats
Running for office	.043	.110**	-.079**	.048	.034	.044
Communicate effectively	.019	.066*	-.057*	.007	-.004	.002
Partisan media	-.047	.020	-.037	-.053*	-.60*	-.059*
Polarized U.S. Congress	-.082**	.000	.040	-.064*	-.051	-.064*
Less Moderate	.005	.036	-.025	-.007	-.005	-.004
Divisive Demands:						
Constituents	.025	.038	-.032	.012	.013	.014
Campaign contributors	-.048	.007	-.019	-.065*	-.071**	-.079**
Lobbyists	-.013	-.020	.012	-.023	-.022	-.027
Legislative party leaders	-.054*	-.059*	-.074**	-.046	-.055*	-.055*
State party leaders	-.028	-.009	.016	-.026	-.023	-.020

*Correlation is significant at the 0.05 level.
**Correlation is significant at the 0.01 level.

the indicator of increasingly ideological legislators as a cause of incivility, none of the rural indicators had statistically significant results.

The final set of potential causes of incivility asked lobbyists what they considered to be the "more divisive demands imposed on state legislators." For constituents, there were no significant associations with the rural indicators used in this study. However, lobbyists from states with larger percentages of upper and lower house seats are significantly more likely to agree that campaign contributors are a source of incivility. The total percent of rural seats also has a statistically significant impact on the perception that campaign contributors are a source of incivility. Both lobbyists and state party leaders as sources of incivility were not significantly related to the rural indicators. However, most of the rural indicators are statistically significant, with legislative party leaders being identified as a source of incivility. The observed correlation coefficients for percent rural population, percent rural area, rural population density, percent lower house rural seats, and percent average total rural seats were all negative and statistically significant. Lobbyists from states with higher percentages of land, rural populations, rural seats in the lower house, and average total rural seats are significantly more likely to identify legislative party leaders as sources of incivility when compared to other lobbyists. In addition, lobbyists from states with higher rural population density are also significantly more likely to identify legislative party leaders as a cause of incivility.

Recommendations to Improve Civility
The third and final set of questions we examine for the potential impact of the rural-urban divide concern recommendations to improve civility during legislative sessions. Table 7.6 provides a description of the questions asked of lobbyists and three possible civility development actions, including eating meals with legislators of the opposing party, changing seating assignments so parties are intermixed, and changing office assignments so parties are intermixed. The survey asked lobbyists about the potential effectiveness of the action and the level of difficulty of implementing each action. Response categories ranged from 1 = low to 5 = high.

As with our previous analyses, Table 7.7 provides correlation coefficients for the civility actions and the various rural indicators. There are few significant correlations evident in the table, but some findings are nonetheless interesting. For the perceived effectiveness of the actions, there are significant coefficients only for changing seating assignments in the legislative assembly. Lobbyists from states with higher rural population percentages, higher upper and lower house rural seat percentages, and overall percent of rural seats in the entire legislature are significantly more likely to see changing seat assignments as an effective action to build civility.

In terms of lobbyist perceptions of implementation difficulty for the three actions, there are two significant coefficients for "meals with opposing party" and "change seating assignments." Lobbyists from states with a high percentage of rural land see implementation of meals with the opposing party and changing seating assignments as having lower implementation difficulty. In addition, lobbyists from lower rural population density states perceive high difficulty implementing meals with opposing parties and changing seat assignments. Clearly more analyses need to be conducted in this area; however, the states that reflect low rural population densities and large percentages of rural lands are located primarily in the western United States, a region where there has been and continues to be visceral conflict over the management of public lands, including major differences relating to the protection of endangered species, natural resource extraction, grazing practices, water allocation, and Native American treaty claims (Wolters and Steel, forthcoming).

We conclude our analyses with some logistic regression models that control for the demographic characteristics and political orientation variables of lobbyists presented in Table 7.1. The models presented in Table 7.8 examine the effects of each of the six rural indicators on the question concerning "norms of fair play" featured in Table 7.2 while controlling for lobbyist demographic characteristics (age, gender, and years as a lobbyist) and political orientations (ideology and party identification). The question lobbyists were asked was "Do you think that norms of fair play are breaking down in the state(s) in which you lobby or advocate for clients?" Response categories provided were 1 = Not Occurring, 2 = Uncertain, and 3 = Occurring. Responses were recoded into a dummy variable with 1 = Occurring and 0 = Else for use in logistical regression models. Dummy variables were then created for gender (1 = female, 0 = male) and party identification (1 = Democrat, 0 = Else; 1 = Republican, 0 = Else; 1 = Independent, 0 = Else). For the models presented in Table 7.8, the dummy variable for Independents is the omitted comparison

Table 7.6. Recommendations to Improve Civility

The following actions have been suggested to enhance adherence to legislative civility norms among state legislators. For each item listed below, please indicate how effective do you think the suggestion would be to improve legislative civility (on the left-hand column). Likewise, please indicate your assessment of how difficult it would be to implement the idea (on the right-hand column). (1 = Low to 5 = High)

a. Eat meals with legislators of the opposing party

b. Change seating assignments so parties are intermixed

c. Change office assignments so parties are intermixed

Table 7.7. Impact of Rural Variables on Recommendations to Improve Civility

	% Rural Population	% Rural Area of State	Rural Pop Density	% Upper House Rural Seats	% Lower House Rural Seats	% Total Average Rural Seats
Legislators' In-session Interactions: Effectiveness						
Meals with opposing party	.030	-.045	.046	.036	.024	.032
Change seating assignments	.102*	.011	.016	.106**	.089**	.100**
Change office assignments	.015	-.008	.016	.033	.037	.034
Legislators' In-session Interactions: Implementation Difficulty						
Meals with opposing party	-.014	-.106**	.131**	.008	.002	-.007
Change seating assignments	-.036	-.074*	.093**	-.027	-.020	-.022
Change office assignments	.054	-.026	.049	.066	.050	.062

*Correlation is significant at the 0.05 level.
**Correlation is significant at the 0.01 level.

variable. It should be noted again that there is much missing data for the demographic and political orientation variables within the lobbyist's survey, which may have an impact on the robustness of these results.

Six separate models are provided in Table 7.8, each with one of the six rural indicators along with the demographic and political orientation variables. Once again, these models will indicate whether it is the characteristics of individual lobbyists that affect perceptions of incivility

Table 7.8. Logistic Regression Estimates for Norms of Fair Play and Rural Indicators[a]

	%Rural Pop	%Rural Area	Rural Pop Density	%Upper House	%Lower House	%Total Seats
	Coefficient (S.E.)	*Coefficient (S.E.)*	*Coefficient (S.E.)*	*Coefficient (S.E.)*	*Coefficient (S.E.)*	*Coefficient (S.E.)*
Age	.008 (.056)	.034 (.056)	.034 (.056)	.016 (.056)	-.029 (.058)	-.017 (.058)
Gender	-.051 (.146)	-.086 (.145)	-.069 (.144)	-.055 (.145)	-.065 (.147)	-.069 (.147)
Years	.001 (.008)	-.003 (.008)	.-.004 (.007)	-.002 (.008)	.003 (.008)	.002 (.008)
Democrat	.220 (.175)	.194 (.174)	.182 (.172)	.203 (.174)	.249 (.177)	.248 (.177)
Republican	-.102 (.191)	-.072 (.190)	-.080 (.189)	-.096 (.190)	-.123 (.195)	-.119 (.195)
Ideology	-.116* (.056)	-126* (.056)	-.118* (.056)	-.115* (.056)	-.118* (.058)	-.113* (.057)
Rural Indicator	.029*** (.005)	.042*** (.009)	.-.007*** (.002)	.019*** (.004)	.026*** (.005)	.023 (.004)
N =	904	904	904	904	904	904
Chi-square =	47.604***	40.455***	26.627***	39.108***	45.168***	
Percent predicted =	59.0%	59.1	54.0	57.5	60.0	58.2
Nagelkerke R^2 =	.068	.058	.039	.056	.067	.064

[a]1 = Occurring, 0 = Else

*p<0.05; **p<0.01; ***p<0.001

in state legislatures and not the rural nature of the state in which the lobbyist works. All six of the rural indicators produced a significant coefficient for this question in Table 7.3, and they also produce significant coefficients for each model in Table 7.8 while controlling for the other variables. The direction of each coefficient is also the same as the bivariate analyses. With the sole exception of ideology, neither any of the other demographic variables nor party affiliation produced statistically significant results. Ideology produced negative coefficients at the .05 level, a finding that indicates that more liberal lobbyists were significantly less likely to perceive a breakdown in norms of fair play when compared to more conservative lobbyists.

For five of the rural indicator coefficients in the models the relationship with perceived incivility is positive, and for the rural population density indicator it is a negative relationship. As we found in Table 7.3, lobbyists in states with higher percentages of rural population, with larger percentages of rural lands, and with higher percentages of lower and upper house rural seats are more likely to perceive that norms of fair play are breaking down when compared to lobbyists in less-rural states. And for the rural indicator of rural population density, the coefficient is negative, indicating that lobbyists in states with lower rural population densities are less likely to say that norms of fair play are breaking down.

Additional multivariate analyses were conducted with the various questions concerning the presence of incivility, the causes of incivility, and actions to increase civility. The consistent overwhelming pattern evident in the results is that if coefficients were significant in the bivariate analyses, they were mostly significant in the multivariate models, even when controlling for demographic characteristics and political orientations of the individual lobbyists. Again, there are a lot of missing data for these variables, so caution should be used in the interpretation of these results.

DISCUSSION

As was discussed in the methods section of the chapter, our indicators of rurality are proxy measures at best, and are not direct measures of rural-urban polarization in state politics and legislative processes. We theorized that states with a critical mass of rural land, rural populations, and rural seats in the legislature would be most likely to experience incivility, as such states can make the legislative process haltingly difficult. This occurred in the Oregon case study noted in this chapter. States that are overwhelmingly urban or overwhelmingly rural may well experience polarization, but dominant coalitions in the legislature may make policy processes less arduous and possibly more civil. Of course, such a thesis would need more sophisticated analyses and more robust sources of data.

Our analyses provide some evidence that the rural-urban divide may well be contributing to incivility in the nation's state legislatures. Lobbyists from more heavily rural states when compared to more urban states are more likely to perceive incivility in legislative processes. They are more likely to report that norms of fair play are breaking down, that the general level of civility during the two most recent legislative sessions has deteriorated, and that incivility among legislators has increased over the last ten years. There is also some evidence that lobbyists from more rural states see that their work has been affected adversely as a consequence of incivility in the legislature.

In terms of the causes of incivility, depending on the rural indicator employed, lobbyists from more rural states identified the election process, the inability of legislators to communicate with opposing parties, partisan media, and general polarization at the federal level as sources. In addition, campaign contributors and legislative party leaders were also identified by lobbyists from more rural states as likely causes of divisiveness. There were no differences between lobbyists from more rural states and lobbyists from more urban states identifying more ideological legislators being elected as a cause of incivility, or state party leaders as the cause.

When lobbyists were asked to assess the possible effectiveness of certain actions to increase civility during legislative sessions, there were no significant differences between lobbyists from rural and urban states concerning meals with the opposing party or changing office assignments to intermix parties. However, when compared to lobbyists from more urban states, lobbyists from more rural states believe that changing seating arrangements to mix up parties in legislative bodies may increase civility. When asked how difficult it would be to implement these actions, those lobbyists from states with higher percentage of rural land see implementation of meals with the opposing party and changing seating assignments as having lower implementation difficulty. In addition, lobbyists from lower rural population density states perceive high difficulty implementing meals with opposing parties and changing chamber seat assignments to intermix parties.

Finally, when examining the impact of the rural indicators on the incivility questions while controlling for demographic and political orientations, the rural indicators were the most important predictors of incivility in the multivariate models. Once more we urge caution in the interpretation of these results given the large number of missing cases for some demographic indicators and for the political orientation indictors. In addition, as with all the analyses presented in this chapter, we must also caution that the rural indicators used here are only proxy measures for the rural-urban divide.

What is to be done concerning the rural-urban divide and creating a more civil legislative process? Returning to the Oregon case study, Clucas et al. (2011) made the following observation concerning overcoming the rural-urban divide (p. 137):

> Thus perhaps the only way in which the state will find agreement is if it can move some policy debates outside the normal political discourse, so that they are isolated from the ideological conflict that has come to define Oregon politics in recent decades. To many Oregonians, the state confronts a variety of problems that need to be solved, from inadequate health care to poor education to fiscal instability. While the rural and urban divide may make it difficult to address these issues, it does not make it impossible to do so if state residents can put aside their disagreements on social values to resolve shared problems. While it may seem simple to focus on the concerns shared by rural and urban Oregonians, the state's political divide makes cooperation a relentlessly difficult challenge.

In this regard, there have been significant attempts—not always successful—to solve problems while taking into proper account differing rural perspectives and contexts. For example, when the Democratically controlled legislature and governor's office in Oregon wanted to raise the minimum wage in 2009, they introduced a three-tiered system with the highest hourly rate for the high-rent Portland metropolitan area, a lower rate for suburban areas, and a third lowest hourly rate for rural locations where the cost of living is substantially lower. This was the direct result of more liberal and urban legislators listening to the concerns of rural legislators with many constituents employed in the natural resource extraction and agricultural sectors.

There also has been rural *and* urban legislative support for K–12 funding throughout the state (everyone wants good schools) and for renewable energy development, such as wind farms, that creates jobs in rural areas and decreases the carbon footprint, which is popular in the state's urban areas. More recently, the COVID-19 crisis has challenged the working norms of legislatures more than ever before, with typical in-person negotiations being transitioned to a virtual setting, if occurring at all. Many legislatures have taken up public health and economic issues that highlight rural-urban divides such as statewide testing capacity, broadband access, economic reopening of counties and more. Of course, success in collaboration is not always achieved, as the previous cap-and-trade bill in Oregon that led to Republican walkouts in 2019 and 2020 demonstrates (Weber et al., 2018). The cap-and-trade bill had extensive provisions to attempt to address rural concerns, but in the end those concessions were not sufficient to bring about consensus and support.

REFERENCES

Alexander, J. T., Anderson, R., Cookson, P. W., Edin, K., Fisher, J., & Grusky, D. B. (2017). A qualitative census of rural and urban poverty. *The Annals of the American Academy of Political and Social Science, 672*(1), 143–161.

Buylova, A., Warner, R. L., & Steel, B. S. (2018). The Oregon context. In E. Weber, P. Southwell, R. Clucas, & M. Henkels (Eds.), *Oregon state and local politics: Innovation and change* (pp. 19–38). Oregon State University Press.

Clucas, R., Henkels, M., & Steel, B. S. (2011). The politics of One Oregon: Causes and consequences of the rural-urban divide and prospects for overcoming it. In R. Clucas, M. Henkels, & B. Steel (Eds.), *One Oregon* (pp. 113–142). Oregon State University Press.

Cramer, K. J. (2016a). *The politics of resentment: Rural consciousness in Wisconsin and the rise of Scott Walker*. University of Chicago Press.

Cramer, K. J. (2016b, November 16). For years, I've been watching anti-elite fury build in Wisconsin. Then came Trump. *Vox.* https://www.vox.com/the-big-idea/2016/11/16/13645116/rural-resentment-elites-trump.

Education Commission of the States. (2018). *Education Commission of the States, census data, Rural Urban Project, breakdown* [Dataset]. U.S. Census Statistical Abstract Digital Files.

Goetz, S. J., Partridge, M. D., & Stephens, H. M. (2018). The economic status of rural America in the President Trump era and beyond. *Applied Economic Perspectives and Policy, 40*(1), 97–118.

Graham, D. A. (2017, March). Red state, blue city. *The Atlantic.* https://www.theatlantic.com/magazine/archive/2017/03/red-state-blue-city/513857/.

Greenblatt, A. (2014, April). Rural areas lose people but not power. *Governing.* https://www.governing.com/topics/politics/gov-rural-areas-lose-people-not-power.html.

Hochschild, A. R. (2016). *Strangers in their own land: Anger and mourning on the American right.* The New Press.

Kurtzleben, D. (2016, November 14). Rural voters played a big part in helping Trump defeat Clinton. *NPR.org.* https://www.npr.org/2016/11/14/501737150/rural-voters-played-a-big-part-in-helping-trump-defeat-clinton.

Lichter, D. T., & Ziliak. J. P. (2017). The rural-urban interface: New patterns of spatial interdependence and inequality in America. *The Annals of the American Academy of Political and Social Science, 672*(1), 6–25.

Macrotrends. (2020). U.S. rural population 1960–2020. https://www.macrotrends.net/countries/USA/united-states/rural-population.

McKee, S. C. (2008). Rural voters and the polarization of American presidential elections. *PS: Political Science & Politics, 41*(April), 101–108.

Monnat, S. M. (2016, December 4). *Deaths of despair and support for Trump in the 2016 presidential election.* Department of Agricultural Economics, Sociology and Education Research Brief, Penn State University. https://smmonnat.expressions.syr.edu/wp-content/uploads/ElectionBrief_DeathsofDespair.pdf.

Monnat, S. M., & Brown, D. L. (2017). More than a rural revolt: Landscapes of despair and the 2016 presidential election. *Journal of Rural Studies, 55*(October), 227–236.

Scala, D. J., & Johnson, K. M. (2017). Political polarization along the rural-urban continuum? The geography of presidential vote, 2000–2016. *The Annals of the American Academy of Political and Social Science, 672*(1), 162–184.

Simon, C. A., Steel, B. S., & Lovrich, N. P. (2018). *State and local government: Sustainability in the 21st century* (2nd ed.). Oregon State University Press.

Smith, N. S., & Hanley, E. (2018). The anger games: Who voted for Donald Trump in the 2016 election, and why? *Critical Sociology, 44*(September), 195–212.

Ulrich-Schad, J. D., & Duncan, C. M. (2018). People and places left behind: Work, culture and politics in the rural United States. *The Journal of Peasant Studies, 45*(1), 59–79.

U.S. Census. (2010). Percent urban and rural in 2010 by state [Data set]. U.S. Census Statistical Abstract Digital Files.

USDA. (2020). What is rural? Economic Research Service, United States Department of Agriculture. https://www.ers.usda.gov/topics/rural-economy-population/rural-classifications/what-is-rural/.

Wolters, E. A., & Steel, B. S. (Eds.). (Forthcoming). *Environmental politics and policy of western public lands*. Oregon State University Press.

Weber, B. A., Fannin, J. M., Cordes, S. M., & Johnson, T. G. (2017). Upward mobility of low-income youth in metropolitan, micropolitan, and rural America. *The Annals of the American Academy of Political and Social Science, 672*(1), 103–122.

Weber, E., Southwell, P., Clucas, R., & Henkels, M. (Eds.). (2018). *Oregon state and local politics: Innovation and change*. Oregon State University Press.

Zimmerman, S. (2019, May 13). Education tax bill passes after deal to end GOP protest. *Eugene Register-Guard*. https://www.registerguard.com/news/20190513/education-tax-bill-passes-after-deal-to-end-gop-protest.

CHAPTER EIGHT

Modeling the Sources of Cross-State Differences in Legislative Civility

Luke Fowler
Stephanie L. Witt
Jaclyn J. Kettler

INTRODUCTION

Incivility in American politics remains a focus of concern for citizens and scholars of the political and public administration systems alike. The year 2020 witnessed an abundance of incivility in all areas of our public life: police brutality toward citizens, protests over police brutality that turned violent, "twitter storms" full of invective toward political opponents, and even physical altercations over the wearing of masks in public spaces in response to the COVID-19 outbreak. The country appears to be in a longer-term trend of increasing incivility. In 2017, 69% of Americans polled believed that the United States had a major civility problem (Andrews, 2017). Other studies point out that the number of Americans who think incivility is a problem has been increasing over time (Weber Shandwick and Powell Tate, 2018). In a recent poll, 90% of respondents said it was "important for politicians to be civil to one another" (Bonn, 2020). This incivility has been linked to negative impacts on voters and their views of democracy. Theocharis et al. (2020) summarize the impacts of incivility thus:

- Incivility in general has negative effects on public attitudes and behaviors.

- Incivility among politicians increases the public's dissatisfaction with political institutions and negative attitudes toward politicians.

- Incivility between citizens online can decrease open-mindedness, political trust, and efficacy, and polarize an individual's view on a topic.

Rising concern about incivility and its impacts has led to the creation of groups dedicated to fostering higher levels of civility among citizens and elected officials alike. These include the National Institute for Civil Discourse (NICD), a group that has worked to heighten awareness of the need for civility in public life and has fostered training for members of state legislatures. The NICD's "Building Trust Through Civil Discourse" program has implemented workshops for state legislators that are facilitated by a Republican and a Democratic member of the legislature to increase collaborative, bipartisan cooperation and to improve civil discourse (Andrews, 2017). Over 500 legislators have participated, and at least one state, Idaho, saw the entire legislature attend the workshop (Andrews, 2017).

Civility can be defined in many ways, but most point out that it goes beyond "being nice." The Institute for Civility in Government defines civility as more than just politeness, though politeness is a necessary first step. It is about disagreeing without disrespect, seeking (and finding) common ground as a starting point for dialogue about differences, listening past one's preconceptions, and teaching others to do the same. (Institute for Civility in Government, 2020)

Participants from the legislative workshops offered their definitions of civility through the NICD website (National Institute for Civil Discourse, 2020):

- "We learned that civil discourse does not mean abandoning one's principles—rather, it means listening respectfully to the one with whom we disagree while advocating our own beliefs and principles—an approach that, when employed, has improved and strengthened our process." (Senator Brent Hill, Idaho Senate Pro Tempore)

- "Civility is more than just having good manners; without it, our system of government cannot function effectively. As citizens, it is our responsibility to expect better from our leaders and from each other. We all benefit when improved civility becomes a mutual priority." (Senator Frank LaRose, Ohio State Senate)

COMPARING STATES

In their superb summary of *Why States Matter*, Moncrief and Squire describe the importance of state governments and emphasize that each state's legislature operates in its own unique institutional and political context (2017). The book opens with an anecdote of how residents on one side of a road in Kansas City are in Missouri and pay Missouri taxes and live under Missouri laws, while residents on the other side of the road live in Kansas and pay a completely different set of taxes and live under a separate set of laws. Moncrief and Squire's work is representative of a body of scholarship that examines the importance of taking state characteristics into account when studying legislative behavior and policy outcomes (Hamm, Hedlund, and Martorano Miller, 2014).

Given the role of states as linchpins in American federalism, state legislatures and the apparent breakdown in civility within legislatures has become a focal point for scholars and political observers alike. Partisan polarization has led to entire party caucuses fleeing the state to avoid or stall bitterly contested legislative votes in Wisconsin, Oregon, and Texas. There are numerous examples of individual incivility as well (see Moncrief, "Legislatures Under Stress," 2018 presentation to the Council of State Governments-Midwest):

- A member of the Texas House of Representatives threatened to shoot another representative (Zelinski and Cervantes, 2017). The confrontation involved issues related to immigration, when a Republican legislator said he had called U.S. Immigration and Customs Enforcement in response to protestors with signs that said "I'm illegal and I'm here to stay." A scuffle then erupted during which the Democratic legislator said he would confront the Republican legislator in the parking lot and the Republican legislator threatened to shoot the Democrat in self-defense.

- A Florida state senator resigned after using disparaging racial and sexist terms in an argument with several other state senators (Burnside, 2017). The Democratic senator referred to fellow senators as [N-word]s and a "bitch" in a conversation over drinks with other senators at the Governor's club in Tallahassee. The Florida Democratic Party demanded his resignation.

- A Republican California state senator was forcibly removed from the chamber by the Senate president during a speech she was giving from the floor (Koseff, 2017). The senator's remarks were critical of the late Tom Hayden's stance against the Vietnam War. Hayden had been memorialized by the Senate a few days before. The senator, whose district included a large number of Vietnamese immigrants, was ruled out of order by the Democratic Senate leadership and removed from the floor forcibly when she refused to stop.

- An Idaho legislator was stripped of her committee assignments after making disparaging remarks concerning why she thought other women legislators received better assignments (Kruesi, 2017). The Republican representative was rebuked by the Speaker of the House after remarking to another female legislator that women only move up in the legislature "if they spread their legs."

In addition to attracting substantial attention and negatively affecting citizens' public trust (Theocharis et al., 2020), growing incivility in state legislatures is also concerning due to its effect on policymaking. Legislative norms for civility help in the negotiation of policy and the resolving of policy disagreements, allowing legislators to reach reasoned compromises in policy deliberations (Uslaner 1993, 2015). As a result, state legislative incivility can lead to gridlock and limit state governments' ability to address policy concerns.

While sometimes overlooked, state legislatures are an increasingly important part of our intergovernmental system in the United States. A decades-long emphasis on devolution has turned many major policy decisions over to state governments and their legislatures (Moncrief and Squire, 2017). As a result, state legislatures have jumped into policy vacuums created by an absence of federal leadership, including action on climate change, marijuana, immigration, pension relief, and health policy. In many cases, states have become the *de facto* policy venue of choice on domestic policy issues. When incivility paralyzes state legislatures, the citizens of our states suffer and our states' ability to meet new policy challenges, such as the COVID-19 pandemic, suffers.

In this chapter we explore several questions related to civility in state legislatures by comparing civility across states. Specifically, we believe that variations in the states' institutional, socioeconomic, and political contexts account for some of these broader trends. In other words, we will ask to what extent civility within legislatures is shaped by the combination of:

- institutional features of legislatures such as professionalism and term limits;

- political and electoral characteristics, such as partisan makeup and electoral competition; and

- socioeconomic and political characteristics of the electorate in each state, such as its political ideology, the proportion of its population that is urban, and the degree of economic inequality present within its population.

To address these questions, we examine results from the National Survey of State Legislative Lobbyists conducted in 2018–2019 in order to obtain a measure of civility in each state. The combined online and mail follow-up survey is the product of a team of researchers from ten universities across the United States. The researchers conducted the survey with the financial assistance of the National Institute for Civil Discourse and the backing of the Thomas S. Foley Institute of Public Policy and Public Service at Washington State University. Responses were obtained from 1,257 lobbyists from all 50 states.

INSTITUTIONAL, POLITICAL, AND SOCIOECONOMIC CONTEXTS OF STATE LEGISLATURES

Institutional Context

Each state legislature is unique, with its own traditions and history, but scholars have identified some key ways in which different institutional designs affect the way legislatures function and what policies they tend to enact. These institutional features create the setting within which behavioral norms are established for legislators. More specifically, individuals will typically choose the path of least restistance, and institutions structure those paths through formal and informal mechanisms. Most obviously, legislative rules of order spell out a formal process for debate, so that compliance is the easist path and deviation from those rules requires extra effort. These structures can also have consequences, intended or unintended, in the strategic political advantage of building and maintaining working relationships with other legislators. Under some circumstances, state legislators may find it easier to isolate themselves within their party caucus than to work toward bipartisanship.

How do the differences in professional and citizen legislatures affect civility in the statehouse? Possibly one of the most-discussed key difference between state legsilatures is their level of professionalism, or whether legislative business is a full- or part-time occupation for legislators. Professionalism is usually measured by the length of the session, the level of legislative compensation, and the numbers of staff employed to assist legislators (Moncrief and Squire, 2017, p. 89). Some legislatures are comprised of part-time members working short sessions and assisted by few paid staff. These are usually dubbed "citizen legislatures." An example of a citizen legislature can be found in Idaho, a state featuring legislative sessions usually lasting around 90 days, offering modest legislative pay of $17,879, and maintaining a small number of staff reserved for leadership and committees. In contrast, a highly professionalized legislature is in operation in California, where sessions last nearly all year and legislators earn $110,459 per year, and they are supported by paid staff (Ballotpedia, 2020).

Professionalism has multifaceted effects on legislatures. First, it changes the relationship between legislators and interest groups. Highly professionalized legislators have staff to conduct their own background research on issues. Legislators serving in less-professionalized chambers must do their own research or rely more upon the information given to them by lobbyists and organized interest groups. Second, previous scholarship indicates that legislative traditions tend to be weaker and socializing among legislators tends to be reduced in professional legislatures as compared to citizen legislatures (Thompson, Kurtz, and Moncrief, 1996; Andrews, 2017). Third, individual members in professionalized legislatures tend to focus more on politics than the mundane (but very important) business of democracy, undermining the formation of interpersonal relationships between members. Accordingly, we expect to find that civility is perceived to be higher in citizen legislatures as opposed to professional legislatures.

Do term limits change the way in which legislators interact with one another, thereby likewise influencing the civility of the legislature? A second institutional characteristic that distinguishes state legislatures from one another is that of variation in term limits. Fifteen states have enacted term limits for legislators, with limitations from as low as six years (Michigan) to a high of 16 years (Arkansas) (National Conference of State Legislatures, 2020). Longer time in office allows legislators to gain more subject-area expertise on policy issues and to develop relationships with bureaucratic staff in agencies over which the legislature has oversight, as well as with other legislators. High turnover in a legislature means more legislators are "learning on the fly" about the policy issues coming before them as they make important decisions. Term limits also force frequent changes in leadership and committee chair positions, key actors in the legislature. These positions are typically based on seniority. Additionally, newly elected members of state legislatures are less likely to be versed in the behavioral norms of their legislature, so they may be more likely to break from estalished tradition. As such, we expect to find that civility is perceived to be higher in states without term limits in comparison to states with terms limits in force.

Political Context

In addition to the institutional differences present across states, characteristics of state electorates also vary in their ideological outlooks and in the competitiveness of state legislative elections. Civility frequently is discussed alongside partisan political conflict and/or partisan polarization, as the underlying political in-fighting is typically identified as a key cause of incivility. As political parties have become more polarized, by definition fewer opportunities for bipartisanship may present themselves, and there may exist less need to build and maintain working relationships with legislators of the opposing party (Rosenthal, 2005; Dodd and Schraufnagel, 2012). Furthermore, citizens have taken on heightened political identities in recent years; previous scholars report that Americans strongly dislike, are less likley to trust, and are less likely to interact with people of the opposing party (Mason, 2015; Iyengar, Lelkes, Levendusky, Malhotra, and Westwood, 2019). Psychologically, much of this behavior is tied to threat responses. Opposing political views can be perceived as an attack on an individual's political identity, which, in turn, elicits emotional responses based on cognitive biases.

Is civility among legislators tied to the ideological profile of the state's electorate? While some state electorates are closely divided along liberal and conservative lines, others lean more liberal and still others more conservative. Those leanings can shape state politics and policy (Berry et al., 2007; Berry et al., 2010; Brace et al., 2004; Wright et al., 1985). In general, core ideological components of conservativism tend to favor authority and hierarchy, group cohesion, and marked resistance to change. As such, previous scholarship finds that conservatives tend to be more sensitive to threats compared to liberals, a sensitivity that lends itself to "closed-mindedness" (Jost, Glaser, Kruglanski, and Sulloway, 2003). Furthermore, other scholars have also found ideological differences in how individuals respond to conflict and threats to groups, with conservatives being more likley to display aggressive behavior (De Zavala, Cislak, and Wesolowska, 2010). This would suggest that groups of conservatives, either as citizens or in legislatures, are more likely to respond to political challenges with emotion that lends itself to incivility. Thus, we expect to find that conservative states are likely to exhibit increased incivility in comparison to liberal states.

How does the level of electoral competitiveness in a state affect civility in its state legislature? Certainly, one of the most direct ways in which elected officials are put under attack is through challenges to their position during elections. As more legislative seats have become competitive in recent years, incumbents have had to raise more campaign funds and spend more time with campaign-relevant issues. These developments increase both the scrutiny legislators receive and the pressure under which they are placed by policy stakeholders (Thompson, Kurtz, and Moncrief, 1996; Abbe and Herrnson, 2003; Rosenthal, 2005). Additionally, political rhetoric used during campaigns and periods of increased media attention may also create obstacles to building bipartisan relationships (Moncrief, Thompson, and Kurtz, 1996; Rosenthal, 2005; Andrews, 2017). Of course, some states are largely one-party control states in which one party holds a supermajority in the legislature. In Idaho, for example, Republicans hold approximately 85% of the legislature's seats. In Hawaii, in stark contrast, Democrats hold approximately 92% of the legislative seats. However, across the 50 states there is a wide range of electoral competiveness between political parties vying to control the legislature. As such, we expect to find that states with less electoral competition are perceived as more civil than states with highly competitive elections.

Socioeconomics Context

Finally, it is nearly impossible to discuss politics without considering the socioeconomic context that shapes it. At a macro level, socioeconomics dictates the parameters of policy problems, and at the micro level it sets the stage for how citizens engage with government. Specific to the interest here, two of the most important socioeconomic measures that have proven key to differences among states in prior research are the extent of urbanization and economic stratification—that is, how geographies and economics are distributed across the population. In the most basic sense, there are two key points of conflict: urban versus rural interests, and interclass conflicts. For citizens, these two dimensions are an important part of their political identities and their perceptions of self, which strongly affect political preferences. For legislatures, these two dimensions affect the intergroup conflicts that must be navigated during the legislative process. Certainly, legislators in states with economic equality and populations concentrated exclusively in urban areas are likely to find easier pathways to solving problems than legislators in states with many different self-identified groups competing over the costs and benefits of new policies.

How does the percentage of urbanization in a state affect civility in the state legislature? Scholars have longed debated the importance of conflicts between urban and rural interests in state legislatures (Alm and Witt, 1997; Pendall et al., 2002; Thomas, 1991). State legislators addressing longtime funding formulas that determine financial "winners and losers" with respect to schools, highways, parks, and other state and local projects often find themselves having to sort out how to balance urban and rural differences in priorities. On one hand, rural interests tend to favor mainating status quo arrangements, while urban interests tend to favor progressive policies focused on emerging problems that tend to arise from population growth. Consequently, urban interests may be perceived as upsetting to life as usual, a situation that can elicit emotional threat responses among rural interests. In contrast, rural interests are rarely seen as a threat to urban life, so legislators from urban areas are far less likely to be upset by the very same debates. Thus, we expect that states with higher rural populations are likely to experience more incivility than states with predominantly urban populations.

How does the degree of economic stratification affect civility in state legislatures? Historically, economic heterogeneity (i.e., diversity) and instability have resulted in policy preferences concentrated within specific social groups, actions that increase competition and conflict over resources. In contrast, when there is relative economic equality and stability, different social groups tend to find more agreement on policies and mechanisms for sharing the benefits of policies (McCarty, Poole, and Rosenthal, 2006). Given that legislatures have enormous responsibility for determining funding for social programs as well as long-term debt projects, a large degree of wealth concentration (i.e., economic inequality) may create decisional circumstances in which there is a higher level of conflict over spending. On one hand, this puts pressure on legislators to find a solution to benefit their constituents; on the other hand, it reduces the potential for compromise. Taken together, economic inequality is likely to create more difficult negotiations, leading some to act uncivilly. Therefore, we expect states with more economic inequality to exhibit higher levels of incivility in comparison to states with less inequality.

ESTIMATING CIVILITY IN STATE LEGISLATURES

To model potential explanations of incivility in state legislatures, it is first necessary to estimate an appropriate measure of civility. Measuring incivility is challenging due to the subjective nature of defining the terms *civility* and *incivility* (Strachan and Wolf, 2012). To address this issue, we use data from the National Survey of State Legislative Lobbyists, which measures individual perceptions of state legislative behaviors expressed by state legislative lobbyists. From this survey we identified 12 items (see appendix for descriptions) that capture perceptions of civility from different perspectives, which we categorized into three mutually exclusive groups: 1) general perceptions of legislative civility; 2) civility of specific legislative process actors (e.g., lobbyists, legislators, average citizens); and 3) state legislators in comparisons both over time and to other state legislative bodies. In general, these items capture perceptions of different aspects of civility as well as balance those perceptions against perceptions of civility in other times and states, allowing for a fairly encompassing measure.

Using this measure, we then make use of a modified Multilevel Regression and Poststratification (MRP) technique to create state-level estimates.

In recent years, a number of scholars have advocated for MRP as a more sophisticated approach to producing state-level estimates from national survey data compared to the more common aggregation approach that relies on calculating the mean for responses from respondents within the same state (Lax and Phillips, 2009a, 2009b; Pacheco 2011; Warshaw and Rodden, 2012; Fowler, 2016). MRP involves a three-step process. Step one is to estimate a multilevel model with fixed effects for individual-level predictors at level 1 and random effects for states at level 2.

From this model, state-level intercepts are calculated that represent comparative differences in dependent variables when individual-level predictors are controlled for. Step two involves producing estimates of the dependent variables for each "person type" in the dataset, and step three applies these post-stratification weights to those "person types" based on states' actual demographic characteristics.

Our focus here is only on comparative civility estimates across states rather than on the public opinion of a specific or general population. Hence, it is necessary to adapt the MRP approach by executing only step one, and not taking the additional steps of estimating person types or applying post-stratification weights. In doing so, the multilevel model controls for individual-level characteristics that may create bias in perceptions of civility (i.e., white men state lobbyists may perceive civility differently than do black women state lobbyists), which addresses one of the primary shortcomings of the aggregation technique. The state-level intercepts then create a functional point of comparison that is unbiased by state-level demographic characteristics, a point of comparison that is indicative of how a hypothetical lobbyist would likely perceive civility within any given state.

In producing our modified MRP approach, we first estimate a multi-level ordered logistic regression model featuring the 12 identified survey items.[1] At level 1, we use a series of variables to control for individual-level characteristics: age, gender, race, partisan affiliation, political preferences on social and fiscal issues, and types of organizations represented.[2] Findings indicate that the models were relatively good fits for the data (see appendix). Demographic factors proved to be the most consistent predictors, with older white men being most likely to perceive high levels of civility. Next, random effects portions of the models were calculated to produce state-level intercepts. Finally, we calculated state means across the 12 survey items, creating a single measure of state-level civility.[3] The civility index has a mean value near zero (3.03e-08), and ranges from -.501 (Oklahoma) to .539 (Massachusetts); thus, it functions in the manner of a standardized variable in that positive values represent values above the mean (i.e., more civility) while negative values are below the mean (i.e., less civility).

Figure 8.1 illustrates the distribution of the civility index across states; states are subdivided into six categories using natural breaks. States with the highest civility index scores (i.e., highest levels of civility) are Massachusetts, Maryland, Utah, North Dakota, Hawaii, and Vermont, while states with the lowest index scores are Kentucky, Arizona, North Carolina, and Oklahoma. Although visual analyses do not indicate any specific geographic patterns, regional averages indicate that the Northeast (.07) and West (.08) are more civil than the South (-.07) and Midwest (-.05). Of course, there are some noteworthy outliers to these overall trends. For example, North Dakota in the Midwest and Maryland in the South have among the highest levels of civility within regions with relatively low levels, while Pennsylvania and Maine in the Northeast, and Arizona and Oregon in the West, have among the lowest levels of civility in regions with relatively high levels. Looking further at subregions, New England

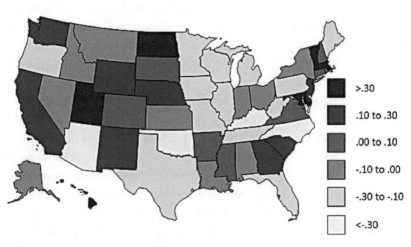

>.30

.10 to .30

.00 to .10

-.10 to .00

-.30 to -.10

<-.30

Figure 8.1. Map of State Civility Index

(.13 for Connecticut, Maine, Massachusetts, New Hampshire, Rhode Island, and Vermont) and the Pacific states (.10 for Alaska, California, Hawaii, Oregon, and Washington) have the highest averages. In contrast, West South Central (-.17 for Arkansas, Louisiana, Oklahoma, and Texas), East North Central (-.16 for Illinois, Indiana, Michigan, Ohio, and Wisconsin), and East South Central (-.14 for Alabama, Kentucky, Mississippi, and Tennessee) have the lowest averages.

EXPLAINING INTERSTATE DIFFERENCES

To provide an empirical test of some of the explanations of civility offered above, ordinary least squares (OLS) regression is used. We use robust standard errors to correct for heteroskedasticity. Our dataset includes cross-sectional data for 49 states; Nebraska was not included due to its nonpartisan, unicameral legislature. Based on previous research, our primary predictor variables focus on measuring political ideology, partisan electoral competition, level of legislative professionalism, extent of term-limit restrictions, economic inequality, and presence of urban/rural divisions (see appendix for descriptions). Additionally, we include a measure of partisan electoral competition to control for the interparty conflict that may also affect civility. For time-variant predictors, we used the most recently available data.

First, the political and electoral context is measured as citizen political ideology and partisan electoral competition. The Berry, Fording, Ringquist, Hanson, and Klarner (2010) citizen political ideology is employed, which uses a continuum from conservative to liberal based on interest group ratings from Americans for Democratic Action and the AFL-CIO Committee on Political Education for members of Congress. Scholars from these groups contend that this is one of the best mechanisms for making inferences about ideological orientations of state electorates. Partisan electoral competition is measured as the portion of elections held during the 2018–2019 electoral cycle in which candidates from both parties appeared in the general elections. Data from Ballotpedia were gathered for this analysis.

Second, we measure states' institutional context with legislative professionalism and term limits. Legislative professionalism is measured as an ordinal variable ranging from full-time, professional legislatures (0) to part-time, citizen legislatures (4). We use the National Conference of State Legislature's classification system, which is based on the amount of time legislatures spend on legislative work, their level of compensation, and the size of legislative professional staffs. In part-time citizen legislatures, legislators spend less than half of a full-time job doing legislative work, receive low compensation, and have little professional staff as compared to full-time professional legislators whose sole jobs are doing legislative work, who are compensated accordingly, and who are supported by large staffs. Term limits are measured using a dummy variable comparing 15 states with term limits for state legislators (1) to those without term limits (0).

Finally, we evaluate the relationship between socioeconomic differences and state civility on one side and economic inequality and urban/rural divisions on the other. Economic inequality is measured with Gini coefficients estimated by the U.S. Census Bureau. Gini coefficients are a measure of statistical dispersion, and they are one of the most common methods of measuring economic inequality at national or regional levels. Urban/rural divisions are measured via percentage of state population living in urban areas.

Table 8.1 displays results from our OLS model. The findings generally suggest that states that are more liberal, have citizen legislatures, feature lower economic inequality, possess high urban populations, witness low partisan electoral competition, and are without term limits are likely to be more civil than their counterparts that are more conservative, operate professional legislatures, are afflicted by high inequality, house large rural populations, experience highly partisan electoral competitions, and have term limits statutes. Notably, the term limits measure is not statistically significant, and citizen legislature is only statistically significant below the 0.1 alpha level; accordingly, the results reported here should be taken with a degree of circumspection. Standardized coefficients indicate that the strongest predictors are electoral competition, economic equality, and citizen legislatures, suggesting there are partisan, economic, and institutional antecedents to the levels of civility in U.S. state legislatures.

While the R^2 statistic indicates our model is a relatively strong predictor of civility across states, it inevitably contains error in predicting civility for individual states. To this end, we use normalized residuals squared to identify states in which there is a high or low amount of residual error

Table 8.1. Ordinary Least Squares Results: Predicting Lobbyists' Perceptions of Legislative Civility in 49 U.S. States (Unicameral & Nonpartisan Nebraska excluded)

	Coefficients	Standardized Coefficients
Political ideology	.004 (.002)*	.276
Legislative professionalism	.071 (.038)+	.293
Term limits	-.035 (.066)	-.066
Economic inequality	-3.498 (1.225)*	-.308
Urban population	.005 (.002)*	.276
Electoral competition	-.417 (.123)**	-.363
Constant	1.204	
N	49	
R^2	.384	

Standard errors in parentheses, *** $p<0.001$, ** $p<0.01$, * $p<0.05$, +$p<0.1$

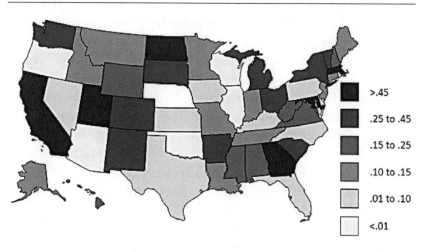

■	>.45
■	.25 to .45
■	.15 to .25
■	.10 to .15
☐	.01 to .10
☐	<.01

Figure 8.2. Map of Normalized Residual Squares. Note: Nebraska not included in predictive model.

between the observed level of civility and the predicted level from our model. Figure 8.2 presents these findings, with darker states suffering from a higher degree of error than lighter states. In comparison to figure 8.1, we find that states with the highest residual error in prediction also have relatively high civility index scores; in other words, as civility increases, the error in predicting civility also increases. This would account for the heteroskedasticity detected by initial diagnostic tests and corrected for with the use of robust standard errors. Theoretically, this would suggest that the predictor variables used in our model explain why incivility emerges in certain state legislatures. However, those explanations are less effective in explaining why civility remains high despite institutional, economic, or political circumstances that may undermine it.

DISCUSSION AND CONCLUSIONS

Civility in state legislatures is about more than a polite set of interactions as legislation is debated. Long-term changes in our federal system have led to state governments taking on increasing numbers of important policy challenges, including climate change, immigration, public health, and racial justice. Rising levels of incivility in state legislatures threaten to impede the ability of states to deal effectively with these and other issues yet to emerge. Everyone suffers when incivility causes a breakdown in deliberation and destroys the possibility of bipartisan cooperation in our state legislatures. In order to examine some of the interstate differences that cause incivility, we used the several questions from the National Survey of Lobbyists to create an index measure of civility and mapped the states by how highly they scored on the civility index. We found that there is a widespread variation in how "civil" the state legislatures are in the eyes of the lobbyists moving legislation in those legislative chambers. While the mapping showed some indications of regional similarities in civility, there are also individual states in each region that are either more or less civil than their neighbors. This may point to the importance of each state's individual/cultural context.

Institutional, political, and socioeconomic contextual differences between states led us to our multivariate analysis. Economic inequality, heightened electoral competition, and conservative political ideology proved to be the most important predictors of incivility across states. However, more professionalized legislatures, imposition of term limits, and presence of rural populations were also correlated with higher levels of incivility, although these findings were not as robust. In sum, a combination of institutional, political, and socioeconomic contexts set the stage for incivility to emerge in legislatures as individual legislators are placed in contexts that encourage them to abandon the norms of civility. These findings are consistent with previous research, as well as with our expectations.

Possibly one of the most important and unexpected findings is that the statistical model was a better predictor of states with low levels of civility than of states with high levels of civility. On its face, this would suggest that while the context of legislatures may facilitate legislative incivility, there are unique characteristics in some legislatures that prevent this from happening. From a statistical perspective, it likely means that there are unobserved variables that are not included in our empirical model. These variables could include a wide range of cultural, social, historical, or individual characteristics. A key factor here, though, is the presence of strong leaders who hold their colleagues accountable for incivility and who emphasize the importance of maintaining decorum within the legislative process. While we believe more research is needed to understand this aspect of our results and the causal pathway that leads to both incivility and civility, it provides an important point of hope that individual leaders can make a difference when it comes to upholding civility in our society.

NOTES

1. Multilevel ordered logistic regressions using an ordinal dependent variable rest on the same logic as multilevel regression using interval dependent variables.

2. Age is an ordinal variable with seven categories divided into decade increments ranging from 29 or younger to 70 or older. Gender is a binary variable. Race is recoded into two categories: white and non-white/all other races. Political preferences were registered on a seven-point scale ranging from very liberal to very conservative. For represented organizations, we use four dummy variables to indicate whether respondents represent business/business associations, professional trade associations, labor unions, or public interest nonprofits.

3. Cronbach's alpha = .85, indicating that the level of internal consistency across the 12 measures was relatively high.

REFERENCES

Abbe, O. G., & Herrnson, P. S. (2003). Campaign professionalism in state legislative elections. *State Politics & Policy Quarterly, 3*(3), 223–245.

Alm, L. R., & Witt, S. L. (1997). The rural-urban linkage to environmental policy making in the American west: A focus on Idaho. *The Social Science Journal, 34*(3), 271–284.

Andrews, A. (2017, July/August). What will it take to rebuild the respectful tone once common in state capitols? *State Legislatures.* https://www.ncsl.org/Portals/1/Documents/magazine/articles/2017/SL_0717-Civility.pdf.

Ballotpedia. (2020). Comparison of state legislative salaries. https://ballotpedia.org/Comparison_of_state_legislative_salaries.

Berry, W. D., Fording, R. C., Ringquist, E. J., Hanson, R. L., & Klarner, C. E. (2010). Measuring citizen and government ideology in the U.S. states: A re-appraisal. *State Politics & Policy Quarterly, 10*(2), 117–135.

Berry, W. D., Ringquist, E. J., Fording, R. C., & Hanson, R. L. (2007). The measurement and stability of state citizen ideology. *State Politics & Policy Quarterly, 7*(2), 111–132.

Brace, P., Arceneaux, K., Johnson, M., & Ulbig, S. G. (2004). Does state political ideology change over time? *Political Research Quarterly, 57*(4), 529–540.

Bonn, T. (2020, February 3). Overwhelming majority of voters say civility is needed in politics. *The Hill.* https://thehill.com/hilltv/rising/481217-overwhelming-majority-of-voters-say-civility-is-needed-in-politics.

Burnside, T. (2017, May 26). Florida state senator resigns over racial slurs in front of black lawmakers. *CNN.* https://www.cnn.com/2017/04/19/us/florida-lawmaker-under-fire-for-racist-remarks-trnd/index.html.

De Zavala, A., Cislak, A., & Wesolowska, E. (2010). Political conservativism, need for cognitive closure, and intergroup hostility. *Political Psychology, 31*(4), 521–541.

Dodd, L., & Schraufnagel, S. (2012). Congress and the polarity paradox: Party polarization, member incivility and enactment of landmark legislation, 1891–1994. *Congress and the Presidency, 39*(2), 109–132.

Hamm, K. E., Hedlund, R. D., & Miller, N. M. (2014). State legislatures. In D. P. Haider-Markel (Ed.), *The Oxford handbook of state and local government* (pp. 293–318). Oxford University Press.

Moncrief, G. (2018). *Legislatures under stress.* Presentation for the Council of State Governments-Midwest, University of Minnesota. Available by written request from author.

Fowler, L. (2016). The states of public opinion on the environment. *Environmental Politics, 25*(2), 315–337.

Institute for Civility in Government. (2020). What is civility? https://www.instituteforcivility.org/who-we-are/what-is-civility/.

Iyengar, S., Lelkes, Y., Levendusky, M., Malhotra, N., & Westwood, S. J. (2019). The origins and consequences of affective polarization in the United States. *Annual Review of Political Science, 22*(May), 129–146.

Jost, J. T., Glaser, J., Kruglanski, A. W., & Sulloway, F. J. (2003). Political conservativism as motivated social cognition. *Psychological Bulletin, 129*(3), 339–375.

Koseff, A. (2017, February 23). California senator removed from floor after criticizing late lawmaker Tom Hayden. *The Sacramento Bee.* https://www.sacbee.com/news/politics-government/capitol-alert/article134515314.html.

Kruesi, K. (2017, January 12). Rep. Heather Scott loses committee assignments after sexual favors remark. *Associated Press.* https://idahonews.com/news/local/rep-heather-scott-stripped-of-committee-assignments-after-sexual-favors-remark.

Lax, J. R., & Phillips, J. H. (2009a). Gay rights in the states: Public opinion and policy responsiveness. *American Political Science Review, 103*(3), 367–386.

Lax, J. R., & Phillips, J. H. (2009b). How should we estimate public opinion in the states? *American Journal of Political Science, 53*(1), 107–121.

Mason, L. (2015). "I disrespectfully agree": The differential effects of partisan sorting on social and issue polarization. *American Journal of Political Science, 59*(1), 128–145.

McCarty, N., Poole, K. T., & Rosenthal, H. (2006). *Polarized America: The dance of political ideology and unequal riches.* MIT Press.

Moncrief, G. F., & Squire, P. (2017). *Why states matter: An introduction to state politics* (2nd ed.). Rowman & Littlefield.

Moncrief, G. F., Thompson, J. A., & Kurtz, K. T. (1996). The old statehouse, it ain't what it used to be. *Legislative Studies Quarterly, 21*(1), 57–72.

National Conference of State Legislatures. (2020). Frequently asked questions about term limits. https://www.ncsl.org/research/about-state-legislatures/frequently-asked-questions-about-term-limits.aspx.

Next Generation. (2020). *Building trust through civil discourse.* A program of the National Institute for Civil Discourse. https://nxtgenusa.org/.

Pacheco, J. (2011). Using national surveys to measure dynamic U.S. state public opinion: A guideline for scholars and an application. *State Politics & Policy Quarterly, 11*(4), 415–439.

Pendall, R., Wolanski, R. M., & McGovern, D. (2002). Property rights in state legislatures: Rural-urban differences in support for state anti-takings bills. *Journal of Rural Studies, 18*(1), 19–33.

Rosenthal, A. (2005). Civility or civil war in legislatures: Is there an in-between? *Spectrum: The Journal of State Government, 78*(2), 22–24.

Strachan, J., & Wolf, M. (2012). Political civility: Introduction to political civility. *PS: Political Science & Politics, 45*(3), 401–404.

Theocharis, Y., Barberá, P., Fazekas, Z., & Popa, S. A. (2020). The dynamics of political incivility on Twitter. *SAGE Open, 10*(2). https://doi.org/10.1177/2158244020919447.

Thomas, C. S. (1991). The West and its brand of politics. In C. S. Thomas (Ed.), *Politics and public policy in the contemporary American West* (pp. 1–20). Albuquerque: University of New Mexico Press.

Thompson, J. A., Kurtz, K., & Moncrief, G. F. (1996). We've lost that family feeling: The changing norms of the new breed of state legislators. *Social Science Quarterly, 77*(2), 344–362.

Uslaner, E. M. (1993). *The decline of comity in Congress.* University of Michigan Press.

Uslaner, E. M. (2015). Congressional polarization and political trust. *The Forum, 13*(Fall), 361–373.

Warshaw, C., & Rodden, J. (2012). How should we measure district-level public opinion on individual issues? *The Journal of Politics, 74*(1), 203–219.

Weber Shandwick & Powell Tate, with KRC Research. (2018). *Civility in America VII: The state of civility.* https://www.webershandwick.com/wp-content/uploads/2018/04/Civility_in_America_the_State_of_Civility-1.pdf.

Wright, G. C., Erikson, R. S., & McIver, J. P. (1985). Measuring state partisanship and ideology with survey data. *The Journal of Politics, 47*(2), 469–489.

Zelinski, A., & Cervantes, B. (2017, May 29). Texas legislator threatens to shoot colleague in altercation. *Houston Chronicle.* https://www.houstonchronicle.com/news/houston-texas/houston/article/Texas-legislator-threatens-to-shoot-colleague-in-11181184.php.

APPENDIX TO CHAPTER 8

Table A.1. Descriptive Statistics of Civility Survey Items

Item	Mean	Standard Deviation	N
Quality of deliberation: In terms of quality of deliberation, how would you characterize your experience with the legislature's deliberation in representing your clients? • Response range: Uniformly poor (1) to uniformly good (5)	3.261	.974	1,236
General civility: Overall, how would you characterize the general level of civility among members of your state's legislature during the two most recent legislative sessions? • Response range: Very uncivil (1) to very civil (9)	5.431	2.090	977
Civility of legislators: Compared to ten years ago, are individual legislators more or less civil today? • Response range: Less civil (1) to more civil (9)	3.571	1.818	971
Civility of legislative leaders: Compared to ten years ago, are legislative leaders more or less civil today? • Response range: Less civil (1) to more civil (9)	3.874	1.931	971
Civility of Actors: Based on your understanding of norms of civility, how civil in behavior do you feel each of the following legislative process actors tends to be in your state: [very uncivil (1) to very civil (5)]			
• You (as a legislative advocacy) [respondent]	4.580	.637	980
• Other lobbyists in your state	3.946	.834	975
• Your state's legislators in general	3.322	.874	979
• State legislators with whom you deal	3.871	.852	979
• State legislators in general in US	2.845	.805	924
• Average citizens in your state	2.907	.926	979
Comparison to Congress: Compared to the US Congress, to what extent do you feel partisan polarization is taking place in your state legislature? • Response range [inversed]: Far more polarized than Congress (1) to much less (5)	2.292	.949	891
Comparison to Other Legislatures: To the best of your knowledge, to what extent do you think partisan polarization is taking place in your own state legislature as compared to other state legislatures? • Response range [inversed]: Among most polarized (1) to among least polarized (10)	5.594	2.226	887

Table A.2. Results from Multi-level Models of Lobbyist Perceptions

	Quality of Deliberation	General Civility	Civility of Legislators	Civility of Legislative Leadership	Comparison to Congress	Comparison to Other Legislatures
Level 1						
Age	.005 (.045)	-.066 (.045)	-.198 (.045)***	-.154 (.045)***	-.010 (.047)	.019 (.046)
Gender	-.347 (.142)*	-.419 (.140)**	-.395 (.138)**	-.478 (.139)***	-.327 (.147)*	-.287 (.141)*
Partisanship	-.346 (.086)***	-.303 (.086)***	-.266 (.084)**	-.167 (.083)*	-.321 (.089)***	-.278 (.085)***
White	-.638 (.252)	-.484 (.257)	-.329 (.244)	-.441 (.241)	.058 (.255)	.193 (.254)
Social issues	.049 (.057)**	-.009 (.056)	-.006 (.055)	-.071 (.056)	-.016 (.060)	.029 (.056)
Fiscal issues	.150 (.058)*	.112 (.057)	.098 (.056)	.140 (.056)*	-.040 (.061)	-.013 (.057)
Business lobbying	-.079 (.057)	-.093 (.057)	.098 (.056)	-.022 (.056(	-.123 (.059)*	-.098 (.057)
Trade association lobbying	-.040 (.051)	.056 (.050)	.019 (.050)	-.021 (.050)	.034 (.053)	.064 (.051)
Labor union lobbying	.007 (.084)	.132 (.088)	.051 (.087)	-.020 (.087)	.172 (.091)	.077 (.083)
Public interest lobbying	.131 (.055)*	.044 (.053)	.001 (.053)	-.001 (.053)	-.053 (.057)	-.061 (.055)
Level 2[1]						
States	.119 (.062)	.654 (.186)	.194 (.088)	.274 (.101)	.416 (.141)	.682 (.198)
N (level 1)	817	813	812	814	789	793
Groups (level 2)	50	50	50	50	50	50
Log likelihood	-1124.758	-1597.511	-1527.116	-1571.763	-1021.767	-1663.310
Pseudo R2	.337	.198	.182	.181	.138	.129
BIC	2350.1	3329.036	3181.523	3270.864	2143.595	3460.135

	Civility: Respondent	Civility: Lobbyists	Civility: State's legislators in general	Civility: State legislators with whom respondent deals	Civility: State legislators in general in US	Civility: Average citizen
Level 1						
Age	.118 (.052)*	.105 (.047)*	-.036 (.047)	.056 (.047)	-.056 (.048)	.140 (.046)**
Gender	.636 (.165)***	.169 (.145)	-.216 (.143)	-.113 (.144)	-.430 (.149)**	-.244 (.141)
Partisanship	.191 (.098)	.059 (.086)	-.142 (.088)	-.032 (.088)	-.047 (.089)	.056 (.085)
White	-.319 (.298)	-.218 (.264)	-.813 (.259)**	-.966 (.266)***	-.224 (.260)	-.423 (.247)
Social issues	-.049 (.064)	.104 (.057)	.035 (.058)	.090 (.059)	.005 (.059)	.056 (.057)
Fiscal issues	-.022 (.066)	-.048 (.059)	.087 (.059)	-.027 (.060)	.118 (.061)	-.118 (.059)*
Business lobbying	-.042 (.064)	-.150 (.058)**	-.081 (.058)	-.068 (.058)	-.063 (.059)	-.059 (.057)
Trade association lobbying	.009 (.058)	.110 (.052)*	.002 (.052)	.055 (.052)	.057 (.054)	.055 (.051)
Labor union lobbying	.166 (.092)	-.084 (.085)	-.035 (.086)	.140 (.085)	.029 (.089)	.067 (.084)
Public interest lobbying	.022 (.062)	.029 (.055)	.020 (.056)	-.042 (.056)	.015 (.057)	-.026 (.054)
Level 2						
States	.015 (.051)	.089 (.070)	.235 (.108)	.139 (.086)	2.24e-34 (2.26e-18)	.113 (.077)
N (level 1)	817	813	816	816	782	817
Groups (level 2)	50	50	50	50	50	50
Log likelihood	-645.355	-970.232	-1025.398	-985.869	-906.258	-1079.472
Pseudo R2	.222	.173	.178	.173	.181	.172
BIC	1398	2047.676	2151.361	2072.304	1905.782	2259.528

1. These are coefficients of variation, estimating the dispersion of observations at this level, not regression coefficients.

Test of Statistical Significance: ***p<0.001, **p<0.01, *p<0.05

Table A.3. Variable Descriptions: OLS models

Item	Mean	Standard Deviation	Min	Max
Civility index: Estimated level of civility	-.005	.241	-.501	.539
Citizen ideology: Berry, Fording, Ringquist, Hanson, and Klarner (2010)'s measure of citizen ideology	52.776	16.035	23.981	97.002
Citizen legislature: Ordinal variable comparing states with citizen legislatures (4) to professional legislatures (0)	2.082	.997	0	4
Term limits: Dummy variable comparing states with term limits for state legislators (1) to those without term limits (0)	.286	.456	0	1
Economic inequality: Gini coefficients of income inequality	.465	.021	.406	.523
Urban population: Percentage of population living in urban areas	73.6	14.716	38.7	95
Electoral competition: Percentage of contested general elections in 2018–2019 cycle	.652	.210	.236	1

CHAPTER NINE

From the Inside Looking In: State Legislative Civility from a Practitioner's Perspective

Karl Kurtz

I t was a different age of communication, information technology, and politics when I started working in and with legislatures in the early 1970s. Photocopiers were considered a luxury (we typed our letters using carbon paper and relied on mimeograph machines to mass-produce documents), fax machines were in their infancy, cell phones did not exist, and there was no internet, no 24-hour news cycle, no social media. Libraries and statute books were our principal resources.

The political parties had no litmus tests for candidates for office. Legislators of both parties were more moderate, and many Republicans in the East and Midwest were more liberal than Democrats in the West and South. Democrats controlled 99% of the legislative seats in southern state legislatures. State legislative election campaigns were mostly low-key affairs fought every two or four years, and few legislative leaders amassed campaign war chests to gain or maintain the majority in their chambers. In all but a few of the largest-population states, legislators relied almost exclusively on central, nonpartisan staff for information and assistance.

Despite assassinations of national leaders, massive marches on Washington for peace and civil rights, the bitterness of the Vietnam war and the political upheaval of Watergate, the 1970s were a more civil time in legislative politics. Democratic and Republican legislators fought with each other on the floor during the day and partied together at night. Legislatures controlled by both parties rode a wave of professionalization that left more time in session, better facilities, larger and more specialized staffs, and streamlined legislative procedures in its wake. In interstate relations, three previously competing organizations of state legislators and staff overcame their past institutional and political differences to merge and form a more powerful and effective National Conference of State Legislatures (1975).

How and when this period of civil politics changed is a story that has been told by others, and I will not repeat it here, other than to say that public cynicism and a lack of trust—between the public and governmental institutions, between parties and among elected officials—has been at the root of growing incivility over the last two decades. Instead, in this reflection, I will examine the role of NCSL in promoting civility, describe what NCSL research has revealed about the state of civility in legislatures, and highlight a few of the most important social and political changes that have particularly affected legislative norms such as comity, courtesy, and respect.

So how are the observations in this chapter "from the inside looking in?" NCSL encourages legislators and staff to view the organization as an extension of their legislature—as a national support team that is inside the system. My 42 years of work for NCSL afforded me both an insider's perspective on legislative life and a perch from which to peer into all 51 of our legislative institutions.

One last introductory comment: The news media and the American public tend to conflate the concepts of political polarization, policymaking (or its converse, gridlock), and civility (or incivility). The common view is that polarization leads to incivility, unproductive obstruction, and policy gridlock. However, these are three quite separate concepts. For example, it is possible to be either polarized or uncivil (or both) and still negotiate public policy. This is not to deny that civility can facilitate negotiation and compromise—only to point out that it is not a necessary condition. In this discussion I will endeavor to separate the concepts of policymaking, polarization, and civility, but in practice it is not always easy to do so, as there is a complex interaction among them.

PROMOTING CIVILITY

In many ways, the very existence of the National Conference of State Legislatures—an organization dedicated to bringing legislators and staff together across parties to share information and ideas about public policy—promotes civility in the legislative process. Legislators and staff who participate in the non-conflictual settings of NCSL meetings can learn to appreciate the perspectives of the other side and get to know each other personally in ways that may not be easy to do in the more charged atmosphere of their own state capitals. They often learn that issues are not black and white, and come to appreciate shades of gray that are present in most policy issues.

NCSL has a number of mechanisms in place to ensure bipartisanship and promote consensus decisions. These include one-year terms for the top elected position (president) of the organization, alternating between the two political parties, having co-chairs of opposite parties for all policy committees, and requiring a three-fourths majority with one vote per state (the same as the requirement for a U.S. constitutional amendment) to adopt public policy positions.

NCSL has a track record of actively promoting civility. Throughout its history, NCSL has assisted legislatures in designing and delivering training and orientation programs for newly elected members, and the importance of civility has been a principal lesson of those programs. For many years, NCSL sent new legislators a brochure, "15 Tips for Being an Effective Legislator" (NCSL, 2011a). One of them, entitled "Don't Burn Bridges," says the following: "It's going to happen. You're going to disagree and become upset and sometimes even dislike another legislator. But remember that today's adversary may be tomorrow's ally, so learn how to disagree without being disagreeable. Don't react emotionally or in anger on the floor to something someone has said."

Working with the Kettering Foundation in the 2010s, NCSL built a network of legislators committed to citizen engagement, civil discourse, and civic engagement. They developed best practices for cross-party consensus-building through community and constituency listening programs, and the foundation compiled a resource list of more than 100 organizations committed to collaborative governance, civil discourse, and deliberative democracy. The idea was rooted in the notion that public incivility contributes to legislative incivility and, conversely, that promoting community civility would lead to greater civility and productivity among state legislators (NCSL, 2018b).

During 2010–11, Massachusetts Senator Richard Moore made civility the theme of his term as president of NCSL. In announcing the initiative, Sen. Moore said, "By promoting civility in legislative business, constituent meetings, and even in the fall political campaigns, state legislators can help to restore collegiality and build consensus for addressing the real problems facing our states and nation" (NCSL, 2010). At Sen. Moore's behest, NCSL approved the following accord giving legislators and legislative staff the opportunity to pledge their commitment to a set of civility principles designed to foster bipartisanship:

> As a member of the National Conference of State Legislatures, we, as state legislators and legislative staff, in order to embrace civility and bipartisanship in our states and through them our nation, pledge our commitment to the following principles for civility:
>
> - Respect the right of all Americans to hold different opinions.
> - Avoid rhetoric intended to humiliate, delegitimatize or question the patriotism of those whose opinions are different from ours.
> - Strive to understand differing perspectives.
> - Choose words carefully.
> - Speak truthfully without accusation and avoid distortion.
> - Speak out against violence, prejudice, and incivility in all their forms, whenever and wherever they occur.
>
> We further pledge to exhibit and encourage the kind of personal qualities that are emblematic of a civil society: gratitude, humility, openness, passion for service to others, propriety, kindness, caring, faith, sense of duty and a commitment to doing what is right. (NCSL, 2011b)

Sen. Moore produced and handed out blue lapel buttons that said "Civility," and they were popular in NCSL circles for a time.

But all these efforts, both symbolic and practical, did not gain much traction with lawmakers and in state capitols. The 2009–2012 period, when NCSL's civility initiatives were in full swing, was a particularly turbulent time in many legislatures. Democrats had won major victories in Congress and state legislatures in 2008 and passed much of their policy agenda immediately thereafter, especially the Affordable Care Act. Republicans bitterly opposed that law, and the backlash spilled over into state legislatures and propelled the GOP to a sweeping victory in Congress and the states in 2010. The emergence of the Tea Party pushed the Republican party to the right, and in majority Republican legislatures the core of the Democratic party was hollowed out, leaving only more liberal, urban members on the fringe. In the Wisconsin and Indiana legislatures in 2011, Democrats drew national attention for staging dramatic and bitter walkouts as Republicans pressed aggressive anti-union measures. The shooting in Tucson of U.S. Rep. Gabrielle Giffords, which included collateral deaths of six other people, placed a tragic exclamation point on the incivility of the time.

Two anecdotes from NCSL's work immediately after the 2010 election illustrate how toxic legislative life had become in some places. An NCSL staffer who facilitated a bipartisan new-member orientation in a midwestern state made a point that new legislators need to move intentionally from campaigning to legislating mode to be effective in their collective work. One newly elected Republican majority member challenged that observation, saying simply, "I'm here to piss off Democrats." When asked, "What if you need some Democrat votes for a bill that is important to you?" the legislator responded that that was a very unlikely scenario. Remarkably, none of the other participants, from either party, said anything in response.

In another state where Democrats had captured the majority in the senate after decades in the minority, the new leaders asked one of NCSL's officers, who came from a state with a tradition of bipartisanship, to speak to a caucus retreat. When she advised them that they should treat the Republican minority in the way that the Democrats wished they had been treated by the Republican majority, an argument broke out between those who agreed with her and those who argued, "It's payback time. Let's get those bastards." In the weeks that followed, the vengeful members of that caucus won out temporarily, but soon lost their majority to a bipartisan coalition.

Against this backdrop, NCSL's and Sen. Moore's well-meaning efforts to promote civility were trumped by the nationalization of party politics and the demands of executive and legislative leaders to hew to the party line and eschew building relations with members of the opposing party. Many legislators gave civility lip (or lapel pin) service, but putting norms of courtesy, politeness, comity, and respect into action meant swimming against the current of the political times. Referring to efforts to promote civility, Alan Rosenthal observed, "These palliatives alone cannot redress the contending forces that are at work in a divided political system" (Rosenthal, 2009, p. 129). Since that time, things have only gotten worse, with the divisive politics of the 2016 election and the subsequent Trump administration.

STUDYING PARTISANSHIP, LAWMAKING, AND CIVILITY

The discussion of civility so far has been about qualities attached to individuals. But the norms of courtesy, politeness, comity, and respect that make up the concept of civility can also be applied to political parties and the legislative institution as a whole. How the majority and minority parties in a legislature treat each other is an important ingredient in the level of civility present in that body.

During 2014–16, NCSL staff, working with a team of political scientists, conducted a study and produced a report, "State Legislative Policymaking in an Age of Political Polarization," based on in-depth interviews in 10 selected legislatures and a national survey of all state legislators. The report concluded that despite evidence of significant—and increasing—polarization in state legislatures, "most of the legislatures in our sample were able to negotiate differences and reach settlements on major policy issues like budgets, transportation and higher education under conditions of political polarization and divided government" (NCSL, 2018a, p. 1). The media focus on controversial legislation and uncivil practices of name-calling and blaming the other side sometimes covers up quiet negotiation and policy settlements. Newspaper stories are seldom written about the 90 percent or more of bills in every legislature that are passed with large bipartisan majorities.

The NCSL study was primarily about the effects of polarization on policymaking. In our interviews, legislators and staff said that civility plays a significant role in the lawmaking process. Legislators in Connecticut, Tennessee, and Washington pointed to strong traditions of civility that mitigated the effects of political polarization on effective lawmaking. Connecticut legislators talked about a "New England sense of civility" that was apparent in a practice of never calling the previous question, thus shutting off debate. In exchange for the right to extended debate, the minority party traditionally did not use the privilege to filibuster or otherwise obstruct legislation. Members of the Tennessee General Assembly reported a similar culture of respect across parties and deference to seniority that allowed the minority party to have a significant role in the lawmaking process. The Washington Legislature used a variety of practices to reduce conflict between majority and minority parties, including a formal "no surprise" rule, collaborative leadership styles, and ensuring that each minority party member got at least one bill passed each session.

Giving the minority party a role in decisions, especially in legislative committees, promotes civility between the parties and gives minority party members a sense of buy-in. By the same token, however, majority parties that suppress and dominate minority parties engender bitterness and distrust from the minority. In our 10-state study, we found examples of chambers with large majorities adopting "Hastert rules" (named after a former speaker of the U.S. House of Representatives)—a practice in which the majority party never brings a bill to the floor without first having obtained a majority within its own caucus. Once this point is reached, all caucus members are required to support the measure on the floor. Debate and deliberation in the chamber thus become *pro forma* and meaningless. It is a useful tool for the majority to enforce its will, but it frustrates and angers the minority party and may invite potentially uncivil retaliation in the form of kicking and screaming to the media—the last resort of a suppressed minority.

Legislative committees are a particularly important venue where minority party members can make their voices heard and influence the outcome of legislation, especially if they do not need to claim credit for their work. A successful midwestern lawmaker and committee chair emphasized that an atmosphere of respect for both sides in committee builds a foundation for more enduring policy settlements. "In a well-functioning committee system, committees give a fair hearing to all sides on proposed legislation, deliberate on the merits of each proposal with active participation by minority party members and screen legislation in their area of policy for the rest of the house" (NCSL, 2018a, p. 14).

Like the effects of the Hastert rule, other efforts to suppress the minority party in committee can encourage incivility among members and in the chamber. There is a growing practice in a few legislative chambers of party caucuses within committees meeting and developing their positions on issues before going into a public committee session. Positions are hardened, the quality of deliberation is strained, and frustrated minority party members feel as if the majority has run roughshod over them. In other chambers, legislative leaders maintain strict control over committee proceedings, thereby often frustrating both majority and minority party members (NCSL, 2018a, p. 15).

Legislators viewed building personal relationships across parties as increasing civility and facilitating lawmaking. A midwestern conservative Republican legislator said that his best friend was a gay, liberal Democrat member of Congress who had served with him in the state legislature. They had sat on the same committees and worked together effectively on legislation. Other examples of deliberate efforts to build opposite-party personal relationships included:

- legislators who made it a point to spend time with every member of the opposing party to learn about their interests, hobbies and past-times, and families;

- a majority party leader who made a deal with a minority party counterpart to cosponsor at least one bill each session;

- intermixing the seating arrangements in some chambers so that members of opposing parties sit together;

- traveling together to committee hearings or state facilities outside the capital or to NCSL meetings; and

- informal issue-oriented caucuses that bring party members together by interest rather than party.

Among the 10 states studied by NCSL, three—Minnesota, Virginia, and Wisconsin—experienced significant stalemates on the state budget in the early- to mid-2010s. The legislators we interviewed from those states reported that the level of incivility increased during such episodes: governors and legislative leaders refusing to meet together, a lack of trust across parties, and complaints by minority parties that the majority had bulldozed them were common themes. Lawmakers did not agree about the long-term impact of these conflicts on civility and trust. Some said that there was a "hangover" that lasted for years afterward. Others said that it was normal majority-minority party conflict, it was no big deal, and in fact the desire to avoid similar gridlock in the future made succeeding legislative sessions run more smoothly as a long-term consequence.

SOCIETAL CHANGES

A few other social and political changes of the last few decades deserve particular mention, or speculation, in explaining the decline of civility in legislatures: term limits, social media and the 24-hour news cycle, the growth of the permanent campaign, the influence of partisan staff, and the pandemic of 2020. These and additional topics of interest are explicitly explored in the preceding chapters of this book.

NCSL conducted another study of the effects of term limits on state legislatures based on research conducted in six term-limited states and three non-term-limited control states in 2002–03. Even at that time, legislators and staff reported reduced socializing and camaraderie among legislators regardless of term-limit status. By reducing the level of experience of legislators, term limits exacerbated tendencies toward displays of bad manners, angry accusations and charges, and lack of respect for the positions of the opposing party (Berman, 2007, pp. 112–115).

Legislators in every state where NCSL conducted interviews for the partisanship and policymaking study complained about the pervasive effects of the 24-hour news cycle and social media. They are frustrated at how easily non-traditional media can spread misinformation. Because every public remark can be instantly tweeted or blogged, many legislators told us that they have become wary of throwing out new ideas or asking hypothetical questions in committee or on the floor. Some said that the quality of deliberation has declined, as members are so absorbed in their electronic devices that they do not pay adequate attention to debate and do not genuinely engage with their colleagues. In states without strong open-meetings laws, negotiation has been driven into closed-door meetings (NCSL, 2018a, p. 24).

These are indirect effects of social media on civility, but social media can also have quite direct effects. Legislators on Twitter or Facebook, like everyone else, can forget that they are talking to real people, making it easy to dash off uncivil tweets or posts in tones they would not use when face-to-face with someone.

A major change in legislative politics over the last quarter century is the pervasive influence of electoral politics. Legislators in safe districts and in small-population states with citizen legislatures still run their own campaigns. These are typically low-key affairs—candidates do not have to raise or spend a lot of money, and the campaign occupies only a few months out of every two or four years. But in larger states, especially where margins between the majority and minority parties are relatively close, the election campaign never really ends. Legislative leaders and the party in the legislature aggressively recruit candidates for office, raise large sums of campaign money, target specific races that are crucial to maintaining or gaining the majority, provide choice committee assignments to vulnerable incumbents, and arrange the legislative agenda and calendar for political advantage. The intensity of partisan politics in "permanent campaign" legislatures spills over and breeds incivility in legislatures. Likening these conflicts to war, Alan Rosenthal has written, "Given battlefield conditions, it is the exception rather than the rule to conduct friendly, even civil relationships with people who are shooting at you" (Rosenthal, 2009, p. 129).

Related to the increasing campaign focus of legislative life is the influence of partisan staff in legislatures in relation to nonpartisan staff. The smaller-population states with citizen legislatures still rely primarily on nonpartisan staff. In about half the states, though, a majority of staff are partisan, and in the largest-population states their influence predominates over that of the nonpartisan staff. Partisan professional staff are committed to keeping their members in office and either maintaining or gaining a majority in the legislature. To the extent that they sharpen the debate and rhetoric, train members in partisan warfare, and emphasize the contrasts between parties, they can contribute considerably to an atmosphere of incivility.

Anything that contributes to a decline in personal relationships is likely also to reduce civility. The tendency for Americans to spend less time socializing with each other, dubbed "bowling alone" by Robert Putnam (2000), has affected legislators as well. In many states, ethics laws that effectively prohibit lobbyists from hosting evening receptions and meals have also reduced cross-party interpersonal relations.

In 2020, the forced social distancing of the global coronavirus pandemic has added another dimension to the difficulty of building personal relationships and civility. Between March and August 2020, two dozen states adopted procedures for remote participation in committees or floor sessions (NCSL, 2020). NCSL staff who are tracking these developments received initial reports of considerable bipartisanship in remote sessions because of the emergency conditions being addressed. As time went on, however, it became apparent that remote communication is difficult in a legislative setting. Some staff have reported that there is less debate and deliberation in online legislative meetings, and the absence of usual nonverbal signals makes communication more difficult. If virtual legislative meetings continue to take place into the future, the implications for civility will bear watching.

In states where legislatures convened in person during the pandemic, ill feelings were caused by differences in attitudes toward masks. Harsh words were exchanged over issues of personal health and public safety. In what might be regarded as an ultimate act of incivility (short of an assassination or old-fashioned duel), a Pennsylvania legislator who had tested positive for COVID-19 notified his own party members who had been exposed to him but not members or staff of the opposing party. Most uncivil acts are words that engender anger and invite in-kind retaliation. But refusal to respect the health and well-being of one's colleagues can cause physical harm.

CONCLUSION

Writing in 2009, Alan Rosenthal said, "The principal effect of incivility is on the legislature itself and how it appears to the public. The legislature as an institution normally has little public support. Incivility, as reported in the media or reflected in campaigns, only makes the legislature's image worse" (2009, p. 129). Having spent much of my career trying to combat public cynicism and distrust toward legislatures, I agree with Rosenthal about the deleterious effects of hyper-partisanship and incivility on the legislative institution. But now, a decade after Rosenthal's prophetic observation, the level of incivility and public distrust has escalated and is threatening all governmental institutions alike—legislatures, executives,

courts, elections, law enforcement, public health…even national organizations such as the NCSL and the National Governors Association are
at risk if elected officials are so divided and bitter toward each other that
they are not willing to participate in bipartisan national organizations.

Despite this somber view of the state of civility in America today, I
would not be true to my calling as a defender and promoter of American
democracy if I did not look for some signs of hope. I remind myself that
most legislators still honor the institution and behave and treat their
opponents with respect. For example, in the midst of the coronavirus
pandemic, two Kansas senators—one a black female academic, the other
a white male from law enforcement—engaged in a moving call for all
Kansans, especially legislators, to listen to and respect each other and
to build a culture of trust. In interviews I conducted for this article, a
long-serving legislative staffer and a former House minority leader in
the Colorado General Assembly commented on how periods of incivility have waxed and waned over time, reflecting on a time in the early
1980s when a militant group known as the "House Crazies" disrupted
legislative norms. Conflicts in today's Colorado legislature seem tamer
than those. Moreover, all the attention paid to conflict and incivility in
our national politics and higher visibility in big state legislatures causes
us to forget that most of the small state citizen legislatures have much
greater levels of trust, respect, and civility and continue to function in
more traditional ways.

The mantra of NCSL's civic education initiative has always been that
representative democracy works—not perfectly, but better than any con-
ceivable alternative. I firmly believe that that remains true. But the waves
of incivility and nastiness in political life today are testing our democracy
in ways that we have only occasionally experienced in our history.

REFERENCES

Andrews, A. (2017, July/August). Breakdown of civility. *State Legislatures Magazine.*

Andrews, A., & Wood, N. (2020). Showing civility when we need it the most. National Conference of State Legislatures. https://www.ncsl.org/blog/2020/06/10/showing-civility-when-we-need-it-the-most.aspx.

Berman, D. R. (2007). Legislative culture. In K. T. Kurtz, B. Cain, & R. G. Niemi (Eds.), *Institutional change in American politics: The case of term limits* (pp. 107–118). University of Michigan Press.

National Conference of State Legislatures. (2010). Civility has appeal. https://www.ncsl.org/aboutus/executive-committee/civility-a-message-from-ncsl-president-senator-ri.aspx.

National Conference of State Legislatures. (2011a). 15 tips for being an effective legislator. https://www.ncsl.org/research/about-state-legislatures/15-tips-for-being-an-effective-legislator.aspx.

National Conference of State Legislatures. (2011b). NCSL executive committee passes civility accord. https://www.ncsl.org/press-room/ncsl-executive-committee-passes-civility-accord.aspx.

National Conference of State Legislatures. (2018a). State legislative policymaking in an age of political polarization. https://www.ncsl.org/Portals/1/Documents/About_State_Legislatures/Partisanship_030818.pdf.

National Conference of State Legislatures. (2018b). "Civil Engagement and Civil Discourse Resources." https://www.ncsl.org/research/about-state-legislatures/citizen-engagement-and-civil-discourse-resources.aspx.

National Conference of State Legislatures. (2020). Continuity of legislature during emergency. https://www.ncsl.org/research/about-state-legislatures/continuity-of-legislature-during-emergency.aspx.

Putnam, R. D. (2000). *Bowling alone: The collapse and revival of American community.* Simon and Schuster.

Rosenthal, A. (2009). *Engines of democracy: Politics and policymaking in state legislatures.* CQ Press.

CHAPTER TEN

Encouraging Civility in State Legislatures: How to Train Legislators, and How to Measure the Results

Robert G. Boatright[1]

INTRODUCTION

Alabama State Representative Mike Ball is one of over 100 state legislators from 27 states who have joined the National Network of State Legislators, a program established by the National Institute for Civil Discourse (NICD). Many of these legislators have worked to develop their own ways to make legislative work more civil and productive. Ball, for instance, has developed his own technique for encouraging comity. He described it to me as follows:

Music can provide a wonderful atmosphere for positive spiritual connections to be made. Since my troubled childhood, playing music has been therapeutic for me. When I was elected to the Alabama Legislature nearly 20 ago, it was only natural that I began taking every opportunity to engage in my favorite form of stress relief. It soon turned into weekly jam sessions around our state capital city with participants and guests of all political persuasions from diverse walks of life. It was at those jam sessions that spiritual seeds were sown that bloomed into deep friendships, strong enough to weather the political turmoil that ensued throughout the years that followed.

My favorite venue for music therapy has been Hank Williams' grave, located just a few blocks from the state house. When the legislative process gets particularly contentious, I sometimes sneak away with my guitar to that special place and sit on the concrete bench at the foot of Hank's grave. It is amazing how well songs like "I'm So Lonesome I Could Cry," "House of Gold," and "Mind Your Own Business" can give one perspective. On occasional nights, I invite colleagues to join me at that special place where animosity is unwelcome, where grudges can be laid to rest. It is a temporary respite from the political, religious, racial, and other differences that create spiritual chasms that prevent us from making the human connections that are necessary to our governing process.

Ball's technique is not necessarily one that could easily be transported to another state. Every state legislature does, however, have legislators who, like Ball, are concerned with the quality of interactions among legislators, but not all states have the resources to do this effectively. One of the goals of NICD has been to develop training for state legislators in how to improve relations among legislators, and to determine how this can be done most effectively.

NICD has worked extensively with the team responsible for the state legislative lobbyist survey described in this book, and we have shared the goal of determining how we can use interstate comparisons of civility so we can figure out what works and how to build upon successful state efforts. The recent retirement of Ted Celeste, who developed and led NICD's legislative civility efforts for nearly a decade, and the recent hiring of Idaho Senate President Pro Tempore Brent Hill provides an opportunity for us to reconsider our efforts and how we can learn from the lobbyist surveys described in the other chapters of this book.

In this chapter I describe the reasons why NICD has worked to improve civility within legislatures, the history of our work with state legislators, and the successes and challenges we have faced in trying to evaluate our work. I use this background to offer some thoughts on the difficulties inherent in studying civility at the state legislative level and on the benefits that such work can provide to political scientists and to practitioners.

CIVILITY AS A PROBLEM IN LEGISLATIVE POLITICS

Incivility has long been recognized as a problem for legislating at the national level. Moreover, many contemporary congressional reform proposals have discussed the relationship between partisan polarization and incivility. In *The Broken Branch*, Thomas Mann and Norman Ornstein (2008) discuss a variety of problems that have plagued Congress over the past two decades. Fewer consequential laws are passed today than during the 1970s and 1980s, few of the laws that are passed have bipartisan support, and when major laws are passed, they do not necessarily have majority support among the general public. Among the many reasons for this dysfunction, they argue, are changes in the culture of Congress.

Before the 1990s, they argue, members of Congress often socialized with each other when Congress was not in session, and they often socialized across party lines. Congressional ethics laws also permitted, for better or for worse, frequent interaction between members and interest groups. Many "odd couple" friendships resulted in landmark legislation. Senator Ted Kennedy, consistently among the most liberal members of the Senate, cosponsored landmark healthcare legislation with conservative Republicans such as Nancy Kassebaum and Orrin Hatch. There were numerous bipartisan caucuses organized around issues without a clear ideological dimension (e.g., the Congressional Autism Caucus) or issues of shared geographic concern (such as, for instance, the Chesapeake Bay Caucus).

Mann and Ornstein contend that during the 1990s members of Congress lost these types of social ties. It became more common for members to spend every weekend in their districts, and the congressional work week was shortened to accommodate this home district travel. While they are all in Washington, members have little time to socialize. Ethics laws were also tightened to discourage some forms of socializing. The culture of the two parties changed, as well; House Speaker Newt Gingrich allegedly discouraged Republicans from fraternizing with Democrats. Eric Uslaner (1993, chapter three) discusses five general explanations for the decline of civility in Congress: the congressional reforms of the 1970s, which were aimed at strengthening the power of liberals in the Democratic Party; divided control of the legislative and executive branches; membership change and diverging values among younger members; the impact of television; and the rise of more ideological interest groups. Uslaner documented this decline by showing changes in members' willingness to cosponsor legislation across party lines, members' disregard for procedural norms, and members' general lack of connection with opposing-party legislators. The problem has certainly become worse since Uslaner's work in this area.

By the late 1990s, civility became something that did not come naturally, but that had to be engineered. Uslaner (1993, p. 23) documents a number of op eds and other steps taken by members of the House and Senate in the 1980s to address this problem, including the establishment of a "Quality of Strife" caucus by a bipartisan pair of senators. In 1996, Representative Ray LaHood (R-IL) held the first of four "civility retreats" for members, aimed at identifying obstacles to civility in the House and at exploring possible reasons for these obstacles and ways to overcome them. These retreats were held off-site, in Hershey, Pennsylvania, were run by trained facilitators, and members were encouraged to bring their spouses and to socialize before and after the training sessions. As Frank Mackaman (2010), executive director of the Everett C. Dirksen Congressional Center, recounts, nearly 200 members attended the first retreat, making it the largest off-site gathering of members of Congress ever convened. However, attendance declined for subsequent events, and the event agendas became progressively more modest. Mackaman concludes that these retreats failed in the end because party leaders and committee chairs were not supportive and because much of the change in the culture of Congress resulted from changes in the institution and in how campaigns for Congress came to be waged.[2]

There remains, however, substantial support for events such as these in the grantmaking community. The Pew Foundation funded the initial retreats. Many civil society organizations, such as the Hewlett Foundation, the Congressional Management Foundation, and the R Street Institute have held similar events and sponsored research designed to identify reasons for congressional dysfunction. Some members of Congress continue to advocate for civility; at the moment, the House has three different civility caucuses.[3] The Harvard University Kennedy School's Institute of Politics continues to host a bipartisan orientation session for new members of Congress, something it has done since 1972.[4] Some academic research has also sought to explore past conflicts in Congress in order to measure more accurately whether Congress is in fact becoming less civil and to ensure that efforts to improve civility do not interfere with legislators' efforts to debate issues vigorously or advocate for their constituencies (e.g., Dodd and Schraufnagel, 2013; Freeman, 2018).

It has proven more difficult, however, to develop training sessions or other programs aimed at encouraging civility in state legislative politics. Studying civility within state legislatures is important for numerous reasons. Research into institutional civility is important simply because of the importance of state legislation in American life. Although the average American is more likely to be able to name his or her U.S. representative and senator than to name his or her state representative or senator, the role of states in responding to the COVID-19 pandemic, among other recent events, has certainly shown Americans how much their lives are influenced by state policy. It is also important because many state legislators go on to seek higher office; according to the National Council of State Legislators, 49% of current U.S. House members and 44% of current U.S. Senators once served as state legislators.[5] Norms acquired early in one's career may shape how a former state legislator acts when he or she reaches higher office.

There are many reasons to suspect that state legislatures are less-civil places today than Congress is. Examples of particularly toxic conflicts have been on display in many states for several years now, as evidenced by recent bitter conflicts in states such as Texas, North Carolina, Oregon, and Wisconsin. There are likely many other examples of partisan conflict that have failed to attract national attention, and there are many examples of intra-party conflict in recent years as well. We have long known, in addition, that the sorts of structural factors that Uslaner described for the U.S. Congress are as important (and perhaps even more important) at the state level. Studies as far back as the 1960s (Lockard, 1966) have contended that changing values in the general public have a greater influence on state legislators than on federal legislators.

We know that many state legislatures are more polarized than is the U.S. Congress (Shor and McCarty, 2011; Clark, 2015, pp. 17, 56). The establishment of term limits in 15 states since 1990 has ensured that the average tenure of state legislators is far shorter than that of members of the U.S. House and Senate (Squire and Moncrief, 2015, p 18). This means that there are fewer state legislators present who can recall when the culture was more collegial, and it means that members have less of an incentive to work to reform the culture of the legislature. Fowler and

Frederking (2000), among others, have shown that when state legisla-tors lose the sense that service in the legislature is a career, the legislature becomes more attractive to people who are there primarily to advance an ideological agenda.

In many states, legislators also lack the ability to develop ties with fel-low legislators. The state may be small enough geographically that there is no reason for legislators to linger in the state capitol on weekends or in the evenings during legislative sessions and interim meetings. In the four states where legislatures meet biennially, legislators may also not see each other frequently enough to develop meaningful connections (Moncrief and Squire, 2013, 40). As at the federal level, some states have moved to restrict the ability of outside groups to sponsor social events for legislators. In addition, the smaller size of state legislative districts compared to fed-eral ones makes it possible for more extreme voices to be heard and, also, for gerrymandering to produce more extreme outcomes (Gray, 2013).

Perhaps most importantly, however, most Americans do not think about the quality of state legislative life as a major matter of concern. Americans know less about what their state legislators do than they know about the U.S. Congress. And polarization and dysfunction in state legislatures receives less attention than do comparable problems at the federal level. This inattention also means that resources simply are not present in some states to develop retreats or training sessions such as what has been done at the federal level.

THE NATIONAL INSTITUTE FOR CIVIL DISCOURSE AND ITS WORK IN STATE LEGISLATURES

The National Institute for Civil Discourse (NICD) was founded in 2012, following the tragic shooting of U.S. Representative Gabrielle Giffords. In 2012, a bipartisan group of American political leaders founded NICD as an institute for research and applied work on civility in American politics and public life. Since its inception, NICD has supported a variety of dif-ferent projects; for instance, it has developed workshops for citizens in several different states, it supports a range of academic research projects, and it has developed a set of online citizen deliberations about public policy aimed at connecting citizens with members of Congress.

NICD's "Next Generation" program is one of the few initiatives that has been a constant part of NICD's work since its founding, and it is important for the organization because it connects applied civility work and research. Next Generation was founded by former Ohio State Representative Ted Celeste, who directed the program from 2012 to 2020. There are three main components to Next Generation: a workshop for state legislators, entitled "Building Trust through Civil Discourse"; a network of state legislators interested in promoting civility and who meet regularly in person and online; and special training sessions for current or former state legislators who wish to become facilitators of future workshops.

As of 2020, NICD has held 27 workshops in seventeen different states and has trained 48 current or former state legislators to work as facilitators. The goal of the workshops is to give state legislators a structured opportunity to explore ways to improve the quality of discourse within their legislature. The workshops also give legislators tools for working with colleagues in the opposing party (and in some cases, for overcoming divisions within their own party) in order to create a culture in which discourse and collaboration are possible. These are not policy-based or issue-based workshops; rather, they are events designed to explore more general obstacles to conducting legislative business.

Scheduling state workshops is a labor-intensive process. Doing so requires support from the leadership of both parties, and it also requires consideration of how workshops fit into the legislative calendar. In many states, NICD workshops have been tailored to particular state legislature-related groups or have been conducted in one chamber but not the other or conducted only for first-year legislators. Decisions must also be made about whether to host workshops on-site or off-site, and whether to work with leadership to determine how much pressure to put on state legislators to attend.

The typical workshop takes a bit more than half a day. Workshops are led by a bipartisan pair of facilitators from another state who are there not to offer advice, but rather to ensure that the workshop stays on task and that the group adheres to the ground rules. After a shared meal, introductions, and the establishment of ground rules, legislators are divided into breakout groups. They begin with a discussion of their "personal journeys." Each legislator is asked to select an event in his or her life that has shaped his or her own values and personal convictions. This event is not expected to be a story about why that person ran for office; rather, it is expected to be a story that will help other legislators understand him or her as a person. Legislators in each group use sticky notes to write down their formative experiences, and members of the group are then given the opportunity to think about each other's comments and to converse about their shared experiences.

Following a short break, legislators (again, still in the breakout groups) are asked to brainstorm comments about the current state of civility in their respective state legislatures, and to use sticky notes again to display particularly noteworthy problems or signature events. After this discussion, legislators are then asked what legislative civility promoting efforts would look like—what tangible steps could be taken in their state to encourage greater civility. In three subsequent short discussions, state legislators identify barriers to their desired state of civility, identify opportunities to bring about change, and propose ameliorative actions they might take. The breakout groups then disband, and all legislators reconvene, at which point members of each group report on their discussions. A list of action items is assembled by the full group, and legislators vote on which actions are the top priorities. The expectation is that legislators will leave the sessions having learned a bit about their colleagues and having made some individual connections. In addition, it is expected that legislators will reach agreement on a plan for how to build upon the workshops, with specific persons on point for taking responsibility for action items. NICD provides a final report to participants after the workshop.

One virtue of these workshops is that, like Mike Ball's sing-alongs, they are designed to address problems, circumstances, and solutions specific to individual states. I had the opportunity to review the comments legislators offered during a recent workshop held in a rural midwestern state. Many of the personal stories were specific to the circumstances of that state—they were, for instance, about the effects of rural poverty, of religion, or of the experience of leaving home for the first time. Likewise, the obstacles proposed at times alluded to particular key individuals, to pressure groups that were particularly powerful in the state, or to the often-dire consequences of majority party factionalism and one-party rule. The solutions proposed, however, are rather easy to generalize. Many participants talked about improving individual relationships and working to change behavioral norms—establishing bipartisan events, sharing meals with legislators of the other party, or mentoring new legislators. Other solutions require some level of institutional change—such as altering the structure of committees or committee hearings, or reconsidering election laws.

Since the beginning of the Next Generation program, NICD has explored how to measure the consequences of these workshops. Doing so is not easy—as the action items above show, many of these changes are matters of personal behavior, not legislation. Similarly, some of the long-term goals of these workshops, such as the passage of more bipartisan legislation, are difficult to connect directly to the workshops. In addition, it is difficult for states to require anyone to attend; some participants have claimed that the people who go are those who are already predisposed to work for civility, while the legislators who are most in need of training tend to stay away. In many states, term limits make it difficult to ensure that the legislators most dedicated to encouraging civility are around to build upon these trainings.

NICD's Director of State Programs Ted Celeste and Next Generation Program Manager Makayla Meacham have conducted several detailed post-workshop discussions with state legislators. They group the desired consequences of NICD's workshops into five categories: the willingness of the state to host follow-up workshops (or for other states to implement them); increased bipartisan interaction, such as friendships, small talk, and district visits; cosponsorship of bipartisan legislation; legislative process improvements, such as alterations in committee and subcommittee decision-making or expanded opportunities for legislators to offer bills or propose amendments; and participation in NICD's National Network of State Legislators. The Next Generation website offers some specific examples of changes states have made in the aftermath of NICD workshops, including a bipartisan adoption bill passed in Ohio; procedural changes in the Ohio Senate; bipartisan agreement on ground rules for abortion legislation in Arizona; changes in chamber seating rules in Maine; and the establishment of a bipartisan choir in Minnesota.

To move beyond anecdotal reports, however, NICD also commissioned an evaluation of the program from the TCC Group, a leading consulting firm that does such work for nonprofit organizations and philanthropic foundations. The TCC Group report included a follow-up survey of workshop participants in twelve different states, and qualitative interviews with legislators from four states where NICD has been particularly active. The TCC Group report concludes that NICD has had an impact on legislators' awareness of civility as a goal, that it has increased legislators' connections with each other, and that legislators who participated in workshops had developed a better sense of their own responsibility for working to increase civility. However, respondents also identified several obstacles to the workshops' success. These included variations in the willingness of the party leadership to "buy in" to the project, term limits, gerrymandering, campaign practices, other institutional features that are largely outside the scope of the civility workshops, and, perhaps most importantly, the often-deleterious imperatives of partisanship. The TCC Group report offered a variety of recommendations about changes NICD might explore, including establishing workshops for legislative staff, seeking the support of state-specific foundations or other organizations in developing workshops, connecting workshops with first-year legislator orientation, and working more closely with party leadership to implement and build upon the workshops.

SURVEYING LEGISLATORS IN IDAHO: A CASE STUDY

The evaluations described above show that if we are truly to understand the quality of life in American state legislatures, it is important to conduct further survey research. This is so for three reasons. First, these evaluations suggest that state comparisons are important—which states have had more success in encouraging a climate of civility? How do rules that vary by state, but are beyond the scope of these workshops, influence legislative conduct? And are there particular events or characteristics of state culture that must be considered when working within any particular state legislature? And second, the evaluations lead us to ask who is in the best position to judge the level of civility within state legislatures. NICD's strategy has been to talk with the legislators themselves, but some of the evaluation comments suggest that staff may have a different perspective. Given the short tenure of many legislators, the lobbyist survey described elsewhere in this book offers another perspective—many lobbyists have much more experience working with the legislature than do the legislators themselves and, of course, some lobbyists are themselves former legislators.

Third, and most consequentially, the evaluations described above do not provide the perspectives on civility of those who have not participated in the workshops. In order to do this, of course, it is necessary to conduct broader surveys of legislators in order to acquire baseline measures. To date, NICD's most successful effort to survey legislators has been conducted in Idaho. This section briefly reviews the response to the Idaho surveys; I then comment on how we hope to expand our surveys, how the results in one state might be put in context, and how these correspond to some of the findings in the survey of state legislative lobbyists described elsewhere in this volume.

NICD, in cooperation with two of the editors of this volume, administered a survey on civility to the Idaho House of Representatives during late November and early December of 2017. The survey was patterned on one that Lovrich and colleagues had given to legislators in the state of Washington during 2009, 2012, and 2013. Question wordings were kept as similar as possible to facilitate cross-state comparisons at a later time. The survey provides a snapshot of life within the Idaho legislature. The ultimate goal is to administer the survey in as many states as possible in order eventually to gain an understanding of legislators' perceptions of civility and bipartisan cooperation nationwide, and to identify reforms that might be promising for the promotion of civil discourse. For the Idaho survey, some questions were slightly adjusted to fit distinct characteristics of the state's legislature. We were aided in our implementation of the survey by professors Gary Moncrief and Stephanie Witt of Boise State University. Links to the online survey were sent to all Idaho House and Senate members. Speaker of the House Scott Bedke and Democrat State Legislator Melissa Wintrow each sent separate emails to members encouraging them to complete the survey.

We received a total of 47 responses to this survey; there are only 70 members in the Idaho House, so the response rate here was quite good—67%. At the time of the survey, 59 members of the Idaho House were Republicans and 11 were Democrats. Although response rates were similar across the two parties, in our judgment the number of Democrats is too small to generate meaningful statistical comparisons across parties. The same goes for gender—there are 23 women in the Idaho House, and response rates for women were somewhat lower than for men. There was, in addition, significant roll-off in the survey; many respondents answered the first several questions but then gave up. We thus shall focus our attention here primarily on the aggregate data, although in our consideration of open-ended responses we do note instances in which partisanship or gender may have been related to the response.

The Idaho survey shows that while legislators report that they are generally satisfied with many aspects of their careers, it is also evident that Idaho legislators of both parties believe that civility can be improved. That improvement requires greater efforts by legislative leaders to model civil behavior and informal actions on the part of legislators to reach out across the aisle and across intra-party factional lines. The findings here should be viewed as preliminary, for two reasons. First, we do not yet know for certain how the quality of discourse has changed in Idaho; we can only know that after subsequent surveys in the state. Second, we are able to make preliminary comparisons with one state, Washington. We will know more about the effects of particular characteristics of Idaho—characteristics such as the lopsided partisan balance, the size of the state and the state legislature, and other cultural features of Idaho and its region of the country—only after we have conducted surveys in states with different institutional and cultural features. The results described below should be seen, then, as a marker for Idaho legislators and citizens, and for those concerned with political discourse in state legislatures more broadly.

Overall Satisfaction with Legislative Service

Overall, legislators provided very positive responses about their satisfaction with their legislative service; as Figure 10.1 shows, 76% of Idaho legislators found their service as legislators to be very worthwhile, and only 6% responded that their service is not worthwhile. Likewise, 76% of legislators said that if they were to live their lives again, they would wish to be a legislator anew, and only one respondent claimed that he or she would not want to be a legislator were he or she to have a chance to reconsider.

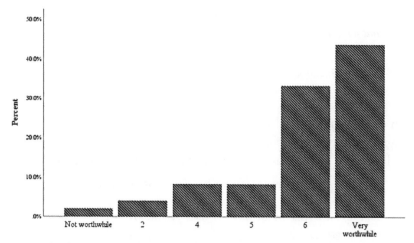

In light of the many demands and stresses of service in legislative office, how worthwhile to you is your service in the legislature?

Figure 10.1. Idaho Legislators' Perceptions of the Value of Legislative Service

We asked legislators to comment on the most rewarding aspects of legislative service. Most respondents discussed the rewards that came from their interactions with constituents:

The opportunity to represent constituents of underserved populations and to advocate for justice.

• • •

Impact on policy (both improving good policy and stopping bad policy in my perspective), more fully understanding the fabric of our society, and hearing from citizens about challenges they face, building friendships (not in the political sense).

• • •

Connecting people who are struggling to find service or justice in systems with appropriate resources to find the answers to their daily problems. For example, one of my constituents with a severe physical and developmental disability was not receiving private-duty nursing benefits which he qualified for. This had a very bad impact on his ability to move in the public realm and was actually against federal law. After a number of meetings, discussions, and letters, the Department of Health and Welfare conceded that he should be getting these services and [said they] would make amends to him and send word to all the service agencies providing service.

• • •

Being a citizen legislator and hoping to make a difference in the freedom and liberty of our state.

• • •

In contrast, most legislators' comments about "the most trying aspects of legislative service" emphasized the difficulties of dealing with problematic colleagues or, in some cases, with disquieting directives from legislative leaders:

Lack of civility, incorrect information circulated by opposition.

• • •

Some of the legislators are there for their personal reasons and not for their constituents.

• • •

Having to deal with personal attacks.

• • •

Listening to debate from legislators that do not know what they are talking about.

• • •

Personal attacks from colleagues and campaigning.

• • •

Working with legislators who do not believe in any type of compromise.

• • •

Colleagues with limited vision who are grounded in "good old boys" club and remain tied to outdated approaches.

• • •

Politics.... trying to work on legislative needs and issues, making good decisions while dealing with the narcissistic demands, personal agendas and attitudes.

• • •

Not being able to change direction the ship is going...it takes a long time to turn around an Ocean Liner. Learning that not everyone thinks the way I do!

• • •

Other legislators who won't rationally discuss issues.

Thus, while the legislators reported a relatively high level of job satisfaction, their frustrations with their colleagues were quite evident. This appeared to be a sentiment shared across the political spectrum; minority party members cited the problems of being in the minority, but majority party members often cited factional conflict within the Republican Party.

Perceptions of Civility

There are concerns, then, about the level of civility in the Idaho legislature today. As Figure 10.2 shows, very few legislators (only 8%) believe that the level of civility has increased; slightly less than half of respondents reported no change, and 43% reported that legislative life has become less civil in recent years. We asked respondents about the effects of this perceived increase in incivility; very few legislators felt that their own commitment to the legislative process, the institution, or their own jobs had been harmed, but many responded that their interactions with their colleagues had been affected. By far the most common effect (noted by 73% of respondents) was that legislators tend to avoid colleagues whom they perceive to be problematic (see Table 10.1).

Our Idaho legislator survey respondents offered many different definitions of civility. Some considerations of civility emphasize what one might call a "surface level" civility—politeness, cordiality, and so forth. Most legislators, though, emphasized their belief that legislative civility included a serious consideration of the points of view of others, and a willingness to break at times with partisan orthodoxy in committee hearings, legislative debate, and informal interactions. As with some of the other questions, many Idaho legislator respondents took particular note of factional conflict within the majority party and the attitudes of, and toward, the legislative leadership:

> *Treating others with honesty, without personal name-calling, belittlement, threats, or aspersion to motive, while at the same time not taking offense to vigorous debate or limiting the depth of debate and exchange of ideas.*
>
> • • •
>
> *If you are equating civility with politeness it [the level of civility in the legislature] is good. If you mean consideration of others and flexibility in views it is not good.*
>
> • • •
>
> *2017 was totally out of control! A wedge within our party…has divided us and almost a third [want] to form a separate "Freedom Caucus." I am totally supportive of this work to assist with bringing our caucus back together…if possible. Mostly disappointed with the disrespect of our leadership.*
>
> • • •
>
> *Your demeanor in and out of public view. Also, how you carry on your personal political newsletters and how you directly influence third parties to carry out your positions.*

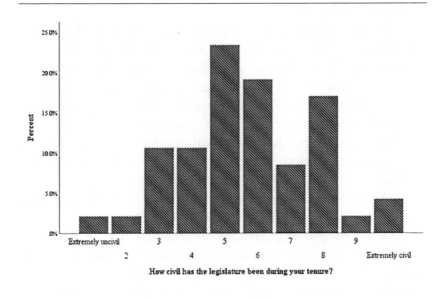

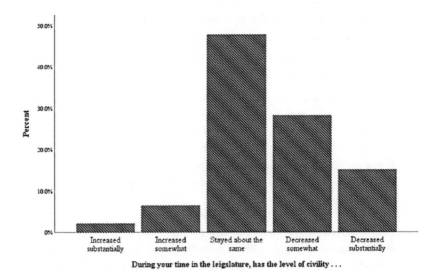

Figure 10.2a. and 10.2b. Idaho Legislators' Perceptions of Changes in Civility over Time

• • •

Civility is more than please and thank you, although these are important. Civility is about providing a fair opportunity for all ideas to come to the table for discussion and a vote. Incivility is blocking an idea from coming forward because of a party affiliation. I think core to civil discourse and behavior [are] honesty and initiative. I try very hard to let folks know what I'm doing so they can prepare. If the press is coming their way, I give a phone call. If there is something I am going to disagree with in public, I try to share that with appropriate parties. Civility includes the thought about who needs to know something and when and how to communicate it. Civility is also about fairness. It also includes considering that I may be wrong about something. Coming to the table with the mindset that I may not have all the info and I may be convinced otherwise.

• • •

To me, civility has two components. The first and most important component is having enough respect for others and the marketplace of ideas to listen to and discuss things with them. The second, and less important—although still important—is to listen and discuss in a respectful and civil manner that allows others to be heard and their views seriously considered. To me all of this (taken together) means that legislative leaders need to stop preventing proposed bills from being heard and considered. Refusing to hear legislation simply silences people, means that there is no listening or discussion, and that there is a fundamental disrespect for competing ideas and the people who espouse them.

These comments from the survey were revealing in several regards. First, the candor of the comments suggests that the survey was an engaging one for many of the legislators. Secondly, it is clear from the content of many of the comments that there is a level of concern about the adverse consequences of incivility on the legislative deliberative process. And finally, there is a clear value to having legislative leadership hear what members are thinking about the way in which they are either promoting civility or increasing incivility.

Partisanship and Interactions across Party Lines

Legislators' interactions with their colleagues tend to be limited to activities conducted while the legislature is in session. Most legislators report formal and social interactions with members of the opposing party while the legislature is in session, but rather few reported social connections with the opposing party outside of the legislative session. A substantial majority of respondents claimed that they know most members of the opposing party, that they respect most of them, that they share common values with the opposition, and that they have at least some friends in the opposing party. Respondents were less likely to respond that they trust or confide in very many members of the opposing party; only 9% of respondents said that they confide in all or most of the opposing party members, and 15% said that they trust most or all of the opposing party members (see Table 10.2). The questions here were arranged roughly to

Table 10.1. Idaho Legislators' Perceptions of the Consequences of Incivility

Has legislative incivility…	
Decreased your work effectiveness?	25.0%
Decreased your legislative work effort?	8.3%
Caused you to worry about incivility?	45.8%
Caused you to avoid certain uncivil legislators?	70.8%
Decreased your commitment to the legislature?	12.5%

Table 10.2. Idaho Legislators' Attitudes Toward the Opposing Party

In reference to members from the other party…	All	Most	Some	Few	None
How many do you respect?	10.4%	60.4%	20.8%	2.1%	0.0%
How many have you met?	79.2	12.5	0.0	2.1	0.0
How many would you consider a friend?	4.2	27.1	37.5	16.7	8.3
How many have interests similar to yours?	0.0	10.4	45.8	33.3	2.1
How many are you willing to confide in?	0.0	8.3	35.4	31.1	16.7
How many have values similar to yours?	0.0	18.8	35.4	31.3	4.2
How many do you trust?	2.1	12.5	58.3	14.6	4.2

Note: "Don't know" responses excluded.

correspond to depth of relationship—that is, they go from mere acquaintance to close friendship. The responses support what we see elsewhere in the survey; most legislators respect most other legislators, and most tend to have some friends in the opposing party. At the same time, it is rare for legislators to trust or confide in these friends, and most members harbor some suspicion toward some members of the opposing party.

Given the lack of a baseline or a comparison group, it is somewhat difficult to know what to make of these responses. This is, in addition, a question on which we would gain a good deal more leverage if the Idaho legislature were less overwhelmingly Republican. Most legislators clearly feel that the quality of deliberation requires some level of bipartisanship; only 15% of respondents claimed that bipartisan dialogue and deliberation are not important for the legislative process. Likewise, when we asked legislators about potential reforms to encourage greater interaction across party lines, the legislators were very enthusiastic about virtually all these prospective reforms (see Table 10.3). They were particularly open to self-initiated, informal efforts such as visiting each other's districts, socializing with others, or reaching out across the aisle as part of the legislative process. They were, however, a bit more skeptical that formal changes, such as mixing offices or seating assignments, would substantively improve the quality of deliberation and dialogue. As with the broader questions, this suggests that legislators primarily see the challenge for bipartisanship and civility to be a matter of personal choices and of the actions of a small number of legislators, not as a larger institutional problem.

The open-ended responses here largely back up this contention. In addition to soliciting opinions on a variety of different reforms, we also asked legislators to explain their views on these reforms, or to offer additional suggestions:

> *The state legislature should have no hand, take no action, in improving legislative relationships.*

● ● ●

> *I don't have any [suggestions]. We have rules of decorum and those should be enforced. Otherwise, we are dealing with adults of wide-ranging personalities and views. If you compare our civility to other legislative bodies such as the British parliament or Congress in the 1800s, we are far and away more civil. Political discourse can be uncivil by nature. Our problem today is not so much*

incivility as it is a drastic change in the way people view some very fundamental issues of life. That brings the polarization that we see, and classes on civility are not going to change that. I think most legislators realize that what goes around comes around, and on any particular issue one day's opponent will be tomorrow's ally, even across party lines. I think the media and certain interest groups have seized on civility as a problem at the legislatures and magnified it, but that is not the problem. From a historical standpoint, I think we have a very civil legislature in an environment where there will always be differing opinions and shifting alliances overshadowed by growing polarization in society.

• • •

Better relations between representatives and senators.

• • •

Reconsider the office assignments so that seasoned legislators are in the proximate areas as new legislators. Break up the political cliques.

• • •

Leadership should meet with each person in the minority party and build a relationship. I would also ask that the Leaders of the majority party discuss with their members to be mindful in including all members in order to safeguard the democratic republic. It is in all our interests to be sure that everyone feels that they have the OPPORTUNITY [caps in original] to be at the table. When people feel blocked or ignored, the opportunity for incivility and revolt increases. When people…don't feel they have anything to lose, they act that way and will do all they can to break a system.

• • •

Legislators have been voted for in their districts; therefore, they are very independent and often unwilling to change the goals and ideas they presented to their constituents for which they were voted for. Even those who differ in the same party. We need to realize all our goals and ideas likely will not be honored and/or become policy; but we still must respect the process and the leadership without creating discontent and animosity in the body.

• • •

There have been some attempts to improve the environment, but it is [sic] very fleeting. In my opinion attempts to educate us with workshops etc. will not work in this age in the political arena. Things have got too personal and dogmatic.

• • •

Those in leadership could speak more positively of the opposition in caucus.

While most legislators (70%) have work-related interactions with members of the opposing party nearly every day during session, and most reported having social interactions at least three to four times per week during session as well, there is little interaction outside of session. Fifty-three percent of legislators reported that they have work-related contacts with members of the opposing party less than a few times a year, and 82% reported that they have social interactions with members of the opposition fewer than a few times a year. In fact, over a third (36%) of legislators reported that they *never* see members of the opposing party socially.

Table 10.3. Idaho Legislators' Support for Reforms to Encourage Civility and Bipartisan Dialogue

Reform	Highly Effective	Moderately Effective	Not Very Effective
Show respect for other people and their opinions	88.9%	6.7%	4.4%
For legislators to be an example of statesmanship	84.5	4.4	11.1
Work with legislators from the other party on joint projects	65.9	18.2	15.9
Being willing to work with someone with whom you disagree	55.6	33.3	11.1
Eat meals with other legislators	55.6	28.9	15.6
Hold social functions which are limited to legislators	54.6	29.5	15.9
Visit other legislators in their legislative districts	52.4	22.2	24.4
Spend time with other legislators outside of the session	47.8	29.3	25.0
Change seating assignments so parties are intermixed	27.3	15.9	56.8
Change office assignments so parties are intermixed	22.7	20.5	56.8

Note: "Don't know" responses excluded.

Civility in Legislative Campaigns

We also asked legislators a battery of questions about their experiences campaigning for office. As some of the comments above show, hostile confrontations during campaigns can have an influence on the conduct of legislative business. Eighty-seven percent of our respondents said that they believe that incivility in campaigns has influenced their working relationships with other legislators, and 67% said that legislative campaigns have become less civil over the past ten years (only one respondent responded that campaigns have become more civil, and the remainder said that there has been no change). Despite these comments, Idaho legislators nonetheless believe that legislative campaigns are more civil than campaigns for the U.S. Congress. Seventy-four percent of respondents believe that the Idaho legislature is less polarized than the U.S. Congress, and only 5% of respondents believe that it is more polarized.[6]

The Quality of Legislative Life

A substantial majority of legislators stated that the legislative workload has increased during their time in the legislature. Seventy-four percent said that they believe that the workload during session has increased, and 87% believe that it has increased outside of session as well. Legislators report working an average of 60 hours while the legislature is in session, and 18 hours when it is not (the median response was 60 and 20, respectively). This heavy workload might be expected to have a number of different effects. It is clear that legislators commit a lot of time to their jobs. A majority (56%) of respondents said that their quality of sleep is "fairly bad" or "very bad" while the legislature is in session. Legislators reported getting to sleep a half-hour later than when they are out of session, and also having somewhat more difficulty sleeping well. Yet when we asked a battery of eleven questions about legislators' quality of life—including questions about work relationships, productivity, quality of family life, and quality of legislators' decisions—respondents gave relatively positive answers. Forty-five percent said that their level of satisfaction with their job was very good or excellent, and 50% said that their personal enjoyment of their jobs was very high.

WHAT WE CAN LEARN FROM SURVEYS OF STATE LEGISLATORS

The Idaho survey will become more valuable once there is an opportunity to conduct surveys in other states. Even at this stage, however, the results suggest three important avenues for research.

Comparing State Legislatures

One of our goals in this project is to be able to make comparisons among states. Many of the survey questions used for our Idaho study were also asked by Lovrich, Benjamin, and colleagues in their surveys of Washington legislators.[7] Responses in the two states are broadly similar. In the 2013 survey, Washington legislators' responses to questions about whether legislative service is worthwhile, whether they would choose to serve in the legislature were they to have a chance to live life over again, and regarding changes in the level of partisanship over the past ten years were similar to those of Idaho legislators. In the 2010 survey, Washington legislators rated the level of civility higher than did Idaho legislators—the mean response on the ten-point scale in Washington was 6.82, and the median was 7. In contrast, the mean response in Idaho was 5.69 and the median was 6. Washington legislators also reported far more social interactions with members of the other party, both during and out of session. Measures of satisfaction with personal life while in the legislature were comparable in the two states. Responses about potential reforms were also quite similar; Washington legislators tended to prefer self-initiated, informal interventions as opposed to changes in legislative rules.

There could be many reasons for the few differences noted. For instance, Washington is a larger state, so more legislators must spend some time living in Olympia as opposed to returning home; the two parties are more evenly represented in the Washington legislature, so there are simply more members of the opposing party to encounter if one is in the majority; and there is no guarantee that circumstances in Washington have not deteriorated since the last survey conducted there. The similarities in responses between these two states, however, suggest that the responses in Idaho are not aberrant. As we gather data from more states, we will be able to gain a better understanding of how state politics and state culture influence civility.

Comparing Training Programs

NICD's Next Generation program is not the only training program for state legislators. The National Council of State Legislators and the State Legislative Leaders Foundation have worked with NICD on various programs, and they have done some of their own trainings as well. There are, in addition, several organizations in individual states that have worked on building bipartisan bridges with legislators, often around particular issues, to improve the quality of legislative deliberations. The Washington State project, for instance, existed well before NICD began its work. Each of these organizations has developed a slightly different model for addressing legislative problems.

Among the organizations that have taken a more consistent approach to improving state legislative capacity is the North Carolina Leadership Forum (NCLF) at Duke University. For the past four years, the NCLF has had a goal of developing the capacity of the state's policy leaders to have effective engagement across parties, policy sectors, and geography by building leaders' dialogue skills and by enabling them to form relationships of trust. Each cohort of leaders attends a series of issue-specific, four-and-a-half-day-long retreats. Legislators can work with policy advocates, state and local officials, foundation leaders, civic group leaders, and others to explore controversial matters of importance to the state. The goal is to enhance understanding of the factors underlying differing perceptions of the nature of problems coming before the legislature and, when possible, to identify solutions on which broad agreement can be reached. More specifically, over the course of several months the program is designed to increase participant understanding of their own and others' views; establish a shared understanding of the nature of important problems and related relevant facts; articulate more clearly the essence of disagreements as well as identify points of acceptance of solutions to those problems; examine and seek to understand the values, perceptions, and experiences that underlie disagreements; build authentic relationships among leaders of different political parties and ideological views; and create a foundation for future collaboration among NCLF participants.[8]

NCLF has held programs for cohorts of policy leaders to discuss jobs, energy, education, and immigration. NCLF leaders have modeled their discussions on work done by the Kettering Foundation and other deliberative democracy groups. As in the case of NICD, they have emphasized the importance of holding events off-site and of working sequentially to build trust and relationships, identify problems, and explore steps toward solutions. Unlike NICD, however, the NCLF has opted to develop longer, policy-specific retreats, and to bring legislators together with other stakeholders.

NCLF has faced some of the same problems as NICD in trying to measure the impact of its events. An internal post-program survey for the last NCLF cohort (on school choice) shows, for example, that over 95% of the participants said that through the program they had formed relationships with one or more people of differing views that they likely would not have formed otherwise. Moreover, all post-program survey respondents agreed that "I better understand the values, opinions or priorities about school choice held by people with different perspectives than mine"; and 96% said they understood the basis of their own views better. Surveys of previous participants in earlier cohorts of the program have produced similar results. While these surveys may show the impact of the program on individual participants, state legislative surveys that are decoupled from these programs can help us to understand the impact of these programs on the legislative environment in a way that evaluations of the program itself cannot.

Comparing the Views of State Legislators and Lobbyists

One of the strengths of this volume is the emphasis on comparing states. For instance, Lovrich and Simon (chapter one) use state-level measures of political culture to explore differences in legislative civility. In chapter two, Schreckhise and Benjamin explore the effects of state legislative professionalism. In chapter six, Giordono, Steel, and McMorris compare states according to their levels of inequality. And in chapter seven, McMorris, Steel, and Giordono compare urban and rural states. All of the comparisons provide context that would be difficult to match in surveys of legislators.

This book is premised on the almost certainly accurate belief that the perspective of lobbyists can reveal characteristics of the states that are not necessarily seen by legislators. At the federal level, it has long been accepted that lobbyists provide crucial information to legislators (Esterling, 2004). Many federal lobbyists are former members of Congress or former congressional staffers, and many lobbyists have worked on Capitol Hill for longer than most members of Congress. There is no reason to think that state legislative lobbyists are different.

At the same time, state legislators can provide crucial information that is not available to lobbyists. A state legislator survey with a good response rate can provide far more detail about the conditions within a state than can a national survey of lobbyists, and well-designed questions can explore some of the same factors that are covered in this book within states. For instance, one might compare the views of legislators from urban and rural districts or compare the views of legislators from districts with high and low levels of economic stratification.

It is also important to note, in addition, that perceptions of civility will vary among legislators. Some of the most salient differences we noted in our Idaho study are attributable to the respondent's party, how long the respondent has been in the legislature, and the ideological perspective of the respondent. Perhaps most consequentially, it is evident in the Idaho survey that men and women have very different perspectives on the civility of interactions among legislators.[9] Many of the differences in opinion are difficult to measure with fixed-response questions but come through in the open-ended responses.

The authors in this volume have solved one major problem: obtaining responses. While we are optimistic about building on our survey work in Idaho, we have faced major coordination problems in our surveying that the lobbyists' surveys can overcome. Just as buy-in from the party leadership is crucial to our workshops, it is particularly crucial to getting legislators to fill out a survey. We were only able to get a good response rate in Idaho because the party leaders sent repeated emails to their members describing the purpose of the survey and asking them to fill it out. We sought to conduct surveys in other states but had to abandon our plans due either to lack of support from the party leadership or an unwillingness on their part to encourage members to complete it. This is a particular challenge if we are to measure civility in states where we have not yet done workshops—if we do want to find out whether our trainings are making a difference, we will have to do surveys well before legislators have worked with NICD. We also have found that it is necessary to create ties to local academics and to organizations that work with the legislature in order to understand our results fully.

CONCLUSIONS

Despite nearly a decade of work with state legislators, our effort to understand civility in state legislative politics is in many ways still in its early stages. We see our effort as a complement to the work described in this book.

The lobbyist survey described in this book offers many insights into how we can work with legislators to improve the quality of discourse. We remain convinced that legislator surveys can provide valuable information for political scientists and reformers about the relationship among state political institutions, state political culture, and legislative productivity and comity. NICD's Next Generation program, now led by Idaho State Senate President Pro Tempore Brent Hill, continues to train facilitators and develop state workshops. NICD also has established Commonsense American, an online citizen forum in which participants are given information on policy problems and connected with legislators at the state and the national levels to discuss their ideas. The problems identified in this book, and in NICD's applied work, are both a fascinating research opportunity and a call to Americans to work to improve the quality of our democracy.

NOTES

1. Thank you to Ted Celeste, Makayla Meacham, Brent Hill, Nadine Wise, Mike Ball, and Leslie Winner for assistance with this chapter.

2. Here, Mackaman offers the ideological views and tactics of Republicans elected in 1994, Democrats' frustration with being a minority party, and conflict around the 1998 impeachment of President Clinton as examples.

3. As Segers (2019) notes, the presence of three different civility caucuses may say something about the nature of the problem in Congress.

4. For discussion see the project website at https://iop.harvard.edu/get-inspired/bipartisan-program-newly-elected-members-congress.

5. See https://www.ncsl.org/blog/2018/11/02/how-many-former-state-legislators-serve-in-congress.aspx.

6. Idaho legislators are not entirely correct in this perception. According to Shor and McCarty (2011), the Idaho State House has become somewhat more polarized over the past decade, but it is less polarized than the average western state legislature (eighth most-polarized of thirteen states). It is, however, more polarized than the U.S. House of Representatives if one compares the median ideology score of Democratic and Republican Party legislators. See also Shor's analysis at https://americanlegislatures.com/category/polarization/page/1/.

7. For a summary of results in Washington, see the Legislative Services Project website at https://labs.wsu.edu/political-interaction/project-results/.

8. Reports from each cohort of the program are available at https://sites.duke.edu/nclf/.

9. This finding is supported by a large literature on the different perspectives of male and female legislators; see, for instance, Osborn and Kreitzer (2014) and Swers (2002).

REFERENCES

Clark, J. H. (2015). *Minority parties in U.S. legislatures*. University of Michigan Press.

Dodd, L. C., & Schraufnagel, S. (2013). Taking incivility seriously. In S.A. Frisch & S.Q. Kelly (Eds.), *Politics to the extreme* (pp. 71–91). New York: Palgrave Macmillan.

Esterling, K. M. (2004). *The Political Economy of Expertise*. University of Michigan Press.

Fowler, L. L., & Frederking, B. (2000). Representation, careerism, and term limits. In W. T. Bianco (Ed.), *Congress on display* (pp. 189–216). University of Michigan Press.

Freeman, J. (2018). *The field of blood: Violence in Congress and the road to the Civil War.* Yale University Press.

Gray, V. (2013). The socioeconomic and political context of states. In V. Gray, R. L. Hanson, & T. Kousser (Eds.), *Politics in the American States* (10th ed.) (pp. 1–29). CQ Press.

Lockard, D. (1966). The state legislator. In A. Heard (Ed.), *State legislatures in American politics* (pp. 98–125). Prentice Hall.

Mackaman, F. H. (2010). *The civility initiative in Congress, 1996–2004*. Dirksen Congressional Center.

Mann, T. E., & Ornstein, N. J. (2008). *The broken branch*. Oxford University Press.

Moncrief, G., & Squire, P. (2013). *Why states matter*. Rowman & Littlefield.

Neblo, M. A., Esterling, K. M., & Lazer, D.M.J. (2018). *Politics with the people*. Cambridge University Press.

Osborn, T., & Kreitzer, R. (2014). Women state legislators: Women's issues in a partisan environment. In S. Thomas & C. Wilcox (Eds.), *Women and Elective Office* (3rd ed.) (pp. 181–198). Oxford University Press.

Segers, G. (2019, January 4). Have an obscure interest? There's a house caucus for that. *CBS News*. https://www.cbsnews.com/news/have-an-obscure-interest-theres-a-house-caucus-for-that/.

Shor, B., & McCarty, N. (2011). The ideological mapping of American legislatures. *American Political Science Review, 105*(3), 530–551.

Squire, P., & Moncrief, G. (2015). *State legislatures today* (2nd ed.). Rowman & Littlefield.

Swers, R. (2002). *The difference women make: The policy impact of women in Congress*. University of Chicago Press.

Uslaner, E. M. (1993). *The decline of comity in Congress*. University of Michigan Press.

CHAPTER ELEVEN

Summary Overview: Insights for Practitioners and Academics

John C. Pierce
Max Neiman

INTRODUCTION

The analyses presented in this work are intended for two distinct audiences. One is composed of participants in the process of state legislative politics in the 50 American states. The second is composed of academics and their students, for whom a preferred subject of study is the state legislative process. For the practitioners of state legislative institutional management, public policy advocates, and scholars interested in state-level comparison of political processes across U.S. states, the advent of gridlock and hyper-partisanship in the U.S. Congress raises two key questions related to civil discourse. First, *is a similar breakdown occurring in the American state legislatures in the ability to reach bipartisan agreements and to demonstrate civility?* Secondly, *to the extent that civility is breaking down in various states, what are the causes of this weakening of norms, customs, and traditions undergirding civil discourse?* The work here also distinguishes between civility and partisan polarization. It is possible for legislatures to manifest high levels of polarization, while also being civil. Civility, in short, might mitigate some of the ill effects of acute partisan polarization.

This book's several analyses of the perceptions of lobbyists as to the level of civility in their state legislatures began with a focus on political culture. The possible role of political culture points us to the path-dependent, historical context within which each state's politics is rooted. Variations in that historical cultural context were hypothesized to produce differences in the level of civility present in contemporary legislative politics. Daniel Elazar identified three cultural strains in the American states, namely moralistic, individualistic, and traditionalistic (1966, 79–116). Much prior research done in political science employing these distinctions in historically based political culture among the states suggests that states possessing a moralistic political culture heritage might exhibit greater civility than either of the other political culture heritage classifications. However, using three distinct operationalizations of political culture, chapter one's findings indicate that none of the three hypothesized strains of political culture acts to buffer the onset of incivility in the 50 U.S. state legislatures. Regardless of political culture, political incivility appears to have penetrated state legislatures and state political life across the entire country.

What of other sets of more contemporary contextual influences to structure that civility? Among those other potential influences is the level of professionalization present in the state legislatures. That possible relationship was examined in chapter two. Indeed, there is a relationship between legislative professionalization and degree of perceived civility. The amount a legislator earns in the form of salary is positively related to the degree to which lobbyists rated their respective legislatures as civil. However, this relationship does not hold for the other traditional components of professionalization. For example, longer sessions as an indication of professionalism are associated with lower civility ratings. Other state-level contextual legislative variables provided additional clues related to civility. One variable that stands out in this regard is a measure of the degree of racial and ethnic diversity present in a state's legislature (Hero, 2007). More-diverse legislatures were rated consistently more civil than less-diverse bodies. This finding is consistent with a very substantial body of literature that suggests diversity of the workforce in a firm is associated with higher levels of productivity and efficiency (Mayer, Warr, and Zhao, 2016). Counterintuitively, chapter two finds that states with more-polarized legislative parties were also rated as more civil. While historic cultural differences among the states apparently do not structure legislative civility, certain differences in the contextual influence of levels of professionalization do make some difference. More data and analysis are required to understand the mechanisms that incline more professional legislatures to be rated as more civil, while those with longer sessions seem less so.

Chapter three turns the analysis inside out, so to speak, looking at whether perceptions of civility are structured by the nature of the interest (rent-seeking or non-rent-seeking) represented by the respondents in the study. The partisan and ideological leanings of nonprofit public interest lobbyists seem to make a difference in perceptions when contrasted to their rent-seeking counterparts. Most notably, nonprofit public interest lobbyists report: (a) more poor experiences in representing clients; (b) a greater sense that legislative norms are breaking down; and (c) fewer nonpartisan areas of policymaking present. Still, nonprofit public interest lobbyists and their rent-seeking counterparts differ relatively little in their perceptions and assessments of civility in state legislatures, although there is some tendency for public interest advocates to see more personal adverse effects of incivility. In this case, is it the nature of the policy domains in which nonprofit public interest lobbyists operate? Are the policy objectives sought by them more fraught ideologically or more likely to catalyze opposition and conflict?

Finally, and perhaps relatedly, nonprofit public interest lobbyists see lobbyists in general as contributing more to legislative incivility than do their counterparts; otherwise, their perceptions of the causes of incivility do not differ much from those of other lobbyists. Again, this could very well be related to the sorts of demands and policy objectives associated with some nonprofit organizations or the generally lower level of wealth that nonprofit lobbyists bring to their work, although available research suggests that differences in lobbyists' resources are only weakly related to legislative "success" (McKay, 2012). Thus, the perception of civility (and perhaps effects of it) broadly speaking is unrelated to the kinds of interests and politics the lobbyists bring to the legislative arena.

Chapter four focused on term limits, along with some institutional and contextual features that could shape civility. The presence of term limits does seem to increase the chances of incivility, although not to a great degree. So once again the suggestion is that other factors might shape matters too. Some doubts are raised as well about whether partisan polarization increases incivility, which is counterintuitive. Also, the impact of term limits on civility may be indirect, explained substantially through its impact on civility via electoral turnover. This is consistent with other research that indicates term limits in a state tend to reduce cooperation and legislative cosponsorship across party lines (Swift and VanderMolen, 2016). Importantly, the analysis presented in chapter four suggests that the states' legislatures are not divided into clear camps, that is, one that is term-limited and remarkably polarized, and the other unpolarized and not term-limited; the mixture of these two dimensions is much more varied. Nor can it be said from the analyses presented that polarization is causing great incivility. Even while incivility might be absent, there can still be major difficulties achieving bipartisan collaboration.

Chapter five highlighted the judgments of an important subgroup of lobbyists—those who had served previously in the legislature and who are known as "revolvers" in the legislative politics literature. This chapter's findings suggest that the work of lobbyists is seriously hindered by uncivil rancor according to revolvers, and that they are desirous of interventions aimed at improved comity among state legislators in the states in which they ply their craft.

It makes sense that lobbyists, insofar as they have served in state legislatures and "revolved" into legislative advocacy from the outside, would want to maintain professional (perhaps even cordial) relationships with one-time colleagues in their own state legislatures. Hence, lobbyists with a background of prior legislative service might well be seen as a potential force for civility-building interventions in the future.

Revolvers see signs of the partisan gridlock and hyperpolarization in Congress having had deleterious effects at the state level. Perceiving current state legislators to be more partisan than those encountered in previous legislative sessions, state revolvers expressed harsher judgments than the rest of the surveyed group of lobbyists with respect to the current state of affairs. As a group, the revolvers also more strongly highlighted the need for enhanced cross-party legislator communication—both among rank-and-file members and among chamber legislative leadership.

Yet the analysis also suggests that term limits, insofar as they affect civility, do so by increasing turnover. That, in turn, increases the number of legislators who are without the experience of forging friendships across the aisle or, perhaps, even among their own copartisans. In their national assessment of states, Olson and Rogowski (2020) find, as have others, that term limits significantly increase partisanship and reduce the effectiveness and productivity of legislatures. With term limits, there are also fewer incentives to invest in relationships, as well as more incentives to pave the way for the "next gig."

Chapter six examines whether income inequality within a state affects the level of civility present in that state's legislature. Income inequality perhaps places more fraught policy issues on the agenda and could plausibly heighten conflict over redistributive issues and provoke ideological debates over social justice. The findings reported in this chapter suggest that the adverse effects of changes in state-level income inequality extend beyond the narrow fluctuations in relative income experienced by individuals and families. Indeed, shifts in income inequality at the state level appear to generate a widespread influence on the political process, ranging from polarization (as shown by previous scholars) to negative perceptions of the conduct of state legislators. These observations both substantiate and extend the findings reported by other scholars. Thus, long-standing welfare-state theories and related empirical evidence suggest that higher income inequality (Meltzer and Richard, 1981) and/or the structure of inequality (Pontusson and Weisstanner, 2018) produce support for key elements of redistributive policy. The findings reported in this chapter suggest that broader shifts in inequality may be intimately connected to the civil discourse-related behaviors of state legislators as well.

Chapter seven assesses the impact on civility of the rural or urban context of the state in which a legislature is found. Lobbyists from more rural states identified the election process, the inability of legislators to communicate with opposing parties, partisan media, and general polarization at the federal level as all being sources of incivility in their own state legislatures. In addition, campaign contributors and legislative party leaders were also more likely to be identified by lobbyists from more rural states as probable causes of divisiveness. On the other hand, there were no differences between lobbyists from more rural states and lobbyists from more urban states in identifying the election of ideologically extreme legislators as a cause of incivility, or state party leaders as a cause. That observation noted, it was also the case that when compared to lobbyists from more urban states, lobbyists from more rural states opined that changing seating arrangements to mix up parties in legislative bodies may contribute to civility.

Chapter eight examines cross-state differences in civility using a multivariate regression approach previously applied in the analysis of cross-state differences in public policy adoption by these same scholars. There is a considerable variation among states in how "civil" the state legislatures are in the eyes of the lobbyists moving legislation in those legislative chambers, hence there are likely to be some factors at play accounting for this variation. The results reported showed marked similarities in legislative civility within geographic regions; that said, there are also individual states within each regional cluster that are either considerably more civil or less civil than their neighboring states.

Economic inequality, heightened electoral competition, and conservative political ideology proved to be the most important predictors of incivility across states when viewed within the multivariate regression analysis wherein all factors are considered simultaneously. In addition, more professionalized legislatures, the presence of term limits, and the presence of rural populations were also factors correlated with higher levels of incivility, although findings for this later grouping of factors were not particularly robust statistically. In sum, a combination of institutional, political, and socioeconomic contexts sets the stage for incivility to emerge in state legislatures as individual legislators are placed in several situational contexts that encourage them to abandon the norms of civility.

Possibly one of the most important and unexpected findings is that the statistical model was a better predictor of states with low levels of civility as opposed to states with high levels of civility. On its face, this finding would suggest that while the context of legislatures may facilitate legislative incivility, there are unique characteristics in some legislatures that prevent this drift toward incivility from happening. From a statistical perspective, it likely means that there are unobserved variables that are not included in the empirical model developed. These variables could include a wide range of cultural, social, historical, or individual characteristics. A key factor here, though, is the presence of strong leaders who hold their colleagues accountable for incivility and who emphasize the importance of civility in achieving the mission of their state's legislature.

It is also possible that the factors that facilitate civility are different from those that create less-civil institutions.

Chapter nine examines legislative civility from the perspective of a political scientist who has spent his entire career as a practitioner. Karl Kurtz notes that having spent much of his professional life trying to combat public cynicism toward and distrust of legislatures, he agrees about the deleterious effects of hyper-partisanship and incivility on the legislative institution. He suggests that the level of incivility and public distrust has escalated and is threatening all governmental institutions alike—legislatures, executives, courts, elections, law enforcement, and even public health. Despite Kurtz's self-described "somber view of the state of civility in America today," he writes that "I would not be true to my calling as a defender and promoter of American democracy if I did not look for some signs of hope." He believes that "most legislators still honor the institution and behave and treat their opponents with respect." Moreover, he suggests that all the attention paid to conflict and incivility in our national politics and higher visibility in big state legislatures cause us to forget that most of the small state citizen legislatures operate with much higher levels of trust, respect, and civility and continue to function in more traditional ways.

In chapter ten, Robert Boatright from Clark University, writing as the director of research for the National Institute for Civil Discourse (NICD), suggests that despite nearly a decade of work with state legislators, the effort to understand civility in state legislative politics is in many ways still in its early stages. He opines that the lobbyist survey featured in this book offers many insights into how NICD can work with legislative leaders and individual state legislators to improve the quality and civility of discourse. While he expresses the belief that more research is needed to understand the causal pathways that lead to both incivility and civility, Boatright observes that this book provides an important source of hope for individual legislative leaders and public interest groups outside the legislature seeking to spread and strengthen civil discourse in our society. Moreover, Boatright argues that legislator surveys similar to the lobbyist survey can provide valuable information for political scientists and reformers about the relationship among state political institutions, state political culture, and legislative productivity and comity. More research is needed to understand these aspects of our results and the causal pathways that lead to both incivility and civility. Commitment to deepening that understanding is present at the NICD and many other nonprofit organizations working to build bridges for bipartisan problem-solving. In fact, individual legislative leaders can make a difference when it comes to upholding civility in our society, and it is hopeful that many of them have volunteered to spearhead efforts in their own states while working with the NICD.

IMPLICATIONS

As noted earlier, there are two distinct audiences for this work. The first of those audiences is the academic/scholarly community and the second is the political/policy community. The latter includes legislators, political party officials, interest group representatives, public agency legislative liaison personnel, and public affairs educators (such as the League of Women Voters and college and university-based internship program coordinators), as well as informed members of the public. For the academic/scholarly community, we focus on the implications for a future research agenda that can better inform all involved and concerned with political civility, including state legislators, legislative staff, interest group representatives, and informed members of the public.

For the second audience, we detail some findings that might enhance the overall quality of discourse and interaction among those subsets of actors engaged in the state legislative policy process. It is anticipated that the survey conducted for this book will serve as a baseline effort for future studies monitoring the state of civility, either in the form of a subsequent nationwide survey or separate surveys conducted in several states following up on efforts to carry out civility-promoting interventions.

FUTURE RESEARCH AGENDA

Although the research presented here significantly advances knowledge about legislative civility, major gaps remain in that knowledge. Filling those gaps will contribute to efforts to create more civil state legislative processes, and perhaps more civil civic life in general. Some feasible research topics that would fill in major parts of our knowledge deficit are sketched out as follows.

First, future research should examine the civility effects of changes in the policy agenda of a legislature, especially as economic inequality intensifies social and political stress. It may be that the more complex and "advanced" a state's economy, the greater the level of inequality, whereby the separation between the beneficiaries and victims of "progress" becomes more obvious. Larger and more complex state economies riven by discontent over rising and pervasive inequality may raise more complex and contentious issues. These, in turn, may foster more disagreement and conflict and perhaps aggravate ideological differences.

Alternatively, deploying sophisticated, professionally facilitated collaborative processes may prove effective in bringing together stakeholders who learn the value of civil discourse and the practical benefits of norm adherence and trust development. Economic inequality can increase the heat of politics around redistributive issues, especially if inequalities are superimposed on racial and ethnic divisions within the citizenry. The extent to which collaborative processes can address these kinds of issues remains to be determined. Civility and civil discourse are perhaps most needed where they are most difficult to conceptualize, initiate, and sustain. Research in this key area of collaborative conflict management and connection to the state public policy process is much needed and fortunately ongoing at different places in the United States (e.g., the William D. Ruckelshaus Center at the University of Washington).

Second, what happens in rural communities as urbanization and suburbanization continue to encroach upon non-metropolitan areas within the states? Insofar as rural communities suffer as a consequence of their declining economic clout and sparser resources, do they tend to cling even more closely to cultural and moral policy issues such as gun rights and conventional sexual preference practices and economically more retrograde policies? Will these divides intensify the erosion of civility and catalyze higher levels of conflict between rural and urban interests? Will a new normal stiffen because of the absence of a common ground? Will the nation's states and communities partition themselves into a variety of lifestyle and morality enclaves with rancorous sound and fury over issues such as abortion, marijuana legalization, or same-sex marriage?

Surely such developments will dissolve civility and its capacity to bond our diverse nation and impede our ability to manage an array of serious policy challenges. We need a much better understanding of currently divisive trends and their sources, their impact on civility, and how to mitigate the ill-effects these are having on the nation.

Third, the effects of legislative incivility are typically derived from observational research. Some of the observations are provided by participants, some by reliance on the perceptions of other external observers such as media personnel—or, as in the case of this study, from indirect legislative process participants such as lobbyists, many of whom have served as legislators or legislative staff. Researchers should develop systematic, empirical measures of civility to see whether they are strongly associated with the *perceptions* of civility that are typically gathered. Perhaps traditional content analysis methods or more advanced artificial intelligence-assisted analyses of word and phase usage in legislative dialogue would provide added insight into and corroboration (or not) of perceptual measures. In a fair number of U.S. states, many important legislative hearings are video-recorded and archived. Research on those archived legislative deliberations could be carried out to assess the extent to which these public actions of a state's legislators have shown signs of declining civility.

Fourth, most of the information gathered about the *effects* of incivility is anecdotal in nature. It would be useful to identify any systematic consequences of variations in incivility that might be present. Such effects of incivility may be related to the efficiency of the legislative process (e.g., getting to closure on budgets and other key bills as opposed to "kicking the can down the road for the next session"), or to the frequency of use of procedural roadblocks (such as denial of quorum, as recently witnessed in the Oregon and North Carolina state legislatures), or to the overall productivity of the legislature as judged by knowledgeable commentators in the press and/or academia. With the independent variable effects assessed here, there may be noteworthy reciprocal effects to be explored and documented as well. For example, heightened turnover among legislators may lead to greater incivility, but then greater incivility may lead to greater turnover.

Fifth, studies of incivility's presence and effects should not be confined solely to cross-sectional slices in time. Longitudinal social science research is critical, especially in documenting the degree to which interventions such as those attempted by the Conference of State Legislatures and the National Institute for Civil Discourse make a difference. It is quite important for both scholars and the practitioners engaged in the process to know whether variations in the larger national political climate are likely to have a major effect on state legislative deliberative processes. Is it perhaps the case that legislative incivility is largely a stable attribute of a state, one largely impervious to external climate effects or the effects of intentional attempts to alter the tenor of the legislative process with respect to civil discourse? Or does the corrosion of civility follow a "conflict escalation" model, in which tit-for-tat responses produce a downward slope toward loss of comity? Only additional, sustained research can answer that question.

Sixth, there might be opportunities to understand more fully the importance of legislative leadership in maintaining decorum within party caucuses and the legislative process. Although legislative leadership is central, one can assume gubernatorial leadership could very well affect the quality and direction of civility (Bowling and Ferguson, 2001). More finely focused research is needed to understand this aspect of the causal pathways that lead to both incivility and civility, and the role that various types of leadership styles might play in this regard. The answers may provide support for the hope that individual leaders (as role models or gatekeepers, or both) can make a difference when it comes to upholding civility in state legislatures. The leadership dynamics may well be quite different in single-party-dominant states than they are in two-party competitive states. In the single-party-dominant states, the presence or absence of major factions (e.g., ideological, regional, urban vs. rural, etc.) likely occasions leadership practices that are either more or less focused on civil discourse. Again, more finely tuned and focused research is needed in this important area. Closely related, of course, is examining changes in rules and practices that enhance or degrade leadership influence (e.g., term limits, party leadership selection processes, or powers of the governor).

Seventh, the data for this study are based solely in the perceptions of lobbyists who have a substantial professional and financial stake in the effective operation of their respective state legislatures. But there are other potential sets of important observers who may or may not have the same stake-based perspectives. Thus, members of the press who concentrate on a state's legislative politics surely offer a different lens on the process of assessing the effects of legislative incivility. It would be informative indeed to triangulate perceptions of a legislature's civility level to see whether there is agreement across sectors of participants—for example, lobbyists and public agency legislative liaison officers, the print and broadcast media press, the judiciary, career legislative staff and caucus staff, and members of the second legislative body. This would have the added benefit of concept validation for the notion that there is genuine substance to the concept of civility.

Eight, the research reported in this book focused on mining data gathered in online and mail surveys of state legislative lobbyists. The primary goal of that major research effort was to obtain representative samples from each of the 50 U.S. states. This effort on the part of over a dozen researchers at ten universities spread across the country resulted in the collection of rich data from a relatively large number of respondents. This was an ambitious undertaking, and some of the insight derived from these data is set forth in chapters one through eight. But such an approach can obscure the richness and detail that would grow out of selected case studies of high-conflict policy disputes over different kinds of specific issues. Thus, subsequent work could vitally be directed at identifying contentious issues, such as state-level pandemic response, and then probing them at some depth for what effect the presence or absence of civil discourse had in the politics arising around COVID-19.

CONSIDERATIONS FOR THE WORLD OF STATE LEGISLATIVE PRACTICE

The findings reported in the survey data-based chapters and observations made by Karl Kurtz and Rob Boatright should provide insight into how one's own state legislative institution is patterned with respect to civility. For example, how is Kentucky different from Vermont, and does that difference matter in how well the legislative deliberative process functions in my own state of Michigan or Nevada? Likewise, in what ways is my own state both similar to and different from other states in my region? The website for this book (https://labs.wsu.edu/outside-looking-in/)

permits any practitioner from any state to contact one of the four editors to learn how to access the survey findings for his or her own state, including the often-detailed comments offered by many of the 1,000+ survey respondents. These products of research are available (comments are de-identified) upon request. Data for one's own state and any other states of interest are available upon formal request. For career legislative staff and legislative leaders, knowing how the lobbyist community views them and their colleagues with respect to matters of civility is valuable information. Rather than relying entirely upon hunches, anecdotes, and rumors, these systematically collected data provide a valuable insight into how people from the "outside looking in" view their state's legislative processes. If there is interest in isolating the views of lobbyists with prior legislative experience, that too can be provided upon request.

Second, for interest group, associational, and nonprofit organizational representatives, these results may help them become more effective advocates for their own constituents' policy goals. For example, the nonprofit League of Women Voters (state-level and local leagues) has a long-standing interest across the entire country in the maintenance of civil discourse in its candidate forums held for nearly all public offices, be they federal, state, or local—and be they partisan or nonpartisan in nature. Similarly, most of the land grant colleges and universities across the nation maintain programs on the topic "youth in government" in their 4-H programs. State legislatures commonly make room for high school youth from across their states to meet legislators and operate a mock legislative session during official session periods.

These activities are of long standing and are firmly centered on the norms, traditions, and customs of legislative life that feature a strong element of decorum, comity, mutual respect, and civility in debate. In Washington, where this research project began, both the League of Women Voters and Washington State University Extension have been able to access and make use of the survey data and comments collected for Washington in their public affairs education work. The same can be said for the public and private colleges and universities which operate legislative internship programs for their undergraduate and graduate students. This book serves, in part, as an open invitation to state legislative practitioners inside of and outside of the state legislatures in other states to make use of data in these ways in their own states.

Third, several of these chapters investigated lobbyists' opinions on what might be effective pathways for change toward greater civility in state legislatures. In many of the survey comments recorded in the study and archived for retrieval, well-considered concrete suggestions are proposed. Ideas for incoming legislator training, bipartisan issue-based caucus formation, suggestions for how legislative leadership can set a tone for civility and decorum, recommendations on how to promote across-the-aisle understanding through hosted home district visits in legislator pairings of urban and rural legislators, and similar ideas are to be found in the data collected. The Washington State University housed website (https://labs. wsu.edu/outside-looking-in/) for this book provides the contact information for the editors and describes the principal contents of the data and resources archived there for use by scholars and practitioners alike.

In closing, please recall that the data from the survey of state legislative policy advocates indicate that there is substantial agreement among these knowledgeable and experienced people that the norms, customs, and traditions of civil discourse long have been important to the successful operation of their respective state legislatures. There is likewise broad agreement that these norms, customs, and traditions are in serious decline, and that this decline is adversely affecting the ability of state legislatures to achieve their goals of making public policy on the basis of productive public deliberation, sound evidence, convincing arguments, and adaptive bipartisan problem-solving. To the degree that practitioners in states beyond Washington have a concern about civil discourse in their state legislatures, this book and associated website offer you research-based resources for taking targeted action in your state.

REFERENCES

Bowling, C. J., & Ferguson, M. R. (2001). Divided government, interest representation, and policy differences: Competing explanations of gridlock in the fifty states. *Journal of Politics, 63*(1), 182–206.

Elazar, D. (1966). *American federalism: A view from the states.* Thomas Y. Crowell Co.

Hero, R. (2007). *Racial diversity and social capital: Equality and community in America.* Cambridge University Press.

Mayer, R. C., Warr, R. C., & Zhao, J. (2016, June). Does employee treatment and workforce diversity impact corporate innovative efficiency? SSRN. https://ssrn.com/abstract=2476543 or http://dx.doi.org/10.2139/ssrn.2476543.

Meltzer, A. H., & Richard, S. F. (1981). A rational theory of size of government. *Journal of Political Economy, 89*(5), 914–927.

McKay, A. (2012). Buying policy? The effects of lobbyists' resources on their policy success. *Political Research Quarterly, 65*(4), 908–923.

Olson, M., & Rogowski, J. (2020). Legislative term limits and polarization. *Journal of Politics, 82*(2), 572–586.

Pontusson, J., & Weisstanner, D. (2018). Macroeconomic conditions, inequality shocks and the politics of redistribution, 1990–2013. *Journal of European Public Policy, 25*(1), 31–58.

Swift, C. S., & VanderMolen, K. A. (2016). Term limits and collaboration across the aisle: An analysis of bipartisan co-sponsorship in term limited and non-term limited state legislatures. *State Politics and Policy Quarterly, 16*(2), 198–226.

Contributors

Nicholas P. Lovrich is Regents Professor Emeritus in the School of Politics, Philosophy, and Public Affairs at Washington State University. He holds the honor of being a Claudius O. and Mary W. Johnson Distinguished Professor of Political Science.

Francis A. Benjamin is Administrative Professional in the Psychology Department and Adjunct Faculty in the Finance Department at Washington State University. He is past president of the Association of Washington Cities and heads up the Political Interaction Lab in the Department of Psychology, which carries out online and mail surveys and experiments.

John C. Pierce is Vice Chancellor Emeritus and Professor Emeritus at the University of Colorado at Colorado Springs and former Executive Director of the Oregon Historical Society. He currently serves as Affiliate Research Faculty in the School of Public Affairs and Administration at the University of Kansas.

William D. Schreckhise is Professor and Chair of the Department of Political Science in the J. William Fulbright College of Arts and Sciences at the University of Arkansas.

FOREWORD AUTHORS

Steven Stehr is the Sam Reed Distinguished Professor in Civic Education and Public Civility and serves on the faculty of the School of Politics, Philosophy, and Public Affairs at Washington State University. He was also the first Director of the Thomas S. Foley Institute for Public Policy and Public Service.

Sam Reed served as Washington's Secretary of State from 2001–2013, and prior to that he served as Thurston County Auditor for five terms. In 2006–2007 he served as president of the National Association of Secretaries of State. His legacy is one of active championing of civility, moderation, and bipartisanship in government.

PREFACE AUTHORS

Craig Curtis is a Professor of Political Science at Bradley University, where he teaches courses in public law and public administration. He earned his PhD in the Department of Political Science at Washington State University and worked on the staff of the Division of Governmental Studies and Services while doing his dissertation research.

James R. Hanni is a resident of Lawrence, Kansas. He has served on the Kansas Historical Foundation Board of Directors and currently chairs the Board of Directors of The Gettysburg Foundation of Gettysburg, Pennsylvania.

Richard Kimball is President of Vote Smart, a nonprofit, nonpartisan voter education organization founded in 1988. Vote Smart staff and volunteers seek to allow reason and civility to regain the advantage in an age when division and faction tend to reign supreme.

Bradley McMillan is Executive Director of the Institute for Principled Leadership in Public Service and serves as Coordinator of the Master's in Nonprofit Leadership program at Bradley University.

Megan Remmel is an Assistant Professor in the Department of Political Science at Bradley University.

CHAPTER CONTRIBUTORS

Robert G. Boatright is Professor and Chair of the Department of Political Science at Clark University and the Director of Research for the National Institute for Civil Discourse at the University of Arizona.

Daniel E. Chand is Associate Professor and Director of Graduate Studies in the Department of Political Science at Kent State University.

Luke Fowler is Associate Professor and Director of the MPA program in the School of Public Service at Boise State University.

Leanne S. Giordono is a Postdoctoral Scholar in the School of Behavioral and Social Sciences at Oregon State University. She holds a PhD in Public Policy from Oregon State University's School of Public Policy and an MPA from Princeton University's School of Public and International Affairs.

Briana M. Huett is a Distinguished Doctoral Fellow and Candidate in the Public Policy PhD program at the University of Arkansas. She is a final-year student in the Masters in Statistics and Analytics program at the University of Arkansas.

Jaclyn J. Kettler is Assistant Professor of Political Science at Boise State University.

Karl Kurtz retired after a 40-plus-year career as a political scientist with the National Conference of State Legislatures. He is now the principal of Legis Matters, a consulting firm dedicated to strengthening democracy. He has been assisting, supporting, studying, and writing about legislatures for over 50 years.

Burdett A. Loomis is a Professor in the Department of Political Science at the University of Kansas.

Claire McMorris is a 2017 summa cum laude graduate of the University Honors College at Oregon State University with a BA in political science and minors in music and Spanish. At Oregon State University, she was a junior inductee to Phi Beta Kappa. Claire currently serves as the Government Relations Coordinator for Oregon State University.

Max Neiman is Senior Research Fellow at the Institute of Governmental Studies of the University of California, Berkeley. He is also Professor of Political Science, Emeritus, University of California, Riverside, and Senior Fellow at the Public Policy Institute of California.

Christopher A. Simon is Professor of Political Science and former Director of the MPA program at the University of Utah. He is coauthor (with Brent Steel and Nicholas Lovrich) of *State and Local Government: Sustainability in the 21st Century* (Oxford University Press, 2011; 2nd edition, Oregon State University Press, 2018).

Brent S. Steel is Professor and Graduate Director in the School of Public Policy at Oregon State University. He has been on the board and executive committee of Vote Smart since the founding of the organization.

Stephanie L. Witt is a Professor and Director of Training for the School of Public Service at Boise State University.

Author Index

Subject Index

Also Available from WSU Press

CIVILITY AND DEMOCRACY IN AMERICA
A Reasonable Understanding
Edited by Cornell W. Clayton and Richard Elgar

In 2011, the Thomas S. Foley Institute for Public Policy and Public Service at Washington State University hosted one of four major conferences held across the country, to initiate discussion about the role of civility in American democracy. Leading scholars from a variety of disciplines participated, concentrating on perspectives from history, religion, philosophy, art and architecture, and media. *Civility and Democracy in America* offers insights from these seasoned experts.

ISBN 978-0-87422-312-5 / $25.95 / Paperback

BARNYARDS AND BIRKENSTOCKS
Why Farmers and Environmentalists Need Each Other
Don Stuart

Rural America faces two dangerous trends—the loss of farms and damage to ecosystems—and the author, Don Stuart, believes a major cause is political deadlock. He proposes a radical solution: collaboration.

ISBN 978-0-87422-322-4 / $28.95 / Paperback

RETHINKING RURAL
Global Community and Economic Development in the Small Town West
Don E. Albrecht

Rethinking Rural traces the environmental and cultural history of the American West, summarizes three emerging issues, and offers guidance to community leaders and policy makers seeking to address the challenges of a new global society.

ISBN 978-0-87422-319-4 / $28.95 / Paperback